This book is
d

PROFESSIONAL
SKI INSTRUCTOR
OF AMERICA

SKIING
RIGHT

BY HORST ABRAHAM

THE PROFESSIONAL SKI INSTRUCTORS OF AMERICA PRESENT

SKIING RIGHT

BY HORST ABRAHAM

WITH A COLLECTION OF ASSORTED ESSAYS AND OBSERVATIONS BY **PHIL BRITTIN, BILL LASH, ABBEY RAND, LOWELL THOMAS, BILL GROUT, DICK NEEDHAM** AND **NEIL STEBBINS.**

A JOHNSON BOOK PRODUCED BY DANIEL PRODUCTIONS

1817

Harper & Row, Publishers, San Francisco
Cambridge, Hagerstown, New York, Philadelphia
London, Mexico City, Sao Paulo, Sydney

PRODUCED BY DANIEL PRODUCTIONS

ART DIRECTOR/DESIGNER: **JOSEPH DANIEL**

EDITORS: **TERI TICHENAL, CHRISTINA THOMAS**

EDITORIAL STAFF: **JURIS VAGNERS, DAWS WILSON, MARIE CLAIR VIERS, SUSAN KOSTER**

P.S.I.A. TECHNICAL ADVISOR: **MIKE DOLAND**

PRODUCTION STAFF: **DEBORAH AUTABO, WENDY ROTHMAN, CHRISTINA THOMAS**

ILLUSTRATION CREDITS: **PAUL BOYLE** — STAR TEST graphics
JOSEPH DANIEL — Conditioning graphics, ATM graphics **BRYAN GOUGH** — Why Ski Anyway? drawings
TOM ZILIS — ATM Mechanics drawings **PSIA** — Early Years etchings

PHOTO CREDITS: **ASPEN HISTORICAL SOCIETY** — 59, 63, 93, 169 **PHIL BRITTIN** — 31
COLORADO SKI MUSEUM — 28, 195 **JOSEPH DANIEL** — 8, 29, 56, 71, 74, 76, 78, 85, 89, 90, 94, 109, 113,
166, 200 **MAMMOTH MTN** — 68 **VAIL ASSOCIATES** — 80, 102, 107, 174, 196
VAIL/PETER RUNYON — 163, 170 **VAIL/JILL VIG** — 55, 114, 158, 203

COVER PHOTO/DESIGN: **JOSEPH DANIEL**

TYPESETTING: **DEBORAH HAVAS, LINDA BEVARD, JO ATKINSON — HORIZON GRAPHICS & TYPE CO.**

PRINTING: **JOHNSON BOOKS**

Copyright © 1983 by Professional Ski Instructors of America, Inc.

ISBN: 0-06-250015-5

LCCN: 83-48651

86 87 10 9 8 7 6 5 4 3 2

To the many students I have worked with who gave me the insights I am sharing in this book and who, because of their enthusiasm and response, have allowed me always to remain a learner.

Inherent in writing a book is the need to present readers with thoughts and concepts arranged in a logical order. In that a book is a monologue, and is inflexible in its presentation once the text is set, individual needs of the reader may not be fulfilled by the order the book is presented.

Those of you wishing to partake in my author's experiences and become familiar with my values and conclusions as they relate to educational processes — read the book as it presents itself.

Those of you who are learners of sports and are preparing to become actively involved in a sport, turn to part four and immerse yourself right away in the practical suggestions. Each development chapter discusses issues from a practical and theoretical point of view. If you stumble across a concept or methodological suggestion that you do not fully understand, check in the corresponding section of the book — there will be clarification.

Those of you using this book for historical, ski mechanical, or sport psychological reference, turn to the segment of the book that interests you. The table of contents will guide you.

TABLE OF CONTENTS

FOREWORDS

PART I - A HISTORY OF SKIING

PART II - A TURN TO THE RIGHT

PART III - PRE-SKI CONDITIONING

PART IV - THE ATM SYSTEM

PART V - STAR TEST

PART VI - SKIING TERMINOLOGY

PART VII - SKIING DIRECTORY

PREFACE

When I was asked if I would be willing to write this book, I accepted the assignment with great enthusiasm. There were thousands of thoughts and ideas in my head that all wanted to be sorted and written down. Once I actually sat down and began to write, the challenge became evident. How do I start? How do I say things that are hard to put into words? How much do I say? What can I assume is known, and to what extent may the reader be willing to accept new and different concepts?

I wrote this book primarily because of my love of learning and learners. But, I also wrote this book because of my concerns that ski teachers are, for the most part, accepting the responsibility of educating without meaningful training. What this book is dealing with merely touches the surface of what is ailing education in general. While attending school, we seldom learn to think from the process of education; from lessons at a ski school we rarely learn to ski and enjoy skiing as a direct result of our skilled instruction. Our value systems as students and as teachers are often so misguided that we expect, exercise and/or insist upon processes that fulfill those requirements, but are otherwise of little or no value. What makes us dreadfully inept during our formal educational process does not usually change when we reach adulthood. Every generation of teachers and parents shapes the potentials of the next generation. Thus, we ensure the perpetuation of conventional concepts that, at their conception, were already archaic. It is my prediction that, though educational institutions will resist such change, there will be a revolution upon our hands that will finally seek to tap human potential in a creative manner, unconstipated by the linearity of systems that currently guide us.

This book explores ski instructional methods that are based upon the still-speculative concepts of brain hemispheric functions; these concepts seem to bring brilliant order to the many 'til now unchartable experiences I have had in teaching, learning and performing. When Richard Sperry received his Nobel Prize in the summer of 1981 for his work on hemispheric brain functions, it was encouraging to realize I had been on the bandwagon before it even *was* one!

Though this book's title, *Skiing Right,* may suggest to the reader that right brain hemisphere functions are the exclusive mode to perform from, that is not correct, nor intended. It means, rather, that a turn to the "Right" is in order to correct the imbalance that our educational and societal emphases of left brain hemisphere functions has generated. The content of this book explores, in thought and practical example, alternate teaching and learning concepts that lean heavily upon the integrated and complementary interaction between both hemispheres. While research on the underlying concepts is still in progress, the practical application (and success) of an integrated approach already has a proven record. Learning takes place faster and with more permanent results, peak performance becomes the rule, rather than the exception. Come, join me in an experiment that you will not regret!

HORST ABRAHAM, 1982

A WRITER'S RESPONSE

When I started skiing in 1959, students in ski school classes often complained that the sport felt "unnatural" to them. Considering the static and sometimes contorted body positions students were expected to assume in those days, it's no wonder that skiing seemed difficult. What's more, there were a thousand things to remember if you wanted to ski like your instructor — weight on the balls of your feet, shoulders downhill, knees bent, head up, uphill ski ahead, hands forward, and on and on. As might be expected, trying to learn the sport in this fashion was more self-torture than fun and, looking back, it seems clear that those who did learn to ski did so in spite of the instruction they received. Many thousands quit the sport in frustration, convinced that they were just too uncoordinated to master it.

Twenty years later ski instructors are beginning to realize that the way to learn skiing (or any sport, for that matter) is not to practice a specific stance or maneuver over and over again until the form "looks right," but instead to concentrate on just a few simple and functional skills that can be felt, repeated easily and remembered by the body. Along with this, they're realizing that the mind plays just as important a role in learning to ski as the body does. It can either slow progress by creating anxiety and/or unrealistic expectations, or it can

dramatically speed up learning by increasing confidence and concentration. Gradual acceptance of these concepts, together with real proof that new teaching methods, based on an understanding of how people actually learn, do indeed work, has started a revolution in ski instruction across the country.

One of the leaders of this revolution is the author of this book, Horst Abraham. What Horst has attempted to do in his work with the Vail Ski School and as chairman of the Professional Ski Instructors of America (PSIA) educational committee, is to fuse concepts from such seemingly diverse disciplines as modern psychology, learning theory, physiology and martial arts into a new way of teaching that makes learning to ski not only faster but more fun, as well. As he says, the modern ski instructor should not only have a bag of tricks but also a book bag — that is, he should not just be a flashy skier with a perfect smile but a real educator on the slopes. In working to change the way skiing is taught, Horst and his colleagues in PSIA are creating a revolution not only in the U.S. but all over the world.

The book you hold in your hand will tell you what that revolution is all about.

BILL GROUT - Skiing Magazine

A WRITER'S RESPONSE

I remember a favorite college class. It was an introductory course in economics and the professor who taught it—his name was Dr. Chang—made it, well, *fun*. When I returned home on school break, I told my friends all about this great class.

"Economics? Man, you must be nuts—that's got to be the most boring stuff in the world."

Well, I suppose the plotting of supply and demand curves isn't the most cerebrally exciting of exercises, but good old Dr. Chang, he just got everyone enthused, reinforced us with economics as a game, then got out of the way and let us learn. In fact, Dr. Chang's approach was the antithesis of what Charles Schultz says elsewhere in these pages: "Try not to have a good time. This is supposed to be educational"—and I learned a lot. In thumbing through the pages that follow, you'll learn a lot, too.

Truth be told, I've always looked forward to another book from PSIA with about as much enthusiasm as a trip to the dentist. But this one, a refreshing look at how we learn—left brain/right brain (the smart side vs. the skilled side), self-discovery, imaging, the creation of a postive self-image—is a dandy.

What makes this book unique, a real supermarket of ski learning and lore, are the warm and entertaining touches that enrich and bring the words to life. It's not an easy thing to write from the heart, as Horst Abraham has so capably done, in penning a work that deals ostensibly with the machinations of ski technique.

To read such passages as "Great ski racers are not reared in ski schools . . . I started to learn when school was over . . . Many teachers didn't learn to ski the way they teach skiing" is refreshing, make that iconoclastic, in a book produced under the imprimatur of the nation's ski instruction establishment. It only shows what American ski instructors are becoming—no longer simply the arbiters of skiing skills and technique but an inquisitive and experimentation-crazy bunch whose unyielding interest is in learning rather than teaching. The distinction is important . . . and I'll leave it to Horst Abraham to tell you why.

You'll enjoy this book, if for no other reason than it reinforces what we've always believed skiing to be—*fun*.

DICK NEEDHAM - Ski Magazine

A WRITER'S RESPONSE

Before my association with POWDER, formal ski instruction was something that offered obvious technical advantages as well as a certain social appeal. At that stage of my career, however, it was not an affordable addition to the cost of a lift ticket and lunch. Consequently, I learned to ski by watching, doing, and even occasionally eavesdropping on large ski school classes where my shabby presence might go unnoticed.

Since POWDER, I have had the good fortune to photograph, interview and ski with some of the best skiers in the world and, since faint heart never won a free ski lesson, I was always quick to importune my illustrious companions for tips to improve what I laughingly called my technique. And a curious thing happened. I discovered that the ability to ski well and the ability to teach skiing well do not necessarily follow upon each other as the day the night. Fortunately, my experiences have also included those exceptional people who can not only do both, but who can significantly improve one's skiing with a single sentence, an example or a simple exercise. I remember Otto Tschudi telling me about hand position at a race camp in Bariloche . . . and Weems Westfeldt making steep bumps seem friendly at Taos . . . and Tim Petrick showing how to complete every turn at Snowbird. I recall watching Gordie Skoog absolutely fly down a field of bumps with his upper body perfectly still and author Tim Gallwey—the guru of non-judgemental instruction—ask his ski instructor, "How'd I do?" just like everybody else who's had a good run.

I guess the point of all these examples is that instruction is not only mental and physical training, it's also a unique personal interaction. What may surprise you the most when you finish this book and seek assistance is that the qualified professional ski instructor of today is not only a scholar and athlete, but a psychologist as well. Within minutes or just a few hours, he or she can not only evalute how you ski but how you learn and what kind of input will work best for you. Thanks to Horst and the P.S.I.A., you can accelerate your learning process through an awareness of the concepts presented here, but don't forget to sign up for a lesson when you want to put these thoughts into action. You'll be amazed what a good instructor can do for you when you're ready to learn.

NEIL STEBBINS - Powder Magazine

A SKIER'S REMINISCENCE

We are told how life is marked by milestones. My first encounter with the real thing was when I was crossing a stretch of the Arabian Desert in 1917. Suddenly we came upon a stone placed there by Roman soldiers nearly two thousand years ago. And then we passed many more as we rode our camels through the Wady Araba on our way to "The Rose Red City" of Petra. While there isn't much connection between the sands of Araby and skiing, I hear there have been a number of major milestones in the history of our favorite sport, especially since World War I. In those days I was first exposed to the sport in the Italian Alps where King Victor Emmanuel's mountain troops were using skis eight and nine feet long, with a single pole. But it wasn't until the Winter Olympics in the Adirondacks in 1932 that I decided here was something I wanted to do. In those days the Olympic ski events were strictly Nordic, cross country, and jumping.

So far as recreational skiing goes here in North America, the first instruction was given by Erling Strom at Lake Placid in the late twenties, four years prior to the '32 Olympics. The big impetus came in 1934 when Katherine Peckett brought the first Austrian pros to America. There were four of them, but the two responsible for our first instruction in Alpine skiing were Kurt Thalhammer and Sig Buchmayr, from Salzburg. They were soon followed by Benno Rybizka, Otto Lang, and others who also came to New Hampshire, and then by a group of their countrymen who were lured to the Sawtooth Mountains of Idaho by Averell Harriman.

This Austrian invasion of course was made possible by the one and only Hannes Schneider as a result of what he had been doing at his school at St. Anton on the Arlberg. Then, in the forties Emile Allais came along with what proved to be an exciting new technique. I'll never forget the dramatic meeting in New Hampshire when Emile was on his first visit to the United States. In Jackson one night after we had all been up to Tuckerman Ravine, I had the pleasure of introducing Hannes and Emile, the two ski giants of those days who had never met. Although

there was much rivalry among their followers, even a bit of acrimony, these two obviously had great admiration for each other.

Since those pre-World War II days there have been other striking advances in skiing, usually brought about by some decidedly uncommon young men most of whom have been my friends and occasional ski companions. Now at long last we are told that what can be termed an "American ski technique" has emerged. Be this as it may it's obvious our American ski schools have been producing tens of thousands of competent and happy skiers, and doing it on a greater scale than on any other continent—this despite the fact that Japan now seems to have more skiers than we have.

One of the difficult-to-explain experiences of my skiing years was at Aspen when I was invited to address the Eighth Inter-Ski International Ski Instructors Congress. Obviously there was nothing important I could tell them, but it was a pleasure to have such an opportunity to express my enthusiasm for skiing and my gratitude to the many ski instructors who have wrestled with the hopeless task of making me "a hot-shot skier." In the White Mountains of New Hampshire, the Green Mountains of Vermont, the Adirondacks, the Catskills, the Berkshires of New York, the Laurentians, I have enjoyed the companionship of these men who have meant so much to American skiing.

I also have roamed the mountains of our western states with them—Colorado, Arizona, Wyoming, Idaho, Utah, Nevada, California, Oregon, Washington. They are on the whole the finest group of men I've ever known. My ski jaunts have taken me to the Alps, the Himalayas, the mountains of Australia and New Zealand, to Japan, and the glaciers of Alaska. Because of the glorious times I have had with the ski pros all over the world, it's a pleasure and an honor to be asked to salute them in the foreword to this important book. (Reprinted from *The Official American Technique—PSIA*, 1964).

LOWELL THOMAS - Honorary P.S.I.A. Member

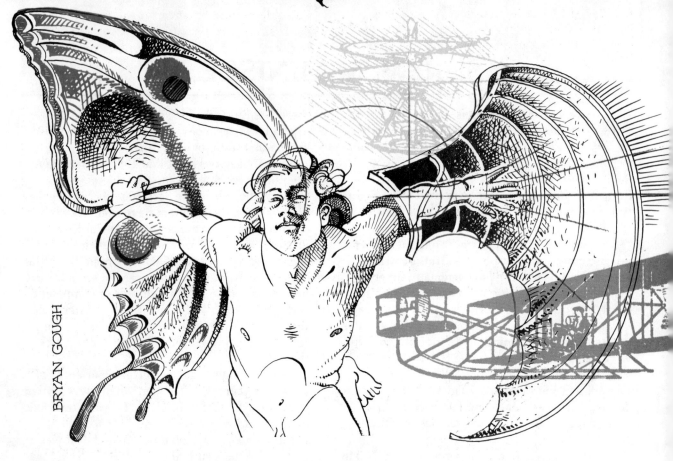

BRYAN GOUGH

WHY SKI ANYWAY?

"Step one in assembling your new Japanese barbeque is to attain peace of mind."
Robert M. Pirsig

Man has always possessed the uncanny ability to adapt a technological device originally invented for utilitarian purposes to attain more abstract ends, particularly for recreation and entertainment (e.g. a powerboat used for waterskiing instead of just for crossing over to the other side of the lake). This characteristic parallels the bicameral concept that claims the left side of the brain is responsible for rational, analytical thinking, while the right side operates more esoteric processes like creativity, emotions and non-analytical thought. In short, one side is for function, the other for fun; hence, vehicles of function like cars, planes, bikes, skis, etc. (products of left side activity) can eventually cross over to become vehicles of fun (a result of right side activity). Intrinsic to the word "function" is the word "fun."

Anchored deep in the recesses of every human being's heart is the covetous desire to fly, literally or metaphorically. Ever since Icarus set the precedent when, with wax wings, he flew too close to the sun (which melted his wings and forced him to return unceremoniously to Earth) man has been painfully aware of his aerial limitations. This doesn't mean he doesn't *try*—quite the contrary; lessons gleaned from Icarus' mishap only gave greater impetus to the drive to design technological devices that would successfully propel the aeronautical dream. One prerequisite of flight is to travel from point A to point B without walking or expending vast reserves of energy, and an endless list of "surrogate" wings has been invented and utilized to approximate this ethereal act. The riding of a horse was probably man's first introduction to a floating motion and rhythm through space that made the idea of non-pedestrian transportation so enticing. Nineteenth century man, in hot pursuit of the feeling, was pedaling his heart out atop bicycles, locomoting along steel rails and chug-a-chugging contentedly behind the wheels of automobiles. Speed was everything, freeing man (at least momentarily) from the shackles of a gravitational existence. These early modes of transport were revolutionary, but still remained earthbound. It was not until Orville and Wilbur Wright made their historic flight at Kitty Hawk in 1903 that Icarus' dream became reality. Finally man had mastered the mechanics and given himself access to the skies. The twentieth century stage was not set for man to explore the mental frontier of metaphorical flight, which has found one of its greatest and most popular expressions in the time-honored sport of skiing.

The popularity of a particular sport is directly related to the accessibility of the technological hardware necessary to participate in that sport, as well as the entertainment value generated by involvement in the sport. To illustrate this point, take a ridiculous case. Suppose there is a sport called "Watching Platinum Tarnish." The technological hardware, in this case platinum, is extremely expensive and inaccessible to most people. Just about the only involvement is passive observation of the tarnishing platinum—most people would rate this zero on an entertainment scale. Because of the outrageous cost and low entertainment value, we obviously do not see a rash of Tarnishing Tournaments. On the other hand, in a sport like skiing, one that incorporates a great deal of left and right brain activity, there is a great deal of interest and therefore, a higher entertainment value.

Skiing is a classic example of the unionization of bicameral thought; a balance is created between technological innovations and humanistic needs, producing a high level of pleasure. Skis were initially developed as a tool that enabled Norwegians to traverse snowfields (human genetics, lacking the ability to evolve 10-foot-long feet, had failed to solve this problem). American gold miners, in the mid-eighteen hundreds, used the wooden "snowshoes" pioneered by their Norwegian ancestors functionally for transportation, but also discovered them to be fun! Zooming down a snow-laden hill after toiling all day in a mine was an exhilarating experience akin to flying. It

was only natural to be curious as to who was the best zoomer, so races were held, crowds gathered and money was wagered (inevitably) on the outcome. Before anybody realized it, everybody was having fun—especially the participants! Skis had made the successful transition from technological tool (that acted as an extension to cover a human inadequacy) to popular, accepted equipment for human entertainment. Thus was born downhill skiing in America. Ever since those early days, advancements in technology have enhanced and influenced the style, technique and attitude of skiing (and vice versa). All of this adds up to make skiing a sport loaded with entertainment potential.

But what makes skiing so appealing? There are several factors that make it such an attractive form of recreation and, to understand this, it is necessary to bear in mind what the definitions of entertainment are, as related to skiing, of course. Good entertainment encompasses the following qualities: a sense of choice, display, risk, monetary outlay, no "redeeming virtues," social interaction and a sense of the uniquely mad. Consider each of the characteristics to see if they apply to skiing, making it a valuable form of entertainment.

1. Skiing offers a SENSE OF CHOICE. You can elect to do it or not do it. Skiing exists in a non-authoritarian atmosphere in which it is up to the individual to groom his/her own sense of self-confidence and accomplishments.

2. Skiing allows individual DISPLAY. Satisfying the ego is basic to the complete health of anyone (provided it is not carried to extremes). Bashing through the bumps, riding the edges of tolerance, "going for it!" are displays that have immediate rewards. Other skiers on the slope or lift can appreciate your level of, or attempt at, expertise and, of course, this gives you a rush. Hitler's organizational genius rested, in part, with his ability to make ordinary people feel extraordinary by involving them in grand displays which they simultaneously participated in and witnessed. Today, the philosophy of skiing as display leans more toward satisfying the criteria of the participant rather than the observer, but few can deny the psychological lift of hearing an unsolicited hoot or admiring word of encouragement when you are "ON," blazing a

BRYAN
GOUGH

path down a slope that Ullr would be envious of.

3. Skiing involves the element of RISK (threat and challenge). Americans like to watch or participate in activities that push the body to limits that might prove to be risky. Consider our Number 1 favorite sport—football, replete with its physical challenges. Even a ballerina or violinist who strains his/her abilities to new frontiers can create movements and notes that will evoke satisfaction, appreciation and even awe in both the performer and the audience. Skiing has its share of risk, threat and challenge; therein lies part of its popularity— flirting with danger and surviving results in returns that may not always be definable verbally, but solving the Rubik Cube Problem in the comfort of your own home does not provide the same sense of elation that mastering a particularly difficult mogul field does!

4. Lately it appears that whatever we participate in requires a MONETARY OUTLAY. We pay to have fun. Skiing is no exception; it extracts monetary remuneration, so subsequently it should follow that the higher the cost of a lift ticket, the greater the level of entertainment it ought to afford. Areas like Vail and Stowe are more expensive but the amenities they provide substantiate the price.

5. Good entertainment usually has no apparent REDEEMING QUALITIES. We indulge in recreation and entertainment to "recreate" and "entertain" that part of ourselves that garners little enhancement from a nine-to-five. The work ethic has redeeming value that contributes to the betterment of society and, at one time, anything else (like entertainment) was a waste of time. But for awhile, recreational activities have been regarded as influential factors in increasing man's efficiency and tolerance for this ethic. We need to "recharge" the right side of the brain, to balance our function with fun.

6. Skiing draws people into a greater SOCIAL INTERACTION; "birds of a feather flock together." Skiing, essentially an individualistic sport, generates a sense of camaraderie and a reason to relate shared experiences with others, creating a common ground for interpersonal exchange.

7. And finally, for entertainment to be enticing, it should be UNIQUELY MAD. Consider golf. There are enough golf courses in the United States that adding up their total acreages would equal the space occupied by the entire state of Rhode Island. And what *is* golf? A game that does nothing more than draw peculiar distinctions between people on the basis of their ability to poke little balls into widely separated holes in the ground! Skiing offers a similar madness in that people go up a hill with the sole intention of coming down it! And, if that's not enough, once down, the individual feels compelled to return to the top (only to face the same situation once again). Skiing is a mobius strip with a few wiggle-wiggles thrown in for good measure. How easily we mortals are entertained . . . but what a fine way to experience self-gratification!

BY PHIL BRITTIN

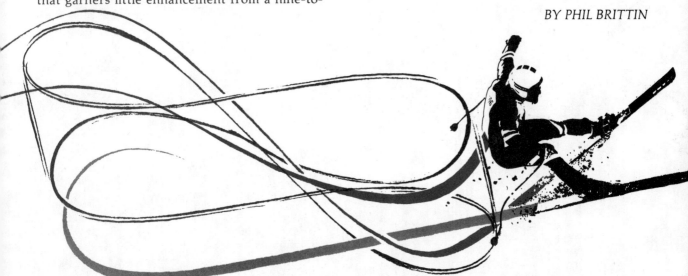

A HISTORY OF SKIING

THE EARLY YEARS

"And the end of all our exploring will be to arrive where we started and know the place for the first time."

T.S. Eliot

Skiing may well be over five thousand years old. Not many sports can make that claim. The word "ski" is the Norwegian name for a snowshoe that was used by the northern nations of the Old World. The name is derived from an Indo-Germanic root; it is found in the English words skid, skip, skiff, slide and skate. The Norwegian word *skilober* is a snowshoe. However, a Dr. Fowler wrote in the Year Book, Ski Club of Great Britain, in 1909, that the word "ski" came from a Germanic and Latin word implying splitting. Thus, ski referred to a split or splitting of wood into the ski shape.

In an unbroken glacial area, from Norway to the Bering Sea, skis, sleighs, skates and snowshoes have helped man cover great distances over snow and ice. These contrivances have been used for thousands of years for hunting, migration, warfare and sport. Early skis were used to prevent sinking into the snow but not necessarily for sliding. It is in the gliding instruments that we are interested and the so-called Hoting Ski is the oldest found. It was dug up by Swedish archeologists in a peat bog in 1921 and its age is estimated at over forty-five hundred years. It is made of pine wood and is wide and short. The Hoting Ski is now in the Swedish Ski Museum at Stockholm.

A stone carving uncovered by Gutorm Gjessing in northern Norway shows a man on skis. This carving is believed to be at least forty-five hundred years old, also. Other finds of that age have been made in Scandinavia and in Russia. The Kalutrask Ski, found in a Swedish marsh, is about thirty-nine hundred years old. The ski is 204 cm. long and is 15 cm. wide at the center. It is of pine wood. A stick, with a hollowed-out blade on one end, was found near the ski.

The Ovrebö Ski is in a museum in Oslo, Norway, and is about twenty-five hundred years old. The Aruträsk Ski, found in Lapland, is fifteen hundred years old.

Prehistoric skis are divided as follows:

(1) *The Northern Arctic Type:* This was wide and short. Straps were attached through vertical holes in the top of the ski. The ski bottom was covered with hide. This ski is still used in Siberia.

(2) *The Southern Type:* This was long and turned up at the top, resembling the skis of the 1930's. It had high side pieces for toe straps and holes for heel bindings. The ski was used in mid-Europe from the Urals to southern Norway.

(3) *The Central Nordic Type:* These consisted of skis of unequal length. The left ski was long and grooved. The right was covered with fur for traction and was called "Andor." The locale where this ski was used is now modern Lapland.

Some of the first skis were frames of pine, ash or birch covered with leather. Pine skis were tarred on the running surface.

Family and hunting scene (opposite page) of Norway from a book by Olaus Magnus, 1555.

THE HOTING SKI
This is the oldest ski. Found in a peat bog in Sweden, it is over 4,500 years old.

THE OVREBO SKI
This ski is about 2,500 years old. It is in a museum in Oslo, Norway.

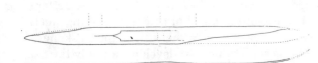

THE ARUTRASK SKI
This ski was found in Lapland and is 1,500 years old.

The first written mention of skiing is from the historian Procopuis (526-559 A.D.). He spoke of gliding Finns — Skridfiner — who raced against nongliding Finns. In 800 A.D., Skadi, the goddess of the ski, is mentioned in literature. In 880 A.D., King Harfagr praised Vighard, who shussed a slope. In 1060 is the first recorded race between Norway's King Harald the Hard and Heming Aslakson the Skier. In 1199, Saxo Grammacticus, the Danish historian, described how Finns skied and waged war on skis.

From 1200 on, skis are mentioned in Norwegian history. They become less evident in the history from 1250-1400. The Russians used skis for military campaigns in 1483. In 1525 there is mention of Norwegian postmen on skis. But it was not until the sixteenth century, when the printing press was widely used, that skiing became widely known. The most famous of ski books is one by Olaus Magnus, the Swedish bishop who was exiled to Norway. He published a book about Norway in 1555, which shows an illustration of hunters skiing. The pictures are not really descriptive because they are an artist's woodcuts and do not represent scenes witnessed firsthand by Olaus Magnus. Nevertheless, the book is considered a fundamental historical source and the illustrations are reproduced in many other publications.

Not until 1650 was a correct picture of a Norwegian ski reproduced. It was published in *Saxo Grammacticus* — a Danish history by Steffanius. An Italian priest, Francesco Negri, wrote a book describing his travel through Scandinavia in 1663 — although the book was not published until 1700. He was the first to describe a turn to a standstill. In 1673 a German, Johann Scheffer, published good pictures of Lapp skiers in *Opera Laponia*. The illustrations show one long and one short ski typical of the Lapps.

In 1689, Valvasor, the German author, made first mention of skiing on the continent and related that the peasants of Krain (Carniola, an

Picture of a Norwegian ski of 1644 published in *Saxo Grammacticus*.

Austrian province) were strong skiers. He stated, "They run downhill on short skis, with a stick in their hands and all the weight of their body well to the rear." He described the skis as wooden boards one-quarter inch thick, six inches wide and about five feet long. They were turned up and had a strap in the center for the feet. Valvasor said he had never seen this invention in other lands (referring to the European continent).

A description of skiing, with good pictures of men on skis, appeared in a book of travels by a Dutch sea captain, de Jong. He described a visit to Norway and the book shows Norwegian troops on skis. The first handbook for Norwegian ski troops was written in 1733 by Jens Henrik Emahusen. A description of skiing is found in Sir Arthur de Capell Brooke's *A Winter in Lapland And Sweden,* 1827. He notes that the "machines" are by no means easy to use where the ground is precipitous.

Lapp skier published in a Latin Work, *Opera Laponia*, in 1673 by Johann Scheffer.

S ondre Nordheim, a Norwegian, introduced ski jumping at the end of a gradient. In 1843 Tromso, the Lapp, won a cross country race using two poles — one with a disk near the tip. The Osier binding was developed by Sondre Nordheim in 1850, and the Norwegian practice of skiing spread all over the world. Norwegian skiers were in Germany in 1853, Australia in 1855 and New Zealand in 1857. In 1865, Lt. Col. Wergeland detailed a history of Scandinavian skiing. It helped to revive skiing in Norway. The first ski races were held near

Christiania, the capital of Norway, in 1866. In 1867, the Winter Sports Association of LaPorte, California, held a race; prizes of $75 were given. By 1868, the telemark skiers appeared in Christiania. Here, Sondre Nordheim jumped eighteen meters without a stick and he swung to a standstill with a telemark, wearing skis of the same length. The Norwegian press, for the first time, discussed ski techniques. In 1870, a downhill race was held in Plumas County, California. The ski club of Christiania was organized in 1877. Meanwhile, in Switzerland (1873) Dr. Herwig used skis in Arosa and Dr. Alexander Spengler was experimenting at Davos. In 1878, the first skiers appeared on the snows of France.

The first exhibition jumping meet was held in 1879 by the Hemmestveit brothers from Telemark; they then opened the world's first ski school. During the 1880's, considerable jumping and cross country competition was taking place. The Huseby Hill competitions were held in 1883, and jumping and cross country became separate events. In the United States, the first ski club had been formed in 1887, at Ishpeming, Michigan and a tournament was held. In 1884, German foresters started using skis and Norwegian students were skiing in the Black Forest. Dr. Fridtjof Nansen, a Norwegian, crossed the southern portions of Greenland in 1888 using sledges and skis; the journey took forty days and covered a distance of five hundred kilometers. In 1890, Nansen's book, *The First Crossing of Greenland,* was published and translated into many languages. We quote the following passage: "Of all the sports of Norway, skiing is the most national and characteristic. As practised in our country, it ranks first in the sports of the world. Nothing hardens the muscles and makes the body so strong and elastic; nothing gives better presence of mind and nimbleness; nothing steels the willpower and freshens the mind as skiing. This is something that develops not only the body but also the soul — it has a far deeper meaning for a people than many are aware of and a far greater national importance than is generally supposed." No book has had greater influence upon skiing than Nansen's work. It was descriptive of equipment, with drawings and methods. Wilhelm Pauleke (German), Colonel Christopher Iselin (Swiss), Mathias Zdarsky (Austrian) and others were greatly influenced by this book. Nansen experimented with various skis and woods, and the Telemark ski design was to be popular for almost fifty years.

Ski literature is important in the evolution of ski technique. Many techniques have been developed in the minds of their creators. But ideas are not techniques until written down, defined, published and made readily available.

Mathias Zdarsky (1874-1946) is considered the father of the Alpine Ski Technique. It was the German translation of Nansen's book that transformed Zdarsky into a skier. The first winter after reading Nansen's book he skied alone — never seeing another skier. In 1896, Zdarsky wrote the first methodical analysis and description of a ski technique, *The Lilienfelder Skilauf Technik*. Zdarsky laid the groundwork for other early ski technicians. He experimented with bindings and skis and eventually designed the binding that bore the name of his hometown — the Lilienfeld binding. Zdarsky was one of the first to teach skiing on a systematic, regular basis. His school was successful — by 1908 it had twelve hundred pupils — and he attributed his success as a ski instructor to discipline.

Zdarsky's skis were short, had no grooves and were unsteady for straight running. He used a single pole (a stick) without a basket or disk applied during turning and skiing to keep the speed down. Although Zdarsky advocated that body weight should not rest on the stick, he pointed out that trailing the stick helped maintain a steady position. Zdarsky, his Lilienfeld technique and binding have long disappeared. The short, grooveless ski was never very popular. Neither was the use of the stick as a brake. Nevertheless, Zdarsky remains in his position as the true father of all Alpine skiing.

BY BILL LASH

TECHNIQUE & TECHNOLOGY

"One machine can do the work of fifty ordinary men. No machine can do the work of one extraordinary man."

Elbert Green Hubbard

It is interesting to explore the development of ski technology and how its growth has facilitated enjoyment of skiing and augmented its entertainment value. Both technology and technique, over time and in a convoluted process, shoulder the responsibility for advancements in the sport.

The ongoing process of developing styles and equipment has always been the synthesis of thought and quality of available materials. On the other hand, sometimes technology has helped to foster style. In the mid-sixties, racing styles pioneered by the French emphasized "sitting back." This technique had been encouraged, in part, by the new plastic boots that gave more lower leg support, accompanied by the introduction of fiberglass skis with stiff tails. Not to be outdone, though, enterprising hotdoggers who capitalized on the sitting back style commanded an important role in the direction of equipment technology. By taping tongue depressors to the backs of their ski boots, they discovered that they could sit back even further on their skis; they were able to pull off new and dramatically "radical" maneuvers. Coupled with the timely spirit of rebellion (prevalent in America during the Viet Nam War era) these hotdoggers created a whole new style of skiing called exhibition/freestyle. Industry technology responded immediately with Jet Sticks and high-top boots that served the same function as the tongue depressors. Because of evolving technique, equipment was demanded upon to adjust accordingly.

This leapfrog process that technique and technology play out with each other is obvious in an event that occured in the early thirties. Rudolph Lettner, a metal worker and skier, was sick and tired of having his all-wood skis torn to splinters by exposed rocks. Applying a bit of technology, Lettner outfitted his skis with metal edges, hoping the armor would increase the life of his hickories. Not only was his experiment a success, but the new edges demanded a change in technique. The carved turn was now a reality, thanks to the better bite of a metal edge. This development led to more angulation of the body and a deeper forward lean (Vorlage) which was characteristic of the Arlberg ski school. Lettner's modest innovation triggered a chain reaction of growth in skiing technique.

This new emphasis on the carved turn

produced a greater awareness of the energy transfer path from leg to boot to binding to ski. It was obvious that increased forward lean created load demands that the old bear trap bindings could not handle. This problem was solved after 1935, as companies like Hvam and A&T developed cable safety bindings that held the boot heel securely in a fixed position. Now skiers could maintain better control over their ski edges and, consequently, worry less about the injurious aspects of a fall, but the increased energy transferal began to take its toll on another link

- Pre 1900's - —1910's— 1920's —1930's— 1940's —1950's— 1960's 1970's —1980's—

As skiing technique advanced so did the evolution of skis. The needs of the serious skier and the success of new building materials put ski design onto the level of high technology, resulting in modern-day boards designed and produced for maximum performance.

in the equipment system . . . boots. As skiing became more aggressive, soft leather boots were increasingly required to accommodate the brunt of the load. To alleviate this problem, steel shanks (in some cases, plywood) were installed in the leather sole to counteract the buckling phenomenon created by fixed heel bindings. Six-foot-long thongs were also painstakingly wrapped around the boots to enhance the ankle support and insure greater contact with the skis. By 1940, it was realized that technological refinements in the leg-boot-binding-ski relationship had to be made. Unfortunately, this insight was put on hold due to World War II; in that era, recreational skiing was forced to a virtual standstill.

Just as the War put a sitzmark on the trail of skiing history, it also produced materials and innovations that could streamline and popularize the sport. After the War, thousands of returning GI's exhibited skiing skills they had learned while training at Camp Hale, Colorado; headquarters for the Army's Tenth Mountain Division (the division trained men for ski mountaineering warfare). Simultaneously, $2-a-pair Army surplus ski boots hit the commercial market. Newcomers could now afford to attempt to ski. A wildcat interest in skiing flourished during the early fifties and a slew of ski areas opened to accommodate new enthusiasts.

On the technological front, things were a poppin' in response to the growing number of skiers. Aircraft engineers like Howard Head left their wartime laboratories and, armed with a knowledge of new materials like aluminum, fiberglass and plastic, began to integrate their understandings into a peacetime economy. Aluminum — lightweight, resilient and strong — had already proven its worth as sheathing on Air Force bombers. Fiberglass, also developed by the Air Force, had just been invented in the late forties as an electronically transparent material ideal for antennas and radar dishes. What was good for aerospace should be just as good for skis, so engineers began constructing them from these versatile materials. The gap between technology and technique narrowed when Howard Head, in 1950, introduced his "Standard" ski, an aluminum sandwich. The revolution was on! The Head Standard sounded a death knell for ash and hickory laminates that had been so popular until the newly-sophisticated fifties. The easy-flexing aluminum ski was virtually indestructible, did not warp (like its wooden

predecessors) and was extremely fast due to its plastic-coated base. Because of its non-torquing characteristics (there was no twisting along the ski's length) the ski could really bite into the slope. However, increased edge control also exacted a change in skiing style. By 1960, technique, at the behest of technology, was using new-found edge control to express Wedeln and Austrian heel thrusts. This, in turn, placed more of a demand on boot performance, an aspect of equipment not, as of yet, up to snuff.

From 1955 to 1965, the quest for better boots paralleled improvements in ski design. Together, boot and ski technology coalesced to define new techniques. In the late fifties, leather boots were stiffer (thanks to people like Bob Lange, who reinforced certain leather boot components with rigid plastic), higher and possessed an increasingly forward pitch. These new designs forced the knees forward, consequently lowering the hips and permitting more knee leverage to be efficiently transmitted to the skis. A skier's posture was also affected; now he could be oriented more squarely over his skis, able to enjoy more stability than the old style of extreme forward lean could afford.

Because of the increased sensitivity available in the new boots, there was a trend toward shorter ski lengths. Rossignol, Dynastar, Dynamic and Sailer fiberglass skis with their stiffer tails, in conjunction with the improved boot designs, promoted the "sitting back" style. Skiers discovered new dimensions in rear-edge control, an advantage that made skiing a dream.

By the mid-sixties, sophisticated boot technology complemented the built-in qualities of the new fiberglass skis. All-plastic buckle boots (like Lange Competitions and Rosemounts) securely anchored the ankle, as well as the rest of the foot, and conveyed load and leverage power to the ski edges lightning-quick. With the increased responsiveness of skis and boots, skiers possessed total edge control and were able to sit back with more confidence. Boot tops got higher in the late sixties and skiing grew more "radical." Foot-conforming flow materials and injected polyurethane foams made much more comfortable ski boots. Anti-friction devices made safety release bindings more dependable. The bond between legs, boots, bindings and skis was emphasized. All technological innovations evolved to the point where skis and boots became extensions of the skier's will; they encouraged new techniques rather than hindering performance.

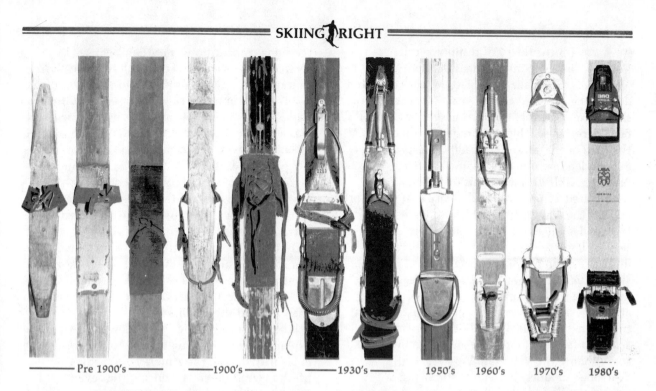

Pre 1900's — 1900's — 1930's — 1950's — 1960's — 1970's — 1980's

Keeping in step with available materials, ski bindings have evolved from simple leather straps to highly mechanized "step-ins." Experts predict the next stage in binding technology will be sophisticated microcircuitry and computerized plates that will electronically release when stress loads peak.

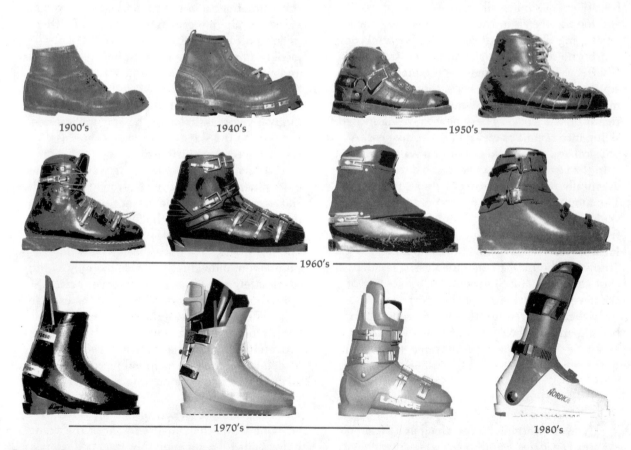

1900's   1940's   1950's

1960's

1970's   1980's

Gone are the days when the well-heeled skier donned heavy leather boot, stood for hours in a bathtub-ful of water and waited until they "dried to fit." Today, lightweight plastics, foams and various petro-chemical derivations have supplemented tortuous leather boots and the agony of "da feet."

With the flurry of technological innovations and a subsequent fractionalization of styles that occurred during the so-called golden years (1950-1970) of skiing, American ski instruction was left rather bewildered as to which technique to advocate. At the turn of the seventies, traditionalists expounded upon "pretty" skiing a la Stein Ericksen. Cliff Taylor and his disciples of GLM (Graduated Length Method) swore that the short ski was the way to go. Then there were the "renegades," just out there doing their "own thing." They probably exerted the greatest influence upon the direction taken by American ski instruction. These "black sheep" began by discarding the authoritarian, ski school atmosphere that stressed stylized final forms as the ultimate goal in skiing. In the spirit of rebellion (as mentioned, the general civil unrest surrounding the Viet Nam War years) they developed uniquely individualistic skiing and teaching styles which collectively were known as freestyle.

Decked out with high-backed boots reaching mid-calf and high-performance skis, the freestylers debunked all theories of ski physics and took to the air in the early seventies. It was an exciting time — hotdoggers like Wayne Wong, "Airborne" Eddie Ferguson and Suzy (Chapstick) Chaffee were pushing newly-marketed equipment to its limits. Helicopters, aerials, mogul bashing, daffys and mobius flips were de rigeur on the slopes. These new moves launched skiing into realms of elevated consciousness. A physical and mental ski revolution was on.

In the seventies, skiers began to deviate drastically from the concept of traditional skiing. The mono-ski made an appearance. People were ski hangliding into the wild blue yonder while freestylers leaped and bounced through ski-space. Helicopters started lifting more and more "snowfield hounds" to once inaccessible regions so they could recapture that pure-skiing feeling of the developmental years of the sport.

By the mid-seventies, the "I-ME" generation had blown the whole sport of skiing wide open. It became a viable, sometimes extreme, expression of the self.

All of this exploration had, of course, good and bad points. A great number of people were learning to ski. This put a strain on ski area capacities. Some enthusiasts abandoned Alpine skiing in favor of the less crowded conditions offered by Nordic skiing. Eventually, freestyle competitions met their demise. Newcomers (even hardcore zealots) disregarding caution, wound up paraplegics (or, in some cases, dead) which branded the wild freestyle with a bad name. It was inevitable anyway, because freestyle was a victim of the very thing that had prompted its birth — over-organization and too many rules.

Apparently, people had to go to extremes before the proverbial "happy medium" was reached. By the end of the seventies, energies settled down and refocused. The ski industry was extremely sensitive to the process of ski technology and concentrated its efforts on comfort and improved safety devices. Innovations like the boot plate and ski brake, assuaged the concern of the skier; he could concentrate more than ever on the act of skiing.

Liberating technology that allowed the mind to explore the act of skiing started to manifest itself in ski instruction; the American Teaching Method (ATM) evolved during the seventies. It was a synthesis of all previous styles, emphasizing the humanistic approach to skiing. It valued understanding rather than the perfection of traditional final forms that had been deemed the ultimate goal in the past. Ski instructors like Horst Abraham were instrumental in furthering philosophies exemplified by the ATM. These ideologies are based on hemispheric research (left and right brain functions) and a humanistic approach to skiing. By 1980, refinements in the ATM were regarded in the ski world as innovative breakthroughs, having applications, not only to the skier on the slopes, but also toward everyday existence.

Today, skiing has come a long way from the gold miners with their twelve-foot-long wooden skis, steadied by a single balance pole, racing down nameless hills in the Sierras and Rockies. Nowadays, the disparities between technology and technique have never been so few; increasing numbers of individuals are able to enjoy skiing more safely and efficiently than ever before. It is yet to be seen if skiing will become the exclusive sport of the wealthy — the economy will determine that. In the meantime, skiing has proven itself an excellent form of recreation loaded with entertainment value, continually adaptable and accommodating to the whims of social and technological change. Will it survive into the twenty-first century? Only time, economics and the enlightenment of the skiing individual will determine that fate.

BY PHIL BRITTIN

EVENTS IN THE GROWTH OF SKIING

THE HISTORICAL EVENT	THE SIGNIFICANCE

1800's Skiing in the U.S. where Norwegian populations are found.

U.S. and Canadian skiing will be years behind Europe. Techniques adapted to rolling hills — not steep Alpine slopes. No heel bindings used.

1854 America's first ski factory began operating out of old "Buckskin" Porter's wood-turning shop at Saw Pit Flat, near Sutter's Mill in California. Porter built twelve-foot-long wooden skis (known as "Racing Propellers") for the gold miners.

Skis (also called snowshoes in the mid-1800's) are manufactured in America as an invaluable means for transportation through snow-laden fields rather than for their recreational potential.

1856 John A. "Snowshoe" Thomson became the first skiing mailman, delivering mail on oak skis to isolated mining communities in the Sierras. His route was from Placerville to Carson, a distance of about 90 miles.

1860 America's first chairlift may have been operating near a town now known as Johnsonville in California. A brochure from the Plumas-Eureka State Park claims that "skiers with their twelve-foot skis, rode ore buckets on a conveyor up to a mine located above the ore mill."

Alpine skiing is more accessible.

1861 The world's first ski club is organized in Kiandra, Australia by Norwegian and Australian gold miners.

Skiing, initially regarded as a mode of transport, is recognized and organized as a sport.

1861 Sondre Auversen Norheim becomes the first ski designer. His innovations: 1. shorter skis (eight feet in length); 2. "waisted" skis, i.e., the area under foot narrower than the tips and tails; 3. anchored heels with a strap made from twisted willow twigs.

Boots immovably affixed to skis gave the skier a greater degree of maneuverability, thereby making skiing more manageable and attractive to beginners.

1864 Fritz Huifeldt invents the first toe iron binding.

1866 Sondre Norheim demonstrates the Telemark turn with a new twist — a parallel stop turn later called the "Christiania," after the old capital of Norway.

Nordheim's turn makes the beginning of the development of new ski techniques.

1867 America's first ski club is formed in La Porte, California.

1879 Tommy Todd averages 88 mph over a 1,804 foot course on Lost Sierra Mountain, north of Lake Tahoe, California. It was thought by witnesses that he was traveling close to 100 mph near the end of the course (unofficially, of course).

This is the first chronicled record of an organized downhill time trial in America, although it is speculated the gold miners had been holding informal races 15-20 years prior to Tommy's amazing feat.

THE HISTORICAL EVENT	THE SIGNIFICANCE
The first official ski manual is published by Jens Emmahusen of Trondheim, Norway, for use by army ski troops.	*The first formalized ski instruction begins.*
1888 Father Fridtjof Nansen and a group of six cross the southern tip of Greenland on skis. Nansen's book, *Paa Ski Over Gronland*, is published two years later.	*Nansen's book, translated into many languages, receives worldwide attention and attracts other skiers, i.e. Paulke, Hoek, Iselin and Zdarsky.*
1890's Wilhelm Paulke, a German, is the first pioneer of mountaineering. Henry Hoek is one of the first Germans to race and one of the greatest ski mountaineers.	*The pioneers are the early proponents of skiing, equipment, mountaineering, etc.*
Christopher Iselin, father of Swiss skiing, founds the Swiss Ski Federation. First Swiss ski club is formed.	
1894 Colonel Bilgeri introduces military skiing to the Austrian Tiroler Corps.	*Bilgeri's experience will prove of value later.*
1896 Mathias Zdarsky experiments with the sport on Norwegian skis in the early 1890s, and in 1896, writes the first illustrated ski manual, *Lilienfeld Schilauf Technik.* He uses short skis and one pole.	*Zdarsky is the father of the Alpine Technique; he contributes the snowplow and stem turn. He writes first treatise on avalanches.*
1901 Mathias Zdarsky is the first person in Austria to have taught skiing on a regular basis. He has 612 pupils.	*His technique is called the "Lilienfeld Technique." His military courses extend to Germany and Switzerland.*
1901-02 French Army organizes first military ski classes with Norwegian instructors. Italian ski club forms at Turin.	*Civilian skiing is still in its infancy.*
1903 Ski Club of Great Britain is formed.	
The Johnston Hardware Company of Bangor, Maine, features for the first time in America "mail-order skis." The catalogue advertises them as "the finest skis of solid native ash, complete with leather harness for $2.95."	*Skis are still considered a tool, but their utilization in America in a recreational way is gaining a greater following.*
1904 Zdarsky has 1,000 students. In later life, survives an avalanche with over eighty fractures; he lives to the age of seventy-two.	
National Ski Association of America is formed by Carl Tellefsen in Ishpemig, Mich. on Feb. 28.	*NSA has sixteen clubs by 1906.*
Victor Sohm holds ski courses in the Arlberg using the Norwegian Technique.	*Sohm teaches Hannes Schneider, who is fourteen years old, to ski.*
Ski-Running is written by E. C. Richardson, C.	*First ski book in the English language.*

THE HISTORICAL EVENT	THE SIGNIFICANCE

Somerville, and W. R. Rickmers.

1905-06 Zdarsky sets a torlau near Lilienfeld, Austria.

Race continues until 1938.

1906 Henry Hoek writes *Der Ski.*

It is Norwegian Technique based on Zdarsky's stem system.

1907 Hannes Schneider receives a call from St. Anton-am-Arlberg, Austria, to be a ski teacher.

With the sport of skiing so young, Schneider has time to practice and experiment.

1908 Fritz Huitfeldt describes a type of slalom in a book called *Kria.*

1909-10 Schneider invents the stem Christiania after he experiments with the Telemark.

Schneider races in Switzerland, wins. Starts his method of instruction.

1910 Colonel Georg Bilgeri, an Austrian army officer who was once challenged to a duel by Zdarsky over a description of a stem turn, writes *Der Alpine Skilauf.*

Bilgeri's book analyzes the Zdarsky and Norwegian ski techniques.

1910-11 Vivian Caulfield writes *How to Ski;* W. R. Rickmers writes *Skiing for Beginners.* Marius Eriksen uses the Telemark turn to be champion of Norway for ten years.

English begin to show influence upon skiing. Caulfield deals a mortal blow to the single stick (pole).

1911 C. J. Luther writes *Der Moderne Wintersport.*

He introduces the term "stem christie."

1912 Teddy Roosevelt, on Jan. 12th at Sagamore Hill, becomes the first U.S. President to ski.

Schneider has a staff of two instructors. The Telemark turn begins to lose its influence in ski technique. However, it is to be taught for twenty-five more years in some parts of the world.

Schneider develops a class system with three stages — beginner, intermediate, advanced. He systematizes the sport so it can be taught.

Skiing is written by Sir Arnold Lunn.

Lunn talks of downhill skiing without a stick.

1916-18 Schneider teaches skiing on a mass scale to Austrian Mountain Troops. The supervision of classes and instructors becomes a necessity of ski school organization.

Schneider discovers need for supervision of instructors and ski classes by director of ski school.

1916-25 A successor to the Telemark turn was the open christie. This was and still is called the scissor christie. It was seen in this country in parts of the West until World War II.

1920 Canadian Amateur Ski Association is formed.

Modern-day ski racing becomes important in Europe and starts in North America.

From 1920-30, ski technique evolution stands still. Turns are made by a stem and weight change.

In the 1920's an Englishman, Sir Arnold Lunn, contributes a lasting significance to skiing. He studies technique and snow,

There is little rotation and no sideslipping. Most skiing is in deep snow. The uphill facilities are limited; there are few skiers by present standards.

and writes books on mountaineering. Lunn revolutionizes competitive skiing. Sir Arnold Lunn's slalom is adopted into the Olympic program.

1923 The first American slalom course is set up by Professor Charles Proctor of Dartmouth College.

1924 The First Olympic Games are held at Chamonix, France; only Nordic events are featured. Not until 1936 are Alpine events included in the repertoire of the Games.

Federation International de Ski (FIS) forms. Ski instructors meet at St. Christoph for a discussion of a ski course.

All instructors and schools adopt the Schneider Arlberg Technique.

First International Downhill and Slalom and first Parsenn Derby founded.

The rapid development of racing — British influence rises.

1925 German and Austrian Ski School directors meet at St. Anton.

1926 First downhill race held in the U.S. at Dartmouth.

Racing becomes an international sport.

Hannes Schneider and Dr. Frank write *The Wonders of Skiing.*

The Schneider influence is now written and published. His influence is felt.

1927 Sir Arnold Lunn writes *A History of Skiing.*

History is now recorded for skiing.

1928 Sir Arnold Lunn organizes the first Slalom Race — the Arlberg-Kandahar.

Erling Strom is America's first and only ski instructor (at Lake Placid, N.Y.).

Strom is one of the pioneers of American and Canadian skiing. He recognizes the potential of Stowe.

1928-30 Rudolph Lettner, a skier and metal worker from Salzburg, Austria, invents and patents the steel edge. Originally he had installed steel edges on his hickory skis with the intent of preventing them from wearing out. He finds, in addition, that the edges provide increased efficiency in narrow-tracked running and turning power.

Rudy's steel edge eventually contributes to the elimination of the deep crouch position in skiing and revolutionizes technique.

1930 The first speed trials, called the Flying Kilometer, are held at St. Moritz, Switzerland. Gustav Lantscher, the winner, is clocked at 66.4 miles per hour.

1931 By 1931, the first ski school in the United States is in operation at Peckett's Inn on Sugar Hill in Franconia, N.H. The school is begun in Decem-

Buchmayr is the first man brought from Europe to teach skiing in the U.S. He teaches the Arlberg crouch with extreme down-up-down motion.

THE HISTORICAL EVENT	THE SIGNIFICANCE

ber of 1929, by Sig Buchmayr. He charges $1 a lesson.

1932   In 1932 F. Schuler's *Ski Mechanics* is published in Switzerland.

This will become the basis for the Swiss Technique.

The first ski trail is cut at Franconia. The Third Winter Olympic Games is held at Lake Placid, N.Y.

The games contribute to the growing interest in winter sports in the U.S.

1932   Norwegian Sigmund Rund, sporting twelve-foot-long wooden skis and a balance pole, schusses the Headwall at Tuckerman's Ravine, New Hampshire, thrilling bystanders (but history remembers Toni Matt, who did a no-turn schuss in 1939 down the steep slope, as conqueror of the ravine).

Like the Winter Games, feats such as these further enhance the popularity of skiing.

1932   The world's first rope tow is invented by Alex Foster and installed at Shawbridge, Quebec. It is powered by a Dodge automobile, jacked up on blocks, with a rope looped around a wheel rim.

Up until now, the greatest obstacle preceding the exhilaration of going down a hill was that one had to laboriously climb up it. The rope tow eliminated the most onerous aspect of the sport.

1933   Theodore C. Cooke erects a 3000-foot-long rope tow on Gunstock Mountain in New Hampshire, claiming it to be the first rope tow operating in America.

1933   The Swiss ski schools organize and a two-week instructor course is held. Fifty instructors and directors attend. This number will increase to one hundred by 1936.

At this meeting is the first attempt to segregate technical knowledge (explanation and demonstration) from methodology. This separation is to enable the teacher to build up lessons logically and in an interesting manner, to pick out the right aspect of the technique and to instruct as individually as possible.

The Swiss ski schools decree: the ski school director has the task of transmitting to his instructors that which is learned in special classes.

The training of ski instructors begins to take on importance.

1933   Adolph Attenhofer develops the first complete all-metal binding that securely holds the heel in place, with "walking" and "skiing" metal hook hold-downs.

This will combine with the steel edge to accelerate technique and racing development. The fixed heel binding provides for more dynamic turning and better edging control on hard-packed ski slopes.

1934   Clinton Gilbert hitches a continuous length of rope to the rear wheel of his Model T Ford and hauls four skiers up a hill near Woodstock, Vermont. The folks around Woodstock claim they have the first operating rope tow in North America.

Oft-disputed as to who really "dunnit" first, the point remains that in the early 1930's rope tows proliferated around New England, luring more and more skiers to the slopes.

1934   Erich Konstamn, an engineer from Zurich,

builds the world's first T-bar. The patent is dated August 17, 1934 and the lift made its debut in Davos in December of that year.

Hannes Schneider, an instructor at St. Anton is teaching the Low Arlberg crouch.

The crouch is awkward, the feet are wide apart.

1934-36   Anton Seelos, Austrian racer and trainer, coaches the French team which includes Emile Allais. Seelos uses a technique with complete body-rotation and counter-rotation with an up-un-weighting.

Seelos makes an important impact upon skiing; Allais learns an almost exclusively parallel turning style from him.

1936   The idea for a National Ski Patrol System starts after founding father Minnie Dole breaks his ankle at Stowe, Vermont.

The Patrol provides vital lifesaving functions at ski areas, alleviating the fears of injured skiers who might otherwise not have been assisted.

The first issue of SKI magazine is published by Alf Nydin in Seattle.

The chairlift is invented by Jim Curran, an engineer with the Union Pacific Railroad. He had designed loading systems for banana boats, so the transition from loading bananas to loading people is easily accomplished. Curran builds the first single chair-lift at Sun Valley in 1936.

The proliferation of chairlifts attracts more people to the sport of skiing.

Max Dercum begins a ski school near Dodge Ridge, California.

1935-36   Dr. F. Hoschek and Professor Freidl Wolfgang start a new approach to teaching skiing. Hoschek's system emphasizes:
  (1) Rotation.
  (2) Up-unweighting.
  (3) Uphill swing (uphill christies) to reach the downhill swing, the parallel swing and the stem swing.

Hoschek's study into the field of instruction will influence methods of instruction in large ski schools by 1938-40.

1936-38   Rotation will be the established technique for skiing by 1938. However, in 1936, others dispute this theory. Four authors write books on the concept of "twisting skiing." One book by Toni Ducia and Dr. Harald Reinl in Austria and the other by two Swiss — G. Testa and Professor E. Matthias. The "twisting technique" was misunderstood and generally rejected. These people were far ahead of their time.

All four authors are from different regions and independent of each other, develop the same fundamental principles for their technique and teaching system. The number of skiers who can demonstrate the technique is too small to make it popular.

Ducia and Reinl help instruct the French team in France. The French do not adopt the Ducia-Reinl technique. They go their own way (the French Allais).
  (1) Up-unweighting is discarded.

The success of Seelos influences the French.

THE HISTORICAL EVENT	THE SIGNIFICANCE

(2) Downward and forward movement with accentuated rotation is the chief characteristic of the French technique.

1937 Austrian ski instructors meet on technique at St. Christoph. Hannes Schneider, Toni Ducia, Dr. Hoschek, Dr. Freidl Wolfgang and others attempt to explore the teaching situation.

There are too many points to be compromised; the time is not ripe for uniformity.

Otto Schniebs has a ski school at Woodstock, Vt. (started 1935) and Whiteface, N.H.; Hannes Schroll School is at Yosemite; Otto Lang establishes schools at Mt. Rainier and Mt. Baker. Sun Valley is built.

Because of publicity, skiing becomes popular in all snow sections of the United States.

Emile Allais, France, wins the FIS downhill and slalom.

Allais' parallel technique startles the world.

Canadian Ski Instructors Alliance is formed.

A change is coming in ski technique.

The Swiss Ski Schools feel too much attention is given toward stemming in ski teaching.

1938 The Swiss, by 1938, have eliminated the notion of extreme forward lean and rotation. Swiss eliminate lower stem — keep body in a high position, weight is placed on the stemmed upper or outside ski.

Swiss feel the most important factor in technique is weight shift to the outside ski of the turn.

The follow through of turns uses a forward drop for unweighting and rotation.

The Arlbergers (Austrian) rotate from the shoulders and use lateral pressure (rotation) to pivot the skis.

Arlberg is extreme forward rotation.

The Swiss use a counter-rotary motion but pivot with the direction of the turn and the skis.

Swiss are more or less square to the skis.

A difference erupts between the Arlberg and the Swiss. Swiss emphasize the sideslipping — which the original Arlberg did not. The Swiss find that less body motion achieves the same result as the exaggerated forward swing. The Swiss find that with less rotation there is less recovery between turns.

Technique becomes a subject of discussion and the modern evolution of ski technique begins.

The French School adopts the Allais Technique.

Allais brings important new concepts to ski teaching:
1. That in ski teaching methods there can be dynamic changes.
2. That these changes often are an indirect result of racing necessities and techniques.

THE HISTORICAL EVENT	THE SIGNIFICANCE

Ski Francais by Allais, Paul Gignoux, and Georges Blanchon is published.

National Ski Patrol is formed.

The first skimobile lift is installed on Mt. Cranmore at North Conway, New Hampshire.

The first Aerial Tramway in the United States is installed at Cannon Mountain, Franconia, New Hampshire.

Sepp Rusch becomes the first Certified Ski Instructor to graduate from the U.S. Examinations held at Woodstock, Vermont.

The certification of ski instructors is recognized as a necessity that assures beginning skiers of receiving high-quality instruction. Previously skiers had no standard from which they could judge the ability and competence of an instructor.

1938 Boots are becoming stiffer, but the use of long thongs is still prevalent as a means to hold the boot to the ski and increase ankle support.

Stiffer boots are a response to the need for increased edge control due to the development of steel edges and fixed heel bindings.

1939 Otto Lang presents the first screening of an American ski movie called "Ski Flight" at Radio City Music Hall (it doubled with "Snow White and the Seven Dwarves").

Hjalmar Hvam markets the Hvam Saf-Ski binding, one of the first safety bindings. Anderson and Thompson (A&T) also market their version of releasable bindings with movable toe pieces and safety cables.

This marks the end of the "Bear Trap" era, and a step in the right direction in the prevention of leg injuries.

1940 The first operating T-bar in America is installed at Pico Peak, Vermont.

1941 Joy Lucas becomes the first female certified ski instructor.

1939-40 The outstanding differences in the Allais approach are:
1. Discarding of the stem position as the basis of learning christies; eliminates the sequence of snowplow, snowplow turn, stem turn, and stem christie.
2. Allais begins with sideslipping; he feels that skidding the skis is most important and should be taught first; he teaches the snowplow later.
3. Hip blocking is used to convey body rotation to the skis.
4. The Allais Technique emphasizes equal weighting of both skis.

The Allais system proves to the ski teaching world the importance of sideslipping, edge control exercises and uphill swings (christies) in ski teaching methods.

Edge control exercises are incorporated into ski school methodology. In the Arlberg method — free rotation — the leverage was dispatched into the ankles and feet. The French use hips to convey rotation to the skis. This represents a mechanical advantage.

1939-46 The war years stop the development of

The lack of skiing and facilities during the war creates a

THE HISTORICAL EVENT	THE SIGNIFICANCE

skiing. Some still occurs in Switzerland, Austria, France, and the United States, but it is limited.

postwar demand for the sport that is phenomenal. In the United States, neither resort facilities nor ski schools are able to meet demands until late 1940s.

Skiing plays a military role in some combat areas, and is used for recreation and the transportation of troops.

Skiing is introduced to thousands of troops during and immediately after the war. It serves as postwar recreation for Allied Occupational Forces in Europe and Japan.

1940 A single chair is installed at Stowe, Vt.

This was the last lift to be built in the U.S. until after WW II.

1942-43 Quartered at Camp Hale, Colo., the Tenth Mt. Division trains troops in skiing mountain warfare.

1946 The first Ski-Snowshoe race is held at Arapahoe Basin in Colorado. First-place winner received a can of cold beer.

The P-Tex (plastic) base is invented by the Swiss firm Muller and Co.

This eliminated the tedious task of waxing and provided a more efficient running base.

The first Coin Operated Racing System (CORS) debuts at Bromely, Snow Valley and Pico Peak.

Aspen, Colorado opens Dec. 15.

1947 Pomagalski invents the Pomalift.

The Poma Lift is fast, efficient and usually allows access to more difficult terrain.

1946-48 Ski resorts in Austria are occupied by France. French instructors train racers and conduct courses for the military.

The French are studied by the Austrians.

The Austrians feel that the French technique is not important as the course of instruction.

French use uphill christies and parallels without the stems and plows.

Austrian teachers begin to follow the basic thought of Hoschek — "on the direct road to swinging."

The Austrians feel that the stem swing is the central point of instruction.

1947 The commercial debut of plastic ski bottoms. The Attenhofer Temporite bottom is manufactured by the Propeller Company; this revolutionary new base is featured on Perma Cam and Northland skis.

The Temporite, along with other plastic bases (Kofix and P-Tex) result in faster skis and the tradition of waxing fades.

First double chair lift is installed at Berthoud Pass, Colo.

THE HISTORICAL EVENT	THE SIGNIFICANCE

Tey Manufacturing introduces the first all-aluminum ski called the "True Flex."

Aerospace technology developed during the War finds applications in the ski industry. Energy is refocused from a wartime economy to one of peacetime.

The Dexdahl Company of Cohasset, Mass. markets the Ski Tree, the first commercially available boot tree designed to prevents boots from warping.

Ski devices, some practical, some comical, began to innundate the ski market, as troops who skied in Europe created a demand for ski products in America.

Groswold and Magnan introduce "ski poles that stretch." As adjustable poles, they can be lengthened for ski touring or shortened for Alpine skiing.

1948 On October 8, the first "Prayer to Ulla" ceremony is held on Mount Baker, Washington. Ulla, a Scandinavian god, is the patron saint of skiers. The "prayer," insuring deep snows and intact bones, is held around a bonfire of "sanctified skis and poles" — those that have been broken while skiing.

Gretchen Fraser becomes the first American skier, male or female, to win Olympic medals — a gold in the slalom and a silver in the Alpine combined at the Winter Games in St. Moritz, Switzerland.

Gretchen's accomplishments inspire thousands to involve themselves in skiing. The Europeans begin to view America as a strong force to contend with in the formerly European-dominated Olympic Games.

Walt Schoenknecht, owner of the Mohawk Mountain Ski Area in Connecticut grew frustrated at the complete lack of snow; over Christmas, he trucked in giant blocks of ice. He crushed and chipped the ice up to cover his bare slope with the slush-like snow.

This was the first conscious, albeit primitive, attempt at artificial snow-making. Three men who had skied Walt's oversized snowcone, Hunt, Pierce and Rickey, were inspired enough the following year to tinker with nozzles that mixed snow and air to make artificial snow. By 1950, Mohawk installed a refined artificial snow-making system patented by Larchmount Engineering.

1948-49 Status of ski techniques in 1948 is summarized as follows:

The Swiss deserve more credit for progress in modern ski technique development. They have always stressed sideslipping. In the late forties the Swiss stress the importance of hips, legs and ankles as a means of effecting turning power.

Swiss: Develop each individual student according to ability. The Swiss do not stress standardization of methodology.

Unweighting is up-down-movement. Uphill stem is used. Turning is done on tips of the skis with unweighted heels. The Swiss use the snowplow and stem turn approach. Shoulder movements are not emphasized.

French: The French technique calls for unweighting with a down movement — followed with a forward lean with rotation. Although the Allais technique stresses equally weighted skis at the start of the

Some advocates of the French over-exaggerate the rotation and forward lean.

THE HISTORICAL EVENT	THE SIGNIFICANCE
turn, the outer ski is gradually weighted more toward the end of the turn.	*The French reach a peak in 1948 with the victories of Couttet and Oreiller at the 1948 Winter Olympics.*
Austrian: The Arlberg stresses sideslipping but with stemming maneuvers. The system uses upper-body rotation with a lower ski stem.	*Arlberg strength is in a transition phase.*
1949 Tyrol Company, of Montreal, Canada markets the Tenderfoot Anklet made from porous foam rubber.	*This device is an early attempt to provide more comfort in ski boot fit. It was a forerunner of the flow-filled inner boots of the Seventies.*
Howard Head markets the aluminum Head Standard.	*Head, a wartime engineer, uses his skills learned from aircraft design, to create one of the first successful metal skis, making use of new materials developed during the war.*
1949-50 Nylon ski boot laces are marketed.	*The "Age of Plastics" dawns.*
1948-50 The increasing number of skiers since World War II produces moguls in quantities that have never before been experienced. The extreme movements of the official French technique do not permit the quick action necessary to change direction through these moguls.	*The need for a great deal of traversing and sideslipping in the French technique makes the technique impractical for teaching at areas with trails only.*
Many new lifts are built in Europe and the U.S.	
The Arlberg technique, with stems, wind-up, and follow-through, is not adapted to mogul skiing.	
Because many of the old teachers have been lost in the war, the new generation of European skiers is largely self-taught.	*The Arlberg technique was satisfactory in its day and does not change.*
1948-52 Some of the younger skiers in Europe begin to ski with a relaxed style and use hip and leg action for rotation. Shoulders are held still.	*Their turns are called counter-shoulder turns.*
At the 1948 Olympics, Nogler, Schoepf, and Mall are watched and imitated by many new racers and skiers.	*Ski school methodology and ski technique is in a static state.*
The Austrians have watched and imitated the French and see the need to develop a new system of racing that will allow faster movements of the shoulders in the bumpy terrain and in slalom running.	*It becomes necessary to ski with the lower body and counterrotation. These updated turns are called reverse shoulder.*
In 1950-52 Toni Spiess, Christian Pravda, Hans Nogler, and Franz Gabl win international victories. All are Austrian.	*The new ski technique is a basis for the Austrian success.*
1950-51 The "new technique" begins to show up in the form of "mambo and wedeln."	*Mambo and Wedeln are used by Allais in Squaw Valley.*

THE HISTORICAL EVENT	THE SIGNIFICANCE
1950-51 Cubco markets a cableless, step-in binding.	*The fledgling ski industry begins to develop a sensitive responsiveness to skiers' needs.*
Rossignol and Kaestle skis, both designed as three-tiered ash laminates, dominate the ski market. By 1960, Kaestle captures 70% of the ski market with its infamous one-year guarantee.	*The late 1950's see a flurry of non-conventional ski designs and materials. The ideas work, but create skis that are stiff and hard to turn. The search for a softer ski is underway. Ski technology affects ski styles, e.g., the stiff-tailed ski encourages sitting back.*
1951 The first International Ski School Congress is held at Zurs, Austria, in order to reach an agreement on a unified technique for the central European ski schools. The congress is called by Austrian initiative, and the Austrian team demonstrates their current "rotation technique."	*The Congress becomes a basic means of international discussion and comparison of ski and teaching methods.*
1952 Andrea Mead captures gold medals in slalom and giant slalom at the Winter Olympic games in Oslo.	*Andrea's feat marks America's first double Gold Olympic Medal.*
1952-53 The first Carrera goggles are sold. Obermeyer markets windshirts. The first ski sweaters and turtlenecks with elasticized necks are imported.	*The appearance of post-war synthetic materials creates a new fashion line — Skiwear.*
1953 The second International Ski School Congress is held in Davos. The Swiss demonstrate their technique based on rotation of the body in the direction of the turn. They show a forward and downward movement of the body toward the tips of the skis.	*The French National School and the Italian National School of Skiing at Sestriere both show uniform techniques, but the Austrians fail to show a unified technique.*
1954 Professor F. Wolfgang, Professor S. Kruckenhauser, Dr. F. Rossner and other Austrian experts are watching the 1954 FIS "with interest." They analyze slow-motion movies of the best racers to help develop new ski technique.	*The new technique with hip and leg action resulting in "the comma" is built into a teaching method by the Austrians.*
Marker introduces the Simplex Safety Binding.	
The Dale Boison Company of Santa Monica, California markets an all-fiberglass ski.	*Both fiberglass and metal begin to supplant wood in ski construction in the fifties. Both are popular because they do not warp, loose their camber or have to be blocked.*
1954 Cadaver legs are twisted and crushed by Dr. Charles Rombold in an effort to garner fracture level statistics for binding manufacturers.	*Safety is becoming a major selling point for binding manufacturers, and a priority for skiers.*
1955 Obermeyer designs the first "flow" boot from a viscous liquid . . . "car grease."	*The search for the perfect foot-conforming material begins.*
Henke Speed Fit buckle boots appear on the market.	*The Henke buckle boot eliminates the cumbersome task of lacing and sets a precedent for the design of future boots.*

THE HISTORICAL EVENT	THE SIGNIFICANCE

Nelson Griggs develops the Nelson Edge Strip — a continuous metal edge for skis. Dr. C. G. Soits had invented the continuous edge called the Soita Angle Edge in the 1930's — but the breakthrough never caught on.

The continuous edge eliminates the old-style, segmented edge with its rust and loose screw problems. The continuous edge also facilitates more effective carving turns.

Harry Holmberg introduces the Hart Alumi-Flyte ski, the first ski made of spring steel, a wood core, aluminum and a plastic casing.

Both Holmberg and Head capitalize on new materials to increase the performance of skis. Wood skis are on the way out, following the path of the dinosaurs.

1955 First stretch pants are made by Bogner.

The baggy, canvas duck look is out until jeans & bib overalls make a brief appearance in the late 60's.

The third International Ski School Congress at Val D'Isere, France, brings to view the new development of ski technique by the Austrians. The Austrian contingent shows its technique to be practical, new and interesting. The Austrians show shortlinked christies. (This system was a new concept that eliminated upper body rotation even in the beginning exercises.)

The theory of movements of the new technique is not clear, but the Austrian demonstration creates an international controversy over technique. A dispute begins, even in Austria, over the new technique and rotation. One reason for eliminating rotation in the elementary stages is that it is not always needed in difficult turns that require an advanced inner shoulder. Thus, rotation is not logical to use in the elementary stages. This new development brings ski schools closer together.

The Austrian system shifts the initial turning impetus from the shoulders to the lower body in all levels of learning, from beginning to advanced. The technique places emphasis on the forward sideslipping, the stem turn and the stem swing. These basics are the central core of ski instruction. They are the basis for advancement to the parallel swings, and the Austrians consider the stem swing the most important turn for general use by all skiers. This was an instructive method advocated by Dr. Hoschek twenty years before.

The Austrians publish Professor Kruckenhauser's *Osterreichischer Schilerplan* — The Austrian Ski Teaching System.

This book makes it possible for the world's ski teachers to study the Austrian technique.

1956-57 There are different expressions of the new technique:
1. Austrians lead to parallel turns through a series of stem exercises. Austrians talk of "comma position."
2. The French lead to parallel from the parallel sideslip positions. French use the term "hip angulation."

The American Ski Schools are thrown into turmoil by the "new technique" — the Wedeln. Early translations and articles by Willy Schaeffler, Clemens, Hutter and others promote the demand for the new technique by the skiing public.

1956-57 Bob Lange begins supplanting certain parts of leather boots with fiberglass.

An early pioneer utilizing new post-War materials, Lange's experiments eventually lead him to develop the revolutionary "Lange Competition" boot in the early sixties.

1957 Jerry Colburn Nunn becomes the first fe-

The Snow Rangers are responsible for avalanche control.

THE HISTORICAL EVENT	THE SIGNIFICANCE
male Snow Ranger to graduate from the Ranger Academy in Alta, Utah.	*Jerry's accomplishment is an early victory for the Women's Movement.*
The first aluminum ski poles are made by Scott.	*The heavier wood and bamboo poles are replaced with lighter and more durable materials.*
Anabel "Ma" Moriarty knits her son Marvin the first three-pointed "Original Moriarty" hat.	*The Moriarty hat becomes the trademark of skiers everywhere.*
The "new technique" confusion in the U.S. is caused by: 1. Bad and incorrect translations. 2. Translations by nonexperts. 3. Personality cult among some ski schools and teachers. 4. Publicity. 5. People writing about technique who are not qualified. 6. Experimental theory. 7. The instructor or school who "want to be left alone."	*The size of the country and the thinking of the progressive ski school heads bring about the demand for some national meetings to discuss mutual problems of technique, method, certification, etc.*
Otto Steiner represents the United States at the IV International Ski School Congress at Storlien, Sweden.	*Steiner attends at his own expense and contributes to the international acceptance of U.S. ski teachers.*
G. Joubert and J. Vuaret publish *Ski ABC* in France; they describe the French version of "angulation —flexion and recoil."	*Translations are soon made in English. The book helps to both clear and confuse the technique question.*
1958 Buddy Werner becomes the first American to win a major European race — the combined at the Lauberhorn.	*Werner is an inspiration to young American racers.*
The Alta meeting of the National Ski Association Ski Instructors Certification Committee; the East and the West meet to discuss and demonstrate technique methods and mechanics. Attending the meeting are: Kerr Sparks, Paul Valar, Jimmy Johnston, George Engel, Jr., Willy Schaeffler, Bill Lash, Alf Engen, Junior Bounous, Ed Heath, Dr. Chuck Hibbard, and Earl Miller. It is agreed to hold annual meetings. This meeting helps to clear the controversy over "the new technique."	*First national meeting of the National Ski Association Ski Instructors Certification Committee where all divisions are presented. It is discovered that the national problem is not only certification but technique, recruiting and training of instructors, and related business problems of ski teaching.*
1958-59 Clif Taylor, considered the father of Graduated Length Method (GLM) graduates his first pupil, Ann Hedges, on a pair of short skis.	*In the next decade, Taylor's teaching method is a boon to thousands who might not have otherwise tried the sport.*
The Official Austrian Ski System is translated by Palmedo. Doug Pfeiffer writes *Skiing with Pfeiffer*. Bill Lash publishes *An Outline of Ski Teaching Methods*. Hutter writes books and articles which are pub-	*These works make available studies that are directed to the ski teacher and the student teacher. Pfeiffer and Lash explore the "whole turn concept" of unweighting — edge change and turning power — which was originally discussed in the 1955*

THE HISTORICAL EVENT	THE SIGNIFICANCE

lished in the U.S. Hugo Brandenberger writes *Skimechanik — Methodik des Skilaufs,* in Switzerland.

Far West Instructor's Manual.

1959 Fifth International Ski School Congress in Poland.

Alpine nations agree to settle all technical arguments by using physical laws.

1. Austrians strong in their approach to teaching.
2. Swiss are not strong, but show better balance.
3. French show "split-rotation" — rotation with uphill shoulder to initiate the turn; shoulders are used in the end phase of the turn.
4. Italians show the best style — relaxed with neutral positions.

Progressive thinking comes out of the Congress. Less up-and-down action is seen in demonstrations; misused terms that are lost in translation are cleared up.

Paul Valar, Franconia, N.H., represents the United States at the Zakopone Congress.

National unity on technique seems an apparent evolution.

A National Ski School Meeting is held in Arapahoe Basin, Colorado, under direction of the NSA Certification of Ski Teachers Committee. Valar reports on the Poland Congress. Each division of the NSA fields a demonstration team. A remarkable national unity of technique seems an apparent evolution.

Instructors from all the divisions begin to work together.

1960-61 The French (Jean Vuarnet, James Couttet, Paul Gignoux, and Emile Allais) develop a natural ski style called "Christiania Leger." In this system, the body remains square over the skis at all times.

An analysis of French competition styles showed that French racers combined elements of their technique with the "heel thrust" movements of the Austrian technique. Critics claim that the French had returned to rotation.

The French produce a movie called *Christiania Leger,* which proves to be some of the world's best ski photography. The film is distributed worldwide.

1960 Over seventy-five instructors meet to discuss teaching psychology, technique, etc., at the National Ski School Meeting in Brighton, Utah.

Divisional demonstration teams show that only minor differences exist in these finished school forms.

Hans Gmoser, an Austrian mountain climber introduces Heli-Skiing to North America as a service featured by the Mountain Holidays Corporation.

As an alternative lift service, heli-skiing becomes extremely popular in the seventies, affording purists in search of untracked powder a broadening of the ski experience.

Kneissel, Sailer and Plymold (now defunct) market the first successful fiberglass skis.

Although not perfected, the incorporation of fiberglass and other petroleum-based materials becomes standard in skis of the future.

1961 In May, 1961, the Professional Ski Instructors of America (PSIA) is formed at the National Ski School Meeting in Whitefish, Montana. All division demonstration teams show final technical forms of skiing.

THE HISTORICAL EVENT	THE SIGNIFICANCE

Bob Parker of Denver takes and studies hundreds of photos of the Whitefish skiers and proves that in the final forms, the different skiers look amazingly similar. Parker suggests that an American Ski Technique exists.

Allais and Perillat demonstrate at Whitefish for the American teachers.

Instructors of the U.S. ask for a clarification of ski techniques. In November, 1961, PSIA is incorporated in the state of Minnesota.

PSIA becomes accepted by organized skiing and the United States ski industry.

1962 Sixth International Ski School Congress is held in Italy at Monte Bandone. The United States fields a team under the direction of PSIA. Six nations demonstrate: French show split-rotation (turn is started with rotation and finished with a reverse). Austrians are less extreme; all nations show a trend toward normalcy in demonstrations.

The United States and PSIA receive international recognition.

1963 Rossignol builds a resin ski (epoxy) that holds up better than the softer, polyester ingredients used in such skis as VR 17's. The product — the Strato 102 — is a phenomenal ski. With its radical side cuts and quick response characteristics, the ski is a favorite of racers and recreational skiers for years.

With advancements in ski technology, ski techniques slowly adjust; there is less vertical movement, more edge carving and quicker turning because of the refined dynamic qualities built into the new skis. Stiffer ski tails, coupled with the French racing technique of sitting back, foster progressive skiing styles (like the jet turn) eventually enabling Killy to "bring home all the Gold" at the 1968 Winter Olympics.

The French fail to agree on a basic presentation of their technique, while the other nations show modified forms of the classic Austrian system.

The Italian demonstration team takes the Congress by surprise with its smooth exposition on the "Italian Modern Technique."

The Italian technique is modified slightly by a French influence.

The PSIA, at its convention meeting in Alta, Utah, studies the films and reports of the VI Congress at Bandone. The American Ski Technique is demonstrated at the Alta convention.

The American Ski Technique receives national acceptance.

The Board of Directors of PSIA defines the Finished Technical Forms based on a three-year study of demonstrations at national meetings.

The technique is separated into three parts: Finished Technical Forms, Ski Mechanics and Methodology.

1963-64 First Annual Amputee Ski Championships are held.

1964 America's Olympic hopeful, Buddy Werner,

THE HISTORICAL EVENT	THE SIGNIFICANCE

is killed in an avalanche.

Billy Kidd and Jimmy Huega become the first American male skiers to win Winter Olympic medals. Both placed in the slalom, Kidd taking a Silver and Huega a Bronze, at the Ninth Winter Games in Innsbruck, Austria.

This is a real psychological boost needed by the U.S. ski team, a team that had consistently placed poorly in the past.

Bob Beattie becomes the head coach of the United States Olympic Ski Team. He continues as coach for the 1968 team.

The PSIA publishes *The Official American Ski Technique.*

Complete revised book shows that PSIA accepts evolution as part of the American ski technique.

1964-65 The first Lange all plastic buckle boots are commercially available.

Boots are becoming higher and stiffer. These innovations affect skiing styles.

1965 The seventh International Ski School Congress is held at Badgastein, Austria. Twenty-two nations attend.

The American team does well. American technique depicts natural positions, total motions and emphasizes the importance of the traverse.

Alpine demonstrations are given by Americans, Canadians, Austrians, Japanese, Germans, Italians and French.

1965-66 Rosemount offers the world's first rear-entry boot.

Comfort and performance in boots and skis are more and more intrinsic goals of the ski equipment industry.

1966 Hermann Goellner demonstrates the first double-aerial flip.

In the mid- to late-Sixties, many skiers are flexing their wings in a style that will become known as freestyle.

Magic Mountain is one of the first ski areas to limit lift tickets.

The popularity of skiing (always on the rise) begins to outstrip ski areas' abilities to handle the growing influx of skiers.

Made from a flexible epoxy material, Lange Competitions, called by the Europeans "Les Plastiques Fantastiques," begin their debut on the racing circuits. Nearly half of the racers in the Tenth Winter Olympics placing in the top ten are wearing the new boots. "Comps," as they are called, are virtually indestructible. They have an elevated heel which puts the racers into what Bob Lange (designer of the boots) calls a "balanced attack" position.

1967 The first World Cup Competitions are staged. Credited with the Cup's inception are U.S. Ski Team coach Bob Beattie, French Ski Team Coach Honore Bonnet and French journalist Serge Lang.

The event is a result of racers' dissatisfaction of being judged by their performance on one run every four years. The Cup rates a skier's performance by a point system accrued over an entire season.

Georges Joubert and Jean Vuarnet publish *How to*

This is the first book outlining the advanced skiing maneuvers

THE HISTORICAL EVENT	THE SIGNIFICANCE

Ski the New French Way (English translation).

so completely.

Eighth Interski at Aspen — seventeen nations see American skiing. The theme: Skiing is for Everyone. Largest congress, with one thousand attending.

Splendid organization. Americans have outstanding performance and choreography in demonstration. Austrians introduce wide-track; French, advanced skiing; Swiss, trick skiing. Lectures given on short skis, graduated length method, Karl Gamma, Swiss, proposes an international ski technique.

International Professional Ski Instructors meeting in Zermatt, Switzerland.

Further international effort to arrive at a universal ski technique.

1968 Jean Claude Killy sweeps the Triple Crown at the Grenoble, France, Winter Olympics.

Killy becomes an overnight success story, capturing the hearts of millions, and is used as one of the best promotional gimmicks to attract interest to the sport of skiing.

Raichle "Red Hot" boots are the center of attention at the Tenth Winter Olympics.

Constructed of fiberglass, with a four-buckle shell, Red Hots are the first ski boots to be on display at the Museum of Modern Art in New York. As part of the permanent design collection, the boots can be viewed along with a baby carriage, a television set and a record player, as examples of 20th Century mass-produced items that are at once functional and aesthetically pleasing.

The first running of the French-American Challenge Cup is held in Aspen, Colorado.

The Cup features a dual slalom which is designed to generate a greater public interest in ski racing and ultimately, attract the financial backing of the television networks.

1968-69 NASTAR begins its first season.

As a program enabling amateurs to taste "the thrill of victory and the agony of defeat," NASTAR proves to be immensely popular nationally among recreational skiers who want to participate in an official racing program.

1969 The first experimental ski trip for Viet Nam Veteran Amputees is held at Soda Springs, California.

International Professional Ski Instructors meeting is held at Cervinia, Italy.

Continuation of progress at the international level. Nations agree to some compromise.

PSIA alters basic principles to allow for down-unweighting and some rotation (axial motion).

Allows for advanced skiing maneuvers.

PSIA has a membership of 4,264. Bill Lash (the first president of PSIA) is succeeded by Will Scheffler.

1970 Revised edition of *The Official American Ski Technique* is published by Cowles Book Company of New York City. (Earlier editions sold thirty thousand copies.)

Includes basic technique, advanced skiing. Greatly expanded.

The first North American Ski Instructors Congress is held at Vail, Colorado.

The congress established a yearly forum for American ski instructors to exchange ideas and discuss teaching methods.

THE HISTORICAL EVENT	THE SIGNIFICANCE

Hans Schmid, a 23-year-old Swiss electrician, demonstrates his monoski; he was inspired to create it by watching skiing amputees.

Herman Goellner performs a forward triple aerial flip on skis.

Freestyle skiing gains momentum as Hart ski movies inspire young acrobats like Wayne Wong, Eddie Ferguson and Scott Brooks to new feats of daring.

Yuichiro Miura becomes the first man to ski down Mt. Everest. He reaches a speed of 93mph, but because of a mishap, is forced to ski part way down on just one ski.

Sylvain Saudan, "Maniacal Master of the Steppes," skis down the northwest slope of the Eiger in Switzerland.

Denver is selected by the International Olympic Committee to host the 1976 Winter Olympic Games. Due to popular opposition, the Games are voted down by Coloradans in a later referendum.

As fate would have it, a snow drought hits Colorado in 1976. The site that would have been used for the Olympic downhill has less than one inch of snow cover.

The first manmade ski hill constructed entirely from garbage is built outside of Toronto, Canada.

Chet Huntley retires as NBC anchorman and announces plans to open his Big Sky Resort in Montana.

Jeff Jobe establishes the first ski-hangliding record by soaring for five minutes, covering 1-3/4 miles, and 3,200 vertical feet at Jackson Hole, Wyoming.

Peter Shields, inventor of the Walk On Boot Tree (which allows skiers to walk with a normal stride while wearing ski boots) walks 362 miles in ski boots from Los Angeles to Mammoth Mountain.

He wins $10,000 from ski filmmaker, Dick Barrymore, who had been skeptical that Shields' invention really worked.

1971 Formation of the International Freestyle Skiers Association. The first National Championship of Exhibition Skiing is held at Waterville Valley, New Hampshire.

Created by SKIING Magazine, the freestyle competitions begin to attract crowds, larger purses and sponsors like Chevrolet.

Aspen, Colorado's new taxi service is composed entirely of Rolls Royces, Bentleys and a few English cabs, for good measure.

Aspen continues to create one of the most popular ski areas in the world.

A restructuring of the PSIA enables "full and certified associate members of each regional association to become voting members of the PSIA."

The PSIA becomes an "umbrella" organization under which the separate regional associations are unified. Due to increased membership, the PSIA is strengthened, more cohesive and financially solvent.

THE HISTORICAL EVENT	THE SIGNIFICANCE
Horst Abraham becomes chairman of Alpine Ski Technique and Education for the PSIA. He develops the American Teaching Method (ATM).	*The 1970's mark a shift to humanistic and alternative learning processes. Ski students are taught a synthesis of styles with emphasis on awareness of self, simple movement and motor skills.*
1972 Sylvain Saudan, ("Maniacal Master of the Steppes," remember?) skis down 20,300 foot Mount McKinley.	
Rosemount introduces their two-buckle boot.	*The seventies see a complete shift to all-synthetic, buckle boots.*
At the Winter Olympic Games in Sapporo, Japan, American Susan Corrock wins the Bronze in downhill and her co-team member, Barbara Cochran wins the Gold in slalom.	*Barbara Ann Cochran's Gold is the first U.S. Olympic Medal in twenty years. Of the 14 U.S. Winter Olympic medals won in skiing, twelve have been awarded to women.*
1973 The first session of the National Instructors Academy is held at Timberline Lodge, Mount Hood, Oregon.	*As a school to teach ski instructors improves teaching skills, the Academy begins to forge a unified American ski methodology — disseminating their philosophies, concepts and programs across the country.*
The Tenth Annual National Amputee Championships are held at Winter Park, Colorado.	*Handicapped ski programs and races are found at most major ski areas.*
1974 The Energy Crisis. Gasoline prices in America by the mid-seventies jump to an unprecedented high of 60¢/gallon.	*Skiers are forced to reevaluate their energy consumption habits. Car pooling and public transportation usage is stressed with lift ticket discounts offered as incentives at many ski areas.*
1975 The American Teaching Method is showcased at the Tenth Interski in Czechoslovakia.	*ATM is demonstrated by the PSIA Ski Team. The Team has evolved during the administrations of Jim Riley, Keith Lange and Warner Schuster. The Team proves to be extremely popular and instrumental in exposing to the ski world the ever-evolving American method at workshops, clinics and symposiums.*
The Burt Binding, the first retractable plate binding, is introduced.	
1976 On December 5th, stuntman Rick Sylvester skis off of Baffin Island's Mount Asgaard, parachuting to safety; he becomes the first man to ski jump 3,300 vertical feet. The stunt is filmed for the James Bond movie *The Spy Who Loved Me*.	
1976-77 The Great Snow Drought. Colorado ski areas lose $78 million.	*As a result, area operators install snowmaking machines as insurance against future dry seasons.*
1978 Salomon features a fully-retractable ski brake. Miller and Cubco had experimented with the idea in the early sixties.	*In the late seventies, many devices are introduced that emphasize safety, helping to prevent skiing injuries.*
Smith Goggle presented a solution to fogged lenses — a built-in electric fan.	

THE HISTORICAL EVENT	THE SIGNIFICANCE
Parablocks, designed by Guenter Schwars, help prevent the annoying problem of crossing ski tips.	
Maple Valley, Vermont features nighttime disco skiing. (. . .Thanks to the BeeGees and John Travolta!)	
Texas A&M students, for the first time, can receive a one-hour credit for skiing on Mount Aggie at College Station, Texas. The 25-foot-high, 50-foot-long manmade ski mountain has been described as "a pickup truck load of dirt dumped in the middle of nowhere covered with astroturf and astropellets."	*Now Texans don't have to go to Colorado to ski.*
1979 In 1979, SKIING Magazine studies reveal that in the past seven years, leg injuries are down 60% and tibia fractures are down 75%.	
Vail institutes lift limits and skiing by reservations.	*The ever-growing popularity of skiing is straining ski area capacities across the country. Limited lift tickets, mid-week package deals and expansion programs are experimented with to solve the overcrowding problems on the ski slopes.*
The American Teaching Method is presented at the Eleventh Interski in Zao, Japan.	*The main emphasis is on "the processes by which students learn rather than specific skills to be taught." ATM is recognized as a major breakthrough in the field of ski instruction and is enthusiastically accepted.*
Gore-Tex is manufactured into ski garments	*Bulky, down-filled parkas succumb to modern fiber technology.*
The world's first octuple (eight passenger) chairlift is installed at Brandywine, Ohio.	
Kirk Hill completes 434 consecutive runs in 63 hours, 50 minutes, covering 195,300 vertical feet at Angel Fire, New Mexico.	
1980 Hub Zemke designs the Hexcel Swallow Tail Ski. Hanson Ski follows shortly with a similar design of the same ski called a Splittail.	*As advancements in technology occur, so do refinements in ski design.*
1981 PSIA organizes a National Certification program. By 1982, only two regional associations have not yet ratified the concept.	*The next step, International Certification, is already on the drawing board.*
1982 There are 350 PSIA ski schools and membership is over 14,000.	
1981-82 PSIA introduces the STAR Test International (Standard Rating Test International) at sixty PSIA member ski schools across the country.	*The STAR tests are a popular innovation. Skiers register for a Bronze, Silver or Gold Star medal. They are run through a standard set of maneuvers and rated by a trained PSIA instructor. High scores enable participants to move up to a higher level.*

COMPILED BY BILL LASH & PHIL BRITTIN

A TURN TO THE RIGHT

LEFT BRAIN/RIGHT BRAIN

"Man's mind, stretched to a new idea, never goes back to its original dimensions."
Oliver Wendell Holmes

Recent discoveries about the function of the brain have exciting implications for novice skiers, racers, coaches and ski instructors. Most of us think of the brain as a single entity, but it is actually comprised of two distinct parts—the right hemisphere and left hemisphere. The hemispheres are connected by a nerve bundle (the corpus callosum) that serves as a communication system between them. The brain hemispheres are mirror images physically, but they have disparate functions. In most people, the right hemisphere controls movement and sensation in the left side of the body and the left hemisphere controls the same in the right side of the body. It is obvious that there is not a symmetry of function: 90% of all people are right-handed. For most people (including the left-handed) the left side of the brain is the dominant hemisphere. Both the hemispheres constantly interact through the corpus callosum. When

necessary, one hemisphere can gradually assume the functions of the other (if the first is damaged, for instance).

Investigators have proposed that the brain hemispheres have different cognitive styles and different ways of perceiving and processing information.

First evidence of the dual qualities of the brain surfaced following reports on stroke or accident victims who had portions of their brains damaged. Patients who suffered damage to their left hemispheres lost the ability to speak, while those sustaining right-side damage did not. Right-side damage reflected loss in perceptual skills and memory. Other evidence came from patients who had their corpus callosums surgically severed in an attempt to alleviate epileptic conditions. Studying these patients, scientists observed that the brain does, in fact, have two separate hemispheric functions. This information sparked research on many levels.

Hemispheric investigation was directed towards "healthy" people to determine if the same split-brained qualities existed. The combined research gave supportive evidence to right brain/left brain theories. Apparently, each hemisphere has "specialized" functions; each side responds differently to the same stimuli, but stimuli are also routed to different hemispheres.

Roger Sperry, of the California Institute of Technology, helped pioneer a great deal of this bicameral research. Along with psychologist Robert Ornstein, neurosurgeon Joseph Bogen and numerous other assistants, Sperry found the implications of right brain/left brain research to reach far beyond the medical field. Sperry maintained that "The main theme to emerge is that there appear to be two modes of thinking, verbal and nonverbal, represented rather separately in left and right brain hemispheres, respectively, and that our educational system, as well as science in general, tends to neglect the non-verbal form of intellect. What it comes down to is that modern society discriminates against the right brain hemisphere."

Most activities use both sides of the brain, but we can think of activities, such as drawing, as coming principally from one specific side. Left brain activities are analytical: thinking, reading, writing, talking, counting and computing. The right brain, oriented towards holistic grasping of complex patterns, can deal simultaneously with multiple concepts and makes the intuitive leaps that complete half-formed associations. Right brain activities are dreams, composition, performance, drawing, craft works and creative thought. The left side of the brain is the "knowing" or "smart" side; the right hemisphere is the "skilled" side. In physical activities such as dance and sports, both sides of the brain interact to control physical movement but the perceptual and information-processing functions required are those of the right brain alone. In skiing, we draw on the right brain capabilities of holistic perception, rhythm, spatial relationships and simultaneous processing of many inputs. Left brain functions are largely uninvolved. The accumulated weight of scientific evidence is not what convinced me of the validity of left brain/right brain concepts. It was rather how results of hemispheric research provided a clear organization to many, so far, unlabeled experiences. Suddenly certain causality chains became very clear. Such research helped clarify my thoughts related to learning and performing. Though many emerging ideas are still speculative, to me, they have a strong intuitive appeal.

What follow are samples of associations, ideas and experiences that seem clearly connected with hemispheric functions. They are not in traditional text form of topic sentences and paragraphs, but rather appear as randomly as they came to my mind. View them without judgement or analysis, but merely as flashes of thought; pretend you're watching a rapidly-moving slide show.

When I draw or paint, I produce mood and lifelike images much better with my left hand than with my right hand (though I am right handed) . . . . when writing, music with lyrics is disturbing to me; instrumental music, on the other hand, is inspiring to my writing, though spelling and grammar deteriorates. Proverbs and stories of ancient China and Japan fascinate me — teachers must learn to use images that rich . . . . dynamic connectedness, wholeness of events are what catch my eye . . . . greatness or grand abilities do not come from following someone else's model, but from developing your own potential . . . . Albert Einstein flunked math . . . . my youngest son *sings* his ABC's—when asked to *say* them, memory fades . . . . as a boy, living in the mountains, I often chose to run home in a dry creek bed to avoid ripping my clothes in the brush; I ran with soft focus, trusting my intuition and feelings to allow me to bound from rock to rock, though I could hardly see in the dark . . . . I doubt I ever would have learned to ride a bike if I had taken a class, taught in traditional fashion . . . . after eight years of English class, I arrived in the U.S. barely able to make myself understood well enough to buy bread . . . . so many great athletes come from the ghetto, ignorant by conventional standards, yet their body-knowledge, their ability and coordination is exquisite . . . . great ski racers are not reared in ski schools . . . . ski schools tend to disseminate knowledge rather than helping people learn to ski . . . . I loved picture books when I was small and not until I found authors who could draw pictures with their words did I enjoy books again . . . . when I have a "gray" day on skis, I can bring myself out of this mood by emphasizing rhythm . . . . I play my guitar or flute to express my moods, not to perform for others . . . . I also ski to explore, to enjoy, not to perform . . . . I do not race . . . . we only become uncoordinated . . . . we only become unintelligent . . . . sports I learned in a "formal" fashion inevitably left me feeling clumsy and uncoordinated . . . . even if I could afford lessons in sports, I opt, rather, to learn them by myself . . . . I give my best at speeches and presentations when I do not work from a prepared text or even an outline . . . . I was very reluctant to write this book—while I knew what I wished to say, the need to put it into words seemed to stifle the generating of thoughts . . . . I never had much use for grammar; when I allow it to dominate my concerns, I lose my ability to speak at all . . . . I started to learn when school was over . . . . I had my best successes as a teacher when I was not intent on teaching . . . . in my teaching I use silly associations, movement, images, metaphors and half-said sentences, sometimes even silence . . . . while students gained much from such interaction, my superiors never liked it . . . . at times I have a vivid image in mind, but I cannot find the matching word . . . . numbers on a clock face do not tell me the time, but the relationship of the hands to one another do . . . . at times we call certain folks primitive, yet we envy their ability to dance . . . . instead of love and caring, we give our children money and gifts . . . .

TRADITIONAL TEACHING

"Schools should not be organized for teachers to teach, but for children to learn."

Briggs, McLean

In earliest childhood, we learn by experience, intuition and inference. No one teaches us to crawl, though we later learn to walk using already-walking people as models. Experts tell us that during the first five years of our life, we learn at a rate never again equalled. During these years, our spatial and sensory abilities are our guides for development. At this time, brain hemispheres are capable of functioning interchangeably. As we grow older, the brain halves become more specialized.

Once we enter school, the educational goals of a sequential and logical world concentrate on the development of left brain functions. Our ability to succeed (to do well in school) is based upon rote memorization, mathematical skills and verbal proficiency. Spatial and holistic skills, are neglected in favor of analytical and linear thinking. Having desks in a circle in the classroom encourages interaction between students, yet conventional classrooms retain the desks in rows facing the teacher. The teacher is the main source of information and evaluation. Many students become bored with task-oriented work and squirm under the pressure of having to perform. Not interested in the curriculum, they combat boredom by investing their energies elsewhere. "Problem students" often are actually rebelling against prescribed, disciplined systems that smother their abilities and desire to learn. Constantly being told what they can and cannot do, these children shun engagement in formal education and replace it with unorthodox experiences of their own.

Contact, interaction and exploration are all concepts that no one would wish to separate from education, yet our educational institutions do not openly develop these qualities. I watched, with great frustration and sadness, the transformation my own children have undergone. They entered school as self-confident youngsters with a sparkle in their eyes, full of immeasurable resources and physical spontaneity, only to become dull-eyed and hesitant to perform. They no longer carried on imaginative conversations; their laughter was replaced with a startling somberness. They no longer allowed themselves to freely surrender to imagination, to jump to conclusions or to offer their perceptions of life.

Most children in school suffer in the same ways, discouraged from drawing conclusions on the basis of fragmented information. They are reprimanded for fantasies and daydreams. The frequent reminder of teachers to "look for all available information" and to "think before talking," is, in part, responsible for the degeneration of right brain skills in children.

Even more worrisome is the education of our educators. Thirty and forty-year-old teachers, equipped with methods considerably older than themselves, have the responsibility of educating members of our society who will be challenged to cope with future issues. Rather than dynamically evolving philosophy, curriculum and practices in continual process, we seem content to maintain a calloused system in which only easily-accessible issues are taught. The main premise of our current educational system seems to be that what cannot be measured should not be dealt with!

Traditional education is a marked contrast to early childhood experiences where learning takes place at an incredible rate through experimentation, observation and trial and error.

I spent my childhood in the mountain hamlet of Tschagguns, Austria, where my family fled to escape the Russian invasion of Austria at the end of World War II. My mother, brother, sister and I lived in a small, one-room home; my father was fighting in the war that eventually would take his life. While all members of the family were at school or working to supplement our meager income, being too small to do either, I tended the chickens we raised. I had much time to explore and play in the surrounding mountains. I spent a great deal of my freedom talking to the old, frail hunchbacked tailor in our village. I would sit for hours listening to the stories of his youth and life in this village. He always sat cross-legged, sewing away with his nimble hands, mending and fashioning clothing for the people of the village. When he died, I experienced a tremendous

confusion about the purpose of life. This man, who was full of tales about people and their thoughts, had made me seriously think about what I wanted to accomplish in my own life. When he was put under the ground, I felt a great loss overcome me. My idea of death was to no longer have a friend to talk with.

Until my entrance into elementary school, the most meaningful things in my life were the bakery, a source of most exquisite things to eat; the cemetery, the place where people, rich and poor, mean or kind, were put to rest; and the river, where my mind wandered, travelling to faraway places through the changing patterns of waves and ripples in their fascinating intricacy.

When I entered school, I fell under the spell of a cowhide bag containing my slate board and slate pencil, as well as a string-tied rag to erase my scribbling with. Seated at narrow bench desks placed upon rough floorboards, creosote sawdust picking up dirt and giving the room a permanent smell, I was totally overwhelmed with the importance of the institution called "school." Our teacher was a sister in a black and white habit; she would dictate and read to us in a high-pitched voice, a delicate singsong. I was in a trance for weeks, filled with wonder and reverence for this new place and the people who were running it. My serenity was suddenly shattered when I was informed, by the same high-pitched voice, that I was not a passing student; I had better start earning my passage by ringing the bells for Mass on Sundays and sweeping the floor after school hours, or shaking june bugs out of the trees in the mornings while they were stiff with frost, so they would not eat the foliage. In return, I would receive the pictures of saints and biblical stories which were required to pass class. I quickly learned the system and managed to get good grades from then on. I became a masterful church bell ringer, swinging myself through the tower cavity with expert elan, tempering the sound of the bells to what I knew the clerical people liked best. Ringing bells, killing bugs and sweeping floors were intrinsically associated with my academic success in those days.

In contrast, I learned about "erosion" and "sedimentation" by playing near the river; I understood "leverage" by clearing a path of fallen trees; I found out about the concept of "horizontal" by building dams in the irrigation ditch; I grasped division, subtraction and addition by watching workers in the neighboring sawmill split logs, saw them into boards and stockpile them in equal rows; I became aware of nutrition by not having access to certain vegetables and fruits for some time, and feeling the pain in my gums and skin disappear when such staples were back in my diet again; I witnessed electricity by watching lightning strike a tree and by accidentally touching a charged wire in the barn. I found out about the speed of sound by experimenting with the echoes in the mountains, yodeling and turning to run as fast as I could before the sound caught up with me; I discovered relative density by melting snow to get water to drink; I experienced displacement, ballast and center of gravity when I built a makeshift boat out of an old barrel and floated in it in a threateningly dark-watered gravel pit. I learned about love and hate when I was taken away from my family for several weeks.

Occasionally carnivals came to our remote village. The combination of music, colourful decoration, people dancing and the gaiety of a crowd that I knew only as somber, stone-faced people, excited me. I loved the carnival, not so much for the variety of activities, but for the general mood it brought. I was content watching from a distance, not really tempted to participate.

Returning to school in the fall brought all this excitement to an abrupt halt. The experiences of summer and curiosity about the unknown ceased with the beginning of each school year. Conformity and submissiveness to arbitrary, but unquestioned, values seemed of importance to my educators. This impression lingered throughout my later education as well.

When I moved from the country, the hidden-away places of Vorarlberg, and moved to Vienna, I traded beautiful mountains for the rubble-heaps of a city that had died. My family and I left a small but functional one-room home full of memories for one that was larger and more comfortable, but scarred with a history that was not ours.

My treasured excursions into the unknown, which had led me into the mountainous wildernesses near my village were now replaced with explorations of the cavernous ruins of bombed-out buildings marked: "Achtung Einsturzgefahr." I came home dust-covered, with tattered clothes, but I did not share my discoveries with my family. Further outings would have been prohibited had I told them of the rifles and ammunition I had found in the woods of the Prater — or the unexploded mine I found shallowly buried in the dust of a path

leading through a thicket. An extra sense had allowed me to not step on it; this same sense made me throw rocks at it from a distance. The mine exploded with a roar of thunder, half-deafening me and lifting me off my feet.

Soon I grew to appreciate my new environment and began moving as I had done when stalking the unknown hare or deer in the country; such action led me back to my sensory world, a world I had missed since leaving my early home.

When school resumed, I found it to be the same as in Vorarlberg, though the rules changed somewhat. It was no longer enough to find out what *one* teacher wanted for behavior and answers; we now had three of them to please. Bell ringing and doing certain favours weren't enough. Having to assume an interest in a teacher's subject became a necessity in order to do well in classes. The kind of activities I enjoyed (music, drawing, social studies, geography, physics and geometry) were not what counted. Latin, Russian and mathematics were heavily-emphasized topics and, because of the way they were taught, I found myself disinterested in learning at all. I struggled with these subjects, consoling myself by excelling in the other classes.

During my first years in Vienna, I visited my grandmother quite often. She had suffered a stroke that paralyzed the entire right side of her body. After many weeks of recovery in the hospital, she came home and was confined to a chair in her apartment. She was unable to speak or walk. For all practical purposes, she was considered a "vegetable." Yet, to some of us, she epitomized warmth and feeling. Though she did not speak or respond in an overt manner when we talked together, I conducted long (though silent) conversations with her. She responded to seeing me, subtly, but meaningfully. The non-paralyzed side of her face would light up, her one eye would glisten and when I caressed her wrinkled, aged good hand, she would respond with a touch. Intuitively I knew that there was a part of her that was very alert, though the obvious manifestations of communication were absent. Often would we sit by the window, looking at the dirty Danube flowing by, watching the greedy pigeons on the window sill gobbling up bread crumbs. We would watch the sunset reflect itself in the windows of the houses across the river, making them seem on fire. We listened to the sparrows chirp. And I knew that this old, apparently useless lady in the armchair was acutely aware of all these happenings. The fact that she could not speak only deepened our understanding.

Upon finishing elementary school and entering *Realgymnasium*, my struggle to deal with what I was beginning to see as the values of the "real world" continued. My efforts to plough through meaningless abstracts of the compulsory curriculum created greater and greater needs to spend time with those things that inspired me. My musical talent was discovered and I was inducted into the school choir. I hid my initial inability to read music with my keen talent for reproducing even difficult passages after only hearing them once, but my interest in singing quickly motivated me to learn to read music.

Enjoying movement, I excelled in physical education. While drills and rigorous technical instructions as they related to high bar routines passed me without much impression, free-form activities like running, ball games, dancing, balancing and the many perceptual challenges of reaction games allowed the instincts acquired in childhood to surface.

My interest in art was fostered by the fact that I could freely express myself. Though my professor *did* divulge to me that he thought my drawing and painting themes odd (I was deeply interested in morbid scenes of swelling bodies in sunken ships, wind-whipped seas, fog-shrouded pasture land and the agonized faces of dying people) he thought that my technical skills were very good. Art became the evidence of how I felt about life and myself.

Oddly enough, it was during those testing years in school that I decided to become a teacher. I based my decision upon the assumption that any subject should be learnable by any person, as long as the methods chosen to teach that subject would allow learning to take place; this was a condition I found so sorely amiss in my own school at that time.

Having made this decision, the mode of education I was processed through suggested alternative methods in my own mind. Thus I experienced an oddly masochistic relationship with the educational system I was subjected to. I honed an interest even in the subjects I had difficulty with in an attempt to imagine how matters could be dealt with otherwise.

I remember thinking *Matura*, the graduation

from Gymnasium, was an outright farce. Graduating students were only capable of regurgitating the information they had been stuffed with, yet they were largely unable to think for themselves. Neither education nor the final test emphasized that creative thinking and doing would play any role in our futures. To this day, I imagine many fellow students who passed the final test with high scores in a "walking harness" (like those used to help severely handicapped children walk upright), symbolically unable to carry their own weight.

Continuing my studies at the University of Vienna, I enjoyed emerging opportunities of supplementing a largely theoretical curriculum with excursions into libraries or study halls where discussions with fellow students enabled me to nurture concrete thoughts drawn from abstract information. My expectations that professors at university level would be skilled, as well as knowledgeable, were soon torpedoed; with few exceptions, they were the epitome of the ivory tower intellectual, unable to convey their understandings and experiences to their students. Lectures were telegram-style deliveries of information; the issue of students "learning" seemed a foreign thought. It furthermore seemed that those few exceptional faculty members who cared for their students, and who were making skilled, genuine efforts towards promoting learning, were not respected by their colleagues.

Field trips into classrooms and the athletic fields became more and more frequent now; such excursions were styled to build practical associations with the theory we were immersed in.

During a "practice teaching" session, I violated accepted procedures by drawing my fellow students into the education process. After introducing the topic, discussion, opinion and reaction towards the issues were solicited. Pictures illustrating the topic were in the background, readily available for reference. At the conclusion of this particular session, I remember an uneasy silence in the room that was only interrupted by a nervous cough. I sensed my fellow students' insecurity about my "failure" to follow the conventional methodological procedure. One student started to clap faintly; gradually others joined in. Then they stood up and applauded wildly, admitting the victory of their feelings over the accepted standard.

THE TRADITIONAL SKI ENVIRONMENT

"Try not to have a good time, this is supposed to be educational."

Charles Schultz

"Tell me what I do wrong." "Did I do any better this time?' "Did I transfer my weight in these turns?" "I did not like my lesson because my instructor did not tell me enough about how to do the various tasks." These are a few typical articulations from ski school students. Without question, they are symptomatic of how people approach the learning of sports.

A statement from Tim McKee, a colleague in the PSIA educational committee, sums up one of the dilemmas ski schools are facing: "We tend to delegate the responsibility for our health to doctors, we delegate the task of explaining life's unknown to religion and we place the responsibility of learning onto our teachers." Our upbringing has conditioned us to evaluate our progress by how our *teachers* evaluate our progress. We are not encouraged to adjust our progress ourselves, or to recognize our own accomplishments. Though there are encouraging changes taking place in some ski schools, the majority are set up in the same manner as the conventional educational system, teaching a person to ski in the same way as he learns the alphabet or the multiplication table. Skiers are taught skiing in a sequentialized manner, mechanical preciseness serving stylish, rather than functional models. Instruction is predominantly oriented towards delivering information (a monologue format of teaching) rather than developing a grasp of what it is that is to be done through joint exploration by student and teacher. Instruction is still largely aimed at parts of a whole, rather than entire, dynamic entities which are then reinforced by isolated practice of certain components. Teaching is largely judgemental; the element of critique is forced into unduly bright light.

Conventional ski teaching in this country survived through the late sixties. In the early seventies, our industry's research about conveying theoretical principles began directing us towards movement awareness as an important aid in acquiring motor skills. The investigation of the mechanical aspects of skiing revealed that the linear progression until then used in ski teaching was best supplemented by "learning skills." The abstract "milestone concept" of linear progression gave way to working more with feel-able skills like turning, edging and controlling pressure on skis. By the mid-seventies, much "housecleaning" was done in ski teaching techniques. We began recognizing characteristic movement patterns that necessitated different methodological emphases. The distinction of turning with both *legs* and *feet* "simultaneously" as opposed to "one after another" made us realize why the conventional progression of teaching skiing stalled between stem christies and parallel skiing—the two kinds of movement are very different from one another and do not "flow" into each other.

The mid and later seventies brought further important realizations to our profession; humanistic development placed more and more value on exploration and interaction between student and teacher, as well as on a greater sensory awareness of what happens to the body. In turn, developing a great versatility of techniques and methods that allow the student many choices developed; a holistically-trained teaching corps was available to choose from. The U.S. was the first ski nation to toss aside the idea of maintaining "one national technique," and this concept has found international following.

Presently, ski schools all over the world recognize the need for more than mechanical explanations and definitions in skiing. Modern-day teaching programs include a wide range of techniques to accommodate the new and/or experienced skier. Shorter skis make it easier to learn to ski. Many instructors are trained to deal with fear and anxiety among students. Instructors are able to change the style of their approach to students. All of this has brought life and variety, as well as appropriate tension levels, into classes. Ski teaching has become more specific, catering to the needs and desires of skiers.

Though most members of the ski education profession have responded to studies on "how people learn," a great many are still essentially uninformed as to the intricacies of this process.

Instructional stereotype and teaching to the subject rather than to the learner or situation are still as frequent in ski schools as they are in the conventional school system. Like so many teachers, I taught within the prescribed, rigid parameters of ski school dogma for many years, but my longing has always been to allow students to experience the same wonder and enjoyment with which I learned to ski . . . .

At age 2½ I was introduced to skiing. My first pair of skis was a pair of board sections with leather thongs to tie my shoes to the wood. Those skis were not built for gliding; they were like snowshoes to prevent me from sinking into the snow when making winter visits to neighbors or to the bakery for bread.

The downhill skiing of my older brother, Werner, and his friends got me interested in the real sport that was beyond the limits of my "shuffle boards." Those people in the village who could afford it had skis made by the local cabinetmaker. This craftsman hand-fashioned skis that were works of art—the grain was perfectly matched, the groove precisely routed. They were beautiful! Families who did not have the money to buy skis had to make their own boards or do without skiing.

My brother had already made himself some skis, and he volunteered to make me a pair. After selecting two boards of similar thickness and grain structure, he began shaping the skis to an outline drawn on the wood. Chisel and plane gave the skis a form with a slight ridge forward of where the feet would be to add strength and beauty. The bending of the ski tips was accomplished by immersing the boards' ends in warm water for a night, then, with vices, forcing them into the desired curve. I helped where I was allowed, but Werner was the master whose advice I strictly followed. When they were finished, my skis were the most beautiful ones I had ever seen—maybe because they were my very own. Ironed-in pine tar gave the running surface the necessary water resistance. Several layers of varnish made the tops shine. I stood the skis up by my bed that night, to stay close to them. I transferred my dreams of flying downhill into them and, when I wore them the next day, they were not just appendages but live extensions of my body.

The main playground for skiers in our hamlet was the outrun of a nearby jumping hill. It offered a packed surface which was a rarity at that time. The distance markers on the landing hill were evidence of one's skiing progress. Beginning skiers inched their way up the hill, those distance markers beckoning them farther and farther on. Equipped with my new skis, I played at the very bottom of the slope; the closest marker was seemingly in the sky! I envied some of the bigger kids skiing from far up the hill; some were so bold they actually jumped off the platform!

After a week of skiing at the bottom slope, I dared ascend to the lowest marker—the 60 meter line. My heart was thumping and my body was rigid with tension. My edgeless skis could barely cling to the steep hill, so I was forced to dig my hazelnut branch poles deep into the snow to keep myself from falling. I stood for ten minutes gathering my courage before I pushed off. I experienced the fatalistic attitude a kamikaze pilot must have had when lowering the nose of his aircraft for the suicidal dive. The acceleration was awesome and the sound of the wind deafening. In the transition to the flat part of the outrun, my knees buckled under the compression load and I fell. I tumbled to a stop, battered and bruised but the pain did not matter. I had reached the markers!

At school, ski trips allowed me to get to know winter in a way I had not known it before. Our outings would lead us to remote alpine valleys with deep snow and steep slopes. We learned about crevasses, hypothermia and snow caves in which to seek shelter. We learned to rely on each other while skiing in a total white-out above timberline. We occasionally had races at the conclusion of such ski weeks. I was quite successful in racing, having grown up in the "school of hard knocks," but my victories were unenjoyable when I saw my friends dejected over their performance. To this day, I keep the prizes from these races over my desk, not to remind me (or anyone else) of my accomplishments, but to reiterate that competition makes losers of all but a few.

By the time I taught skiing in Westendorf, Tirol, I had a very distinct philosophy on the subject. Skiing was a mixture of physical excitement, mystique and mental exhilaration that evoked a deep feeling of well-being; I felt that skiing had strong therapeutical value. In turn, I knew I was obligated to allow those I taught to experience the sport in a similar way. I was exhausted after teaching my first class of beginners; the day of total involvement left me drained. This happy bone-weariness is the way I like to feel at the end of a day of teaching. It tells me that I have done a good job.

My concern for students made it difficult for me to worry about the "it is Monday, it must be time to side slip" syndrome. Though my return rate of students was very high, I was "let go" from many ski schools for "doing my own thing." Kitzbuehel was one of those schools.

Kitzbuehel is a lovely town nestled in the Tirolean Alps. The age of the city is apparent from the fortress-like walls that surround its inner core; tall stucco buildings line the streets, their facades decorated with frescos, their gables leaning towards one another as if seeking support. I stayed in this town far longer than I should have.

The ski school was run in an authoritarian manner. Work assignments were not based on qualities as a teacher, but on whether or not you belonged to the local "group." We had meetings three times a week, 200 sweaty bodies crammed together to hear the leaders of the school announce new policy or conduct. Sometimes a "kangaroo court" was held, with some poor bloke who had violated the ski school law standing in front of everyone, to be either fined or fired. These "court cases" were brief and fierce, the victims having no chance for rebuttal and suffering humiliation for weeks thereafter. Iron discipline was maintained.

I left the ski school in Kitzbuehel because I failed to adhere to progression and timetable in my teaching approach. This same thing happened again in St. Anton and Zermatt. At this stage, I had emerged from a romantic association with skiing and ski instruction to becoming intensively engaged in researching learning theory and ski mechanics. Aided by my access to the libraries at the University of Vienna, I approached my profession scientifically. It was an arduous process investigating skiing and ski teaching in light of the arbitrary assumptions that the sport was historically based upon.

The courses I took to get my Austria State Instructor Certification are vaguely in my memory. I *do* remember a series of hot, blistering days on the glaciers above Obergurgl, practicing skiing while roped to other skiers, learning to rappel and to build rescue sleds. On the occasion of one outing, we came across the frozen-in corpse of a First World War soldier as we cooled off in a glacier's mouth.

I also remember the final written exam in St. Christoph. After a tension-filled session of questions about methodology and ski technique, I was alone in the study hall, with light slowly fading outside. Professor Kruckenhauser, the Dean of the Austrian Academy, returned my paper, pointing at the segment dealing with "how to make a parallel turn" and suggested that I rework it. The silence of the room was overwhelming. The answer to this question might influence the outcome of my great investment of time and money. After about an hour, Professor Kruckenhauser came back to the now almost totally dark room. I stared at my notes. Though I could no longer see the writing, I knew they contained succinct definitions and a thorough analysis of the sequences of events in a "parallel turn," even to the point of including a mathematical equation of the forces at work and some graphic illustrations of the vectors. I looked up and saw the professor silhouetted against the feeble light from the window. In a kind voice, he asked me once again about the characteristics of "parallel turning." After ten minutes of telling him all I knew, he gently interrupted me and said, "All this will enable you to see clearly as a teacher, but don't forget that for the student, all the contemplations are reduced to just one simple thing: 'Turn both feet.'" He put his arm around my shoulder as we left the room.

When I left Europe, it was a symbolic departure from all those things that were preventing me from contributing to the field of skiing. I left Vienna by train. I hadn't told anyone that I intended to leave home for good, but the look in my mother's eyes as I reached out the train window to touch her hand in farewell told me she knew.

I had a mission to accomplish and my destination was Aspen, Colorado. I arrived just when the Austrian counter-rotation technique was beginning to replace the older Arlberg technique. Inadvertently I became a showpiece and trainer for this transition in Aspen. At the time, I never dared to express my discomfort at doing just the sort of thing I came to the U.S. to escape. The relatively open-minded working environment in Aspen, combined with the "always ready to try new things" American attitude, was a splendid laboratory. I started to write and, in doing so, I improved my linguistic skills as well as allowing myself to study the logic of my own thinking.

In 1969, I attended the French National Academy. I was impressed by the strong emphasis on a methodology which was very practically oriented. Skiing to the theme of the French school at that time, "toute neige, toute terrain" (all snow, all terrain), I pushed my abilities, picking up on what I had virtually lost in the style-oriented Austrian school. Function once more surfaced as the predominant guideline. Bringing my experiences home, I was ready to "strike out on my own."

An opportunity to test many of my new-found concepts came when Curt Chase, the director of the Aspen Ski School, gave me a chance to run the ski school under his direction at the neighboring area of Snowmass. I could then try out not only mechanical and methodological ideas, but I also was able to create what I considered to be a desirable working environment in which the instructors were treated with as much encouragement and consideration as I expected them to show to their students. There was excitement and energy in the air; the highly-motivated staff eagerly explored new things.

When in 1970, I was offered the position of technical director in the Vail ski school, I declined. My friends, and roots, were in Snowmass. However, when the offer came again in 1971, I accepted. My mission did not change. I knew that taking the job in Vail, and simultaneously assuming the position as PSIA educational chairman, would force me to forego the promotion and salary advancement that are bestowed upon managerial, but not educational, positions. This deprivation persists to this day, but the personal growth and satisfaction gained through my work are certainly worth the sacrifice.

My first action as the PSIA national educational chairman was to diversify. Instead of concentrating only upon technique, I involved people in the fields of biomechanics, to learn more about how the human body moves and performs; in learning theory, to understand more about learning itself; in sociology, to comprehend people and the market situation. The team of PSIA took a fresh look at existing instructional premises and consequently, the ATM (American Teaching Method) began to take shape. The U.S. contribution to "Interski" (an international meeting of all skiing nations in order to share findings in the field of ski instruction) in Stribske Pleso, Czechoslovakia, in 1976, was met with wrinkled foreheads from our European counterparts. Not only did we *not* have one linear progression, not only did we *not* adhere to one technique, but we presented our thinking under the umbrella of "skill development," demonstrating how skills are polished throughout the process of learning to ski and how those skills provide a unique continuum throughout the growth of a skier. Rather than referring to abstract terms, we proved how skills were of kinesthetic (feeling) value to the learner. Our dealing with "edging," "turning" and "pressure control" were not well received.

Not until the Interski congress in Zao, Japan, when we showed the *relationship* between the learning process and the skills, and also clarified the humanistic tendencies of our teaching approach, did the international forum respond to our innovative theory.

What was evident from our presentation was that the era when someone could take a "part-time attitude" towards teaching was gone. What we made clear was that it was time that we, as teachers, concerned ourselves with the question of "how people learn" and that we should develop a strong basis of understanding about how our instructional intervention could be useful to the learning process.

The general response was: "It sounds really nice, but how can we bring our instructorship (that largely consists of people who have not 'enjoyed' 'higher' education) to subscribe to such standard?" The consideration that "building theoretical knowledge and analytical skills through academic schooling was a good way to go but it is not essential" was dismissed.

The level of shallow association and ignorance in ski instruction was hiding globally behind a smokescreen of what is commonly called "macho" image. I came to the sad realization that to seek alliances in the international forum was unrealistic. In order to get things done, Americans had to work on their own.

Coming across the research done on hemispherical brain functions helped me clarify many ideas about learning and performing. The American Teaching Method is a process that strongly embraces humanistic learning theory. Experiential learning, movement awareness, mental rehearsal, imagery and non-judgemental learning are strong emphases in the PSIA approach to working with people. Our training programs are constantly readjusted to meet the demands of an evolving market, while maintaining a strong basis in the less-rapidly changing "fundamentals" of ski instruction. The new generation of ski instructors is closer to the idea of being educators than the majority of older instructors used to be. Teachers nurturing an understanding of underlying concepts are more effective and less stifled in their approach. Utilizing mental aspects of learning and performing, this new generation of instructors is able to promote greater enjoyment and more lasting successes for their students. Leading the skier beyond the mechanical realm of skiing is the real challenge of modern ski schools.

MY IDEAL SKI SCHOOL

"When all you have is a hammer, everything in life looks like a nail."

Abraham Maslow

The ski school of my dreams is owned and operated by the teachers working in it. It seems that the vested interest in the well-being of the operation and the quality of services offered would be ensured by such a relationship. Even in a ski school that is owned by a company or individual, the teachers should take an active part in the daily processes on all levels.

In addition to teaching, instructors would be rotated through other positions: coordinating customer traffic, instructor training, marketing and operational functions like ticket sales and bookkeeping. Certain key functions of managerial and financial nature would have the assistance of an expert consultant.

The physical plant of my "Training Center" (I would call it that rather than "ski school") would include a spacious health center, several lecture halls of varying sizes, audio-visual studios and lounges that invited people to linger, converse, relax and read. The Center, furthermore, would have various libraries specializing in such topics as diet and exercise, psychology, exercise physiology, mental health, etc. The facility would have a large gym adjacent to a pool for swimming and diving, with jacuzzis and saunas, smaller studios for dance, martial arts and film/theater performances. Even if the latter "extravagances" were not attainable, there should at least be common rooms where films, videos and slides could be shown and beginner orientations could be held. Larger rooms would have to accommodate pre- and post-skiing sessions in warmup, stretching and relaxation techniques. Students at the Center would be divided into groups, not only by skiing ability, but by personal preferences about teaching styles as well as by their general rate of learning.

Classifications would be made after each individual viewed video tapes of different levels of skiing performance to allow for more accurate self-evaluation; a computer would aid in the sorting of customers' preferences.

Novice skiers would begin their day indoors. Gentle warming-up sessions would be followed by relaxation exercises which, in turn, would be followed by previewing the day's events on film. The fit of boots and bindings would be ensured at this time. Instructors and students would meet and get to know one another. The basis for rapport and trust could then ensue.

The earliest on-skis lesson would take place on a cone-shaped hill with a continuous, graduating pitch all around. Escalator-like uplift ramps would transport students to the top of the cone. A separate area for the beginners would be a "terrain garden," a conglomerate of manmade landforms that would facilitate the honing of certain skills. People would be assigned teams of instructors on a 1 to 6 ratio. Each individual could determine his own pace of learning and at what level of aggressiveness/cautiousness he would like to function. The general atmosphere of the instructional process would be non-pressured, supportive, encouraging and caring. Through the instructor's skill and the choice of terrain and task, students could quickly become confident of their abilities.

Beginning through intermediate classes would be provided to develop and refine the skills necessary to handle easy and intermediate terrain in all but extreme snow conditions. All advanced programs would be run under specialty titles such as: "Super Class—Get to know this mountain with a guide," "Bump Skiing," "Deep Snow," "High-Speed Skiing," "Out-of-Bounds Touring," "Zap Class" (getting more confident and demanding the most of yourself) . . . the skier could decide what to pursue.

Certain programs would be all-embracing and would include exercise workouts, skiing, health club usage, film reviews of personal performance, equipment clinics and social gatherings like dances.

Specific practice slopes on the mountain would be designed as "check-up islands." These slopes would be fenced off from general traffic, and their layout would make it easier to effect performance changes within a rather short period of time. Different portions of these slopes would have quality music piped in to encourage skiing to rhythms; permanently mounted video cameras would be trained on certain corridors of the slope, so that at the end of his performance the student would be able to slide right into a booth that allowed him and his instructor to review his technique. Two-way communication devices could be worked into these "training islands" to aid in shaping and solidifying specific performance characteristics. Fast-moving double poma lifts would allow teacher and student to confer "on the fly."

Students would get "homework" in the form of a particular film loop that they would be able to play whenever convenient. They would also receive a card reminding them to view the material and practice mental rehearsal in conjunction with it during the off-season. Exercise recommendations in preparation for the upcoming ski season would also be included in the set-up.

In conjunction with the health spa facilities, the Training Center would offer programs on holistic health, stress management and meditation, and exercise and dance classes. Specialists in fields like nutrition, exercise physiology and psychology would visit, giving lectures and workshops. Skiing would be only one of the many experiences offered at the Training Center. The Center would operate year 'round and would do consulting work for other training centers around the world.

Instructors would be employed at the facility year 'round. The experience of the instructors at entry level would be a teaching background, above average skiing and sporting skills, and fine social ease and the urge to expand personal abilities. Teacher training would be an evolving affair, with guest speakers and domestic training staff constantly providing new experiences and challenges to personal improvement. Instructor training would expand into topics like applied teaching skills, skiing skills, anatomy, physiology, physics, dynamics and psychology.

The working environment of the teachers would be enhanced by airy, light locker rooms. The entry hall would be the place to store boots; its grated wood floor would allow moisture to drain. Boots would hang on vent pegs that gently circulated air through them.

The ski room would be next in the chain of conveniences for the teachers. Ski racks would line the walls, allowing each teacher the space for several pairs of skis. The center of this room would be occupied by a series of work tables with effective vises and heating elements that contained the right wax (in liquid form) for each particular day. Belt systems would be available for reconditioning skis after heavier use or damage. Industrial vacuums would allow for easy and quick cleaning of the wax and file shavings after a tuning job was complete.

In the locker room itself a well-ventilated area would be provided to allow wet clothing to be hung freely. A washer and dryer would enable teachers to launder their undergarments and socks for the next day. Private locker space for personal paraphernalia would be available to each instructor. Adjacent to the locker room would be the showers, the sauna and the jacuzzi. The day's fatigue would transform into a pleasant feeling of relaxation in the process of "cleaning up." A change of clothing would make it possible to meet customers directly after work. For instructors with no immediate obligations, a small weightroom would allow them to maintain muscle tone.

Teachers could relax in comfortable lounges close to the enrollment area. Reclining chairs would allow them to elevate their feet while they waited for their customers. Earphones, with a selection of music, and a variety of magazines would make the waiting time more enjoyable. In the event of pre-booked lessons, the instructor would have a detailed personality data sheet in order to fully prepare for each individual student.

A teachers' library would encourage the instructors to spend time "brushing up" on certain issues pertaining to teaching; the selection of books would be a complete inventory of classic and contemporary publications covering the wide variety of ski-related topics. Books would be available to check out, as well.

An employee cafeteria serving a variety of foods at reasonable prices would be available. A monthly bill could be deducted from each instructor's paycheck.

Employees would earn a salary appropriate to their expertise and the influence they might have upon the return rate of customers. This salary would allow them to live in the community where they were employed, rather than feeling like a commuter from a different social environment. This would foster harmony and a greater community feeling.

For the customer, similar storage and changing facilities should be provided. Massage and medical consultation would be offered by the staff. Evening cross country activity would exist as an alternative to structured exercise program. Lighted tracks in a variety of lengths would appeal to anyone's needs. A nearby indoor ice rink could become a social hotspot before dinner, allowing people to build up an appetite in a convenient meeting place.

Because of the quality of service and the experience such a set-up would encompass, customers might have to book their vacations in advance. The season could essentially be booked out, leaving a small segment of lodging and service arrangements open for "walk-in" business. Administration could be further facilitated by a process of central billing. Every customer would be issued an electromagnetically charged pass to be worn around his neck, which, in turn, would be the passport to lifts, purchasing commodities, food, drink, lessons, rentals, etc. Customers would either pay upon departure or request to be billed later. Installment payments would also be available; the Center could charge interest for outstanding charges as a bank would. People would "line up" for such an experience!

Though parts of this dream are already a reality at some ski areas, I wonder whether the holistic concept of a "training center" could ever become a reality. Some of the ideas seem futuristic, but all of them are possible with our existing know-how and finances. I am, furthermore, convinced that this type of a Training Center could be a financial success. Someone with influence and capital must be convinced to share my dream!

PEAK PERFORMANCE

"Memories are myths, you don't remember facts, but how you perceive them."

Anonymous

Bernard Russi, a great downhill racer, once described his experience on a most-challenging section of the Kitzbuehel downhill as a visit with extraordinary tranquility. Having studied this notorious segment of the course, he dreaded the steep fall-away and its tremendous ripples, knowing that he would hit them at over 50 mph. To his amazement, as he came to the spot during the race, he felt light, relaxed; time seemed to slow down. It was as if he was seeing himself in a film running at slow-motion. He was perfectly aware of his body, of sailing through the air, of the changing pressure on his skis as they twisted and bounced.

Climbing a mountain near my home in Austria, I was about halfway up and struggling to overcome a rock face when I heard a loud rumble warning me of an approaching thunderstorm. A crack of lightning sparked a surge of energy in me and I began climbing

with a skill and speed beyond my known capabilities. With static electricity literally making my hair stand on end, I discarded all my metallic gear and continued in a free-climb. Grips I would never before have trusted became secure ledges. I swam over an impossible traverse pushing inward on the finest fissures. The mountain receded beneath me as I slithered up its treacherous side, completely oblivious to potential dangers. I was never scared and it seemed the most normal thing in the world.

I returned to that area many times after that day and, each time, that experience seemed impossible. I would stare in wonder at that rock face. Had it really happened?

There are countless stories of similar athletic experiences. In essence, they are no different from the feelings great composers, scientists and philosophers sense when they go through extraordinary enlightenment in their field. Many recreational runners tell stories of transcending agony to arrive at a feeling of lightness and litheness; running is effortless, as if the feet are not even touching the ground. The common denominator for all these experiences is that people succumb to a state of thoughtlessness, abandoning intellectual associations to the task at hand, and surrendering to a euphoria that cannot be generated through conscious thought or action. It does not take "greatness" to reach such a state.

Incredible feats are identified by psychologist Abraham Maslov as "peak performance." According to Maslov, peak performance is accompanied by a trance-like state of mind. Movement seems to slow, the mind becomes extremely calm, effort subsides as output increases. It is a period of rallying of mental and physical resources that plateaus in a cool, non-judgemental mode of perceiving only "what is." The element of effort is absent and tension is merely functional, appropriate to the situation. Athletes involved in various sports have reported "peak performance" experiences. Many tennis players describe times when the ball, coming at them at 100 mph or more, seems to be transformed into a large, fuzzy grapefruit-sized object; the ball slows down or even stops, as if waiting to be hit.

"Peak performance" is the dominance of right brain capabilities. To come closer to it in skiing, we need to wake up the right brain, to allow ourselves to learn more quickly and to fully employ our existing skills. Since the right side of the brain has been largely neglected since childhood, it takes time and skill to unearth its qualities, but by revitalizing right brain functions, we can begin to explore our true potential.

Physical movement is a right hemisphere function, so we can stimulate the right brain by moving. There is a Chinese proverb that says:

"I hear and I forget,
I see and I remember,
I do and I understand."

Experiments have confirmed this. Experts tell us that people generally remember:

10% of what they READ
20% of what they HEAR
30% of what they SEE
50% of what they HEAR and SEE
70% of what they SAY and WRITE

and 90% of what they DO.

Doing, alone, rarely promotes learning. "Practice makes perfect" is a misnomer. Awareness, another right brain function, must accompany practice in order to achieve results. The clearer the awareness of the situation, the more learning that can take place.

Awareness is being alert to your self and your surroundings. A skier attempting to overcome a particular problem in his technique will have great difficulty until he has a physical understanding of what it is that he's doing wrong. One instructor at the Vail Ski School was able to ski any snow on any terrain, but he had one idiosyncrasy that was disturbing; he swung his hips when turning. He attended various workshops where he was told about this flaw in his style. After unsuccessful attempts to remedy the problem, he saw a video of himself skiing. It was a great surprise to everyone to hear him exclaim: "Oh, *that's* what I'm doing!" With this realization, he was finally able to correct his undesirable habit.

The two ways of "knowing"—intellectually vs. intuitively—are, unfortunately, not distinctive to many people. I have often heard students exclaim, "I know what I am supposed to do, but I don't seem to be able to do it." To make things worse, these skiers often reject attempts to awaken their awareness. Instead, they insist on more explanation and eventually leave the lesson satisfied, with a sense of having increased their knowledge, but with no improvement in their skill.

Awareness can be general (listening, feeling and watching without expectation) or specific (dealing with one particular aspect of the situation). It can be internally directed toward what is going on physically or mentally; it can be external, directed toward what is happening outside the body. Experts ski with general external awareness, taking in what happens around them. They may momentarily switch to a more specific internal focus as the situation demands, but they soon return to a general approach. Picture a ski race: the racer is warming up, stretching out, mentally reviewing the course. He is called to the start. Exploding out of the gate, he's off. His body responds automatically through fined-tuned reflexes. He focuses ahead, intent on the upcoming turns. Every once in awhile, a tactical thought will come to his mind—"slow down for the fall-away left turn, then let the mother's honk," but he will immediately switch back to the whole picture when he's in the clear. Ifs, shoulds and oughts don't clutter a winner's mind.

While the expert skier is in a state of general external awareness, the beginner is most effective using general *internal* awareness. He attends mostly to the feelings of his own body, the rhythm and intensity of his movements, the speed, the fears, tensions, elation and confidence. He will shift to a specific external awareness when needed. He hits a patch of ice and his awareness shifts from rhythmic turning to increasing edge angle and thus preventing a slide. (When performance is interrupted by anything that threatens balance, the attention of the skier will be immediately diverted from a general to a specific level.)

Novices often go wrong in trying to control their movements with a constant, specific internal awareness. They engage the left brain functions of analysis and sequence to construct a string of commands for their bodies: these orders interfere with holistic coordination of physical movement, which is a right brain function.

Picture a beginning skier. He is at the top of a beginner's slope. His friend, an experienced skier, has told him, "It's easy! All you have to do is stay in a snowplow and shift your weight to the downhill ski. Don't lean into the hill. Bend your knees and turn, but don't look at your skis. Relax!" The novice says, "HUH?" The expert friend repeats the same instructions, only *louder* (maybe beginners are deaf). Coerced into starting down the hill, the beginner, rigid with tension, tries to do all the things his friend has told him. He ends up going straight down the hill faster and faster, wobbling from side to side, until he finally loses his balance and crashes, falling over backwards. His friend skis down to him and says, "I *told* you not to lean *backwards!*"

Obscuring a person's awareness with too many instructions will make him so preoccupied that he can't even stand up on his skis! They call it "paralysis through analysis." Experiment with your own awareness as you ski to find your own most functional level. Make distinctions between sensory/environmental awarenesses, general/specific awarenesses, and external/internal awarenesses. Develop a broad perspective, but don't try to take in so many things that your mind grows cluttered. Learn to focus your thoughts toward the desired effects.

These exercises in awareness can be done alone, but are more fun and beneficial with a skiing friend. At various times while skiing, ask yourself the following questions and share responses.

• What is foremost in your mind right now? The answer may be a *general* feeling like "cold," "tired," "bored," "enthusiastic," or a *specific* aspect of your experience such as the feel of the snow, the rush of the wind or the rhythm of the turns.

• Are you scared? How do you know? What are the areas of tension in your body?

• What differences do you feel between smooth, rounded, rhythmic turns and abrupt, choppy ones? What do you do differently? Does your speed vary between left and right turns? Assess the intensity as you go from turn to turn; say aloud, "a little—medium—a lot." Does it vary? Why? Are the turns the same? If not, what makes them different?

• Can you experiment in the same manner with edge angle, fore/aft pressure change, up/down movements and any other noticeable characteristic of your technique?

• How do your changing moods affect your skiing and ability to progress?

THE ART OF IMAGING

"A picture is worth a thousand words."

Fred R. Barnard

Imaging, a right brain function, is the use of mental pictures to aid performance. It helps to have a visual image before attempting a new movement. That image can be conjured up from a description, from pictures or from observation. The more vivid the image, the easier it will be to emulate. Images fade rapidly; to retain its accuracy, the image must constantly be refreshed.

A big part of learning how to ski is learning how to observe. Select appropriate models and view them in general. Look for rhythm, cadence, harmony and flow. Allow every possible association; feel the mood of your model as well as the forces he is reacting to. Occasionally you can choose a specific aspect of the skier's movements, focusing on detail. Concentrate for awhile before fitting this element back into the general picture.

Imaging is preparation for action. Either summoning mental pictures of a performance or concentrating on an image to affect mood or movement can dramatically enhance your execution. Visual rehearsal is one form of this practice; you watch a movie of yourself in action. Replay your mental movie until it runs smoothly and continuously. Closing your eyes will reduce distractions and allow you to concentrate. Practice at home. Picture yourself doing a sequence of turns in a selected environment you want to prepare for, i.e., a steep slope, deep snow, high speed, etc. Experience the run in perfect harmony, with flawless technique, flow, rhythm and confidence. The ability to make these impeccable runs is the privilege of your imagination. Enjoy it!

Visual rehearsal not only aids mental preparation but actually stimulates the muscles needed for the movement. The more real the mental image, the greater the benefit of such practice. Initially you will see the action as if watching a film—essentially as a bystander. Gradually attempt to cast *yourself* as the performer. Watch yourself from the front, side and rear. *Feel* the wind and the snow, the pressure exerted on your skis, each movement and reaction. Actually hear your jacket flapping in the wind and the sound your skis make as you turn. This sensory association will make the image more powerful.

For decades, top athletes have been using this type of visual rehearsal to prepare for competition; its psychological and physiological benefits are well established. In 1962, Gerhardt Happel, an Austrian soccer star, was asked what made it possible for him to shoot penalty shots with such incredible force and speed. He replied, "When getting ready to shoot the soccer ball, I picture myself from underneath, as if watching my footprints on a glass surface from the level below. When I make my inrun, I concentrate upon the image of sinking my balancing leg deep into the soccer field turf while picturing my swinging leg to whisk the ball with the speed of an express train. The rest just happens."

Another form of imaging is "role playing." You can ski like a slithering snake, a fierce tiger, a stately bishop, a floating feather. The power of suggestion depends on your willingness to identify with the image you select.

Once, when working with a timid skier who seldom strayed from gentle terrain, I suggested he "become" Phil Mahre, World Cup Champion. I told him that he had just won a medal at Lake Placid, that he was one of the best skiers in the world, that he was confident and that he loved skiing fast. While we were having this exchange, we skied through a difficult section of terrain and snow. His total immersion in this image made his skiing as strong and supple as could be expected from a skier at his level. He had skied a run that he had never dared ski before. He had become Phil Mahre; he enjoyed the challenge of the hill.

Another time I worked with a lady who had been badly injured the year before. She was scared stiff. Starting out on very easy terrain, I asked her what animal she identified with "aggressiveness." "The gorilla," she finally decided. "What would a gorilla ski like?" I asked. She hunched over, letting her arms dangle and lowering her stance. She began turning with greater movement and strength. Bounding from ski to ski, she flashed down the hill. I also skied like a gorilla. We took a breather and I asked her what a gorilla would *sound* like when skiing. Suddenly the air was filled with the most incredible screams of belligerence I've ever heard. Head-shaking people on the lift no doubt wondered who the two drunks loose on the slopes were. However, her skiing ability took a phenomenal leap as she caught hold of the image. We regained human form at the bottom of the hill and laughed at how silly we must have looked to other people. There wasn't a trace of fear associated with her injury for the rest of our lessons together.

Imaging awakens the right side of the brain; in its various forms, it can be a powerful tool for a skier at any level of expertise. It helps us believe in ourselves and relax our anxieties. Through practice and a willingness to surrender to the image, this technique is one of the most useful tools any athlete can acquire to improve his performance.

HOLISTIC LEARNING & JUDGEMENT

"Our loudest critics will be those who are bitterly afraid and internally torn in their own struggle for a meaningful fulfillment in life."

Anonymous

Too often skiing is taught by components. The teaching plan directs instructors to work on one skill at a time. When an accepted level of performance in that particular area is achieved, the student is "allowed" to progress. People take lessons for an entire week but sometimes learn only the unintegrated aspects of a turn. The problem is not limited to ski instruction; whether you take a lesson in golf, tennis, dancing or squash, your coach generally instructs you using a series of directives: "know your grip," "get the step," "the swing is led by the hips," "the skis are turned by transferring weight and edging. . . . "

Holistic perception is a function of the right brain; learning physical movements in a sport like skiing is facilitated by this approach. Consider the components of a turn. You start the turn by moving upward and when the skis are light, you gently pivot them in the desired direction. At this point, edge change takes place through an altering inclination of the body; weight transfer coincides with the edge changing movement. All of those words describe just the *very start* of a turn! We could continue and dissect the controlling and the finishing phases of it, not to mention the mechanics involved in connecting turns, but who would care to remember all of those instructions, let alone keep them in a proper sequence and timing? With a totally mental approach, "flow" is impossible. Regarding a movement as a whole, rather than as many parts, can make learning considerably easier. The ability to move is a sensation, not an explanation.

Waking the right side of the brain is a process that engages us holistically; spatial and non-verbal faculties must help us learn and perform. This new way of perceiving releases existing skills and increases the rate at which we learn. As we have seen, the right side of the brain has been largely neglected since childhood, so it will take time, patience and practice to unearth its qualities and employ them in our endeavors.

Tapping into methods like rhythm in skiing, exploring rather than being directed, appealing to feeling, awareness and intuition, we build a strong basis from which we can develop confidently, rapidly and autonomously.

While we know that optimal results in learning are achieved by using both hemispheres, the real key to learning is to teach skillfully to the "right side of the brain." Spontaneity and intuitiveness make learning a joy and when people enjoy what they are doing, they progress much more quickly. Teaching to the right side of the brain (as well as to its partner) takes advantage of vast, otherwise untapped, resources. It is a holistic process; first students learn to learn, then they learn to ski.

Give yourself the freedom to make mistakes; do not judge yourself (or others) on "errors" committed as a normal part of learning. The common attitude toward an "error" is that it is something bad, an abnormality, a deviation from the *right* path. Too often we attach emotional importance to our mistakes, allowing them to adversely affect our self-esteem. We too often misconstrue them as personal failures.

Making judgements (right or wrong, good or

JUDGEMENT PARAMETER

JUDGEMENT PARAMETER

Performance vacillations are few and are judgementally curtailed by self or instructor. "Experiencing" (a prerequisite for learning) is essentially suppressed.

bad) engages left brain functions that can obscure our sensory feedback. Consider a typical situation: a skier falls in view of the crowded chairlift. As soon as the shock of his fall fades, he feels he must make excuses: it was the binding or the nasty snag uphill that must have tripped him. Swearing at himself for his stupidity and lack of coordination, he gets up and quickly brushes off the evidence of his fall. Still embarrassed from the incident, he hacks his way downhill, only to fall again. His emotional reaction to the initial fall didn't allow him to recognize the reason for it; nor was he able to

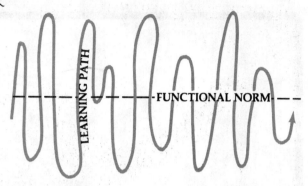

Experimenting goes largely unchecked thus allowing a wide basis for the learner to glean from. Rather than trying to prevent the student from straying from what might be the most functional technique, an instructor can actually draw this person into unusual practice, introducing the functional norm by choice rather than by directive.

regain his composure and concentration for a renewed attack. If we can manage to stop judging ourselves emotionally, we will be free to learn from the mistakes and problems all people face.

Too often, beginning skiers and/or their instructors place arbitrary limitations on their performance. Students oriented in this way are so afraid of making mistakes, they won't experiment and consequently, they do not advance beyond what they are currently doing.

Without the contrived boundaries of perfection, a learner feels encouraged to explore and experiment. From a vast range of experiences, he will eventually be able to select his own functional technique for a particular situation. He is also able to cope with less desirable performance incidents simply because "he's *been* there." This is a trial-and-error process in which the error is not a "bad" or punishable experience, but an information source.

So, experiment with "errors." Try out "mistakes," so the correct method can be recognized. If you only *know* one way, how can you be sure it's the right one? Single-solution approach totally ignores the flexibility required to cope with the ever-changing situations encountered in skiing. A marksman, sighting in a rifle, is operating in a non-judgemental way. He will carefully stabilize the rifle and fire at the target, aiming at the bull's-eye. He doesn't expect his shots to *hit* the bull's-eye; he looks to see where the shots hit and adjusts his scope accordingly. He does not throw his rifle down in disgust or call himself a bad shot. He repeats the process over and over, reading the pattern each time to further adjust his sights. By viewing his actions this way, he can correct the rifle and, ultimately, hit dead center.

SELF-CONCEPT

"They say I am always playing myself. I have played all these different parts — but of course I am always myself!"

Bette Davis

We are who we *think* we are and we can do what we *think* we can do. "Suggestilology can revolutionize teaching and learning," to quote Dr. Lazanov from the Institute of Suggestilology in Sophia, Bulgaria. Suggestilology has to do with self-perception and self-communication. Most of us know that we can talk ourselves into having a bad day or convince ourselves that we cannot do something. Few of us talk ourselves into "good" days or into believing we *can* do something. The adjacent diagram shows the perpetuating effect of our self-concept. Our perception of self is the basis for self-talk, which, in turn, influences output, which creates self-image, more self-talk, etc.

Negative self-image is epidemic in skiing. Inextricably tied to the values of right and wrong is a lack of confidence that undermines performance. To change the outcome, you are compelled to alter your self-image.

When discussing self-image, I often ask people whether they think of themselves as athletic or non-athletic as far as skiing is concerned. Frequently, they reply that they do not perceive themselves to be "natural athletes." I ask them to point out a "natural athlete" if one skis by. I then pursue the identified "natural athlete" to ask whether he perceives himself in that light. He usually shares the same self-doubt.

Low self-esteem results from constantly comparing ourselves to what we are not. This unrealistic comparison and its consequent senseless attachment to self-worth distracts us from the reality of a situation. Since awareness is the path to change, we must not allow negative self-image to interfere with our awareness.

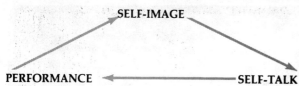

SELF-IMAGE

PERFORMANCE ← → SELF-TALK

Many athletes pursue the image-building process differently. Some very successful ones never need to attend to this issue since what already makes them successful, in part, is their belief in themselves.

I have found that the most accessible way to improve "crumbled self images" is by taking inventory of what a person can currently do. Some of the students I inherited at times were reluctant to discuss what they could do, wanting to stick to their self destructive talk of what "they could not do." At times I also realized that such learners spent little or no time in the here and now, thus always belittling the past or doodling self-chastizingly in the future — "Gee, I really want to ski like Stenmark, yet, look at me. What a clutz I am." One way or another, I would bring the skier to take stock of what he or she can do.

The next step then is to find out what short- and long-term goals that skier wants to accomplish. We then go through a process that I have begun to call: Goal Identification/Goal Selection. We then will proceed to determine what we wish to accomplish in one, two, three lessons; what we want to be able to do in a week. The important issue in this process is to isolate realistic goals that lie within the reach of the student from a physical and psychological point of view.

The next step then is to make a commitment to work towards those goals.

Self image will rise the moment we actually reach a goal the student and I have set ourselves. Keeping careful inventory of where we have been, where we are and where we are going, we should also leave ourselves the option of changing our goals. This process will soon help learners to focus upon concrete tasks and the experience of skiing and will divert them from the self-destructive process of self-belittling.

The process of "image building" can be achieved by the teacher with setting the student up for successes. Careful selection of terrain and snow, skillful selection of tasks and a keen, supportive eye for improvement which is observable will soon boost the learner to self sufficiency.

Seemingly insignificant, but very effective techniques for image building also include: working with the student as an equal, using video tapes of successful skiing experiences to reinforce the behavior and boost the ego, encouraging the learner to wear something that makes him or her feel good, making sure the skis are waxed and tuned so successes will come with minimum effort and using the learner who has accomplished a goal as a model for others.

TURNING "RIGHT"

"We do not see first, then define. We define first and then see."

Walter Lippman

Most ski instructors and coaches are products of an educational system that emphasizes left brain capabilities. It is not surprising, then, to find that they also teach skiing in a left brain mode. Paradoxically, many of these teachers did not learn to ski the way they teach skiing. Most people I know in the profession learned the sport largely from experimentation, observation and just "going out to ski."

Traditional education is based upon the behaviourist learning theory—it contends that acquisition of a new skill is the result of repeated trials with differential reinforcement of responses (reward or punishment). The frequency of the desired response is gradually increased as the organism associates its performance with positive reinforcement. Behaviouristic theory separates tasks into parts; each segment of the ultimately desired outcome is stressed by itself. The theory is fine for controlled experiments using laboratory animals, but is inadequate in dealing with the individual differences and situational effects of human learning.

A————B————C————D————E————F——→

This is a linear, conceptual model. Concept A is followed by concept B, which in turn is followed by concept C, and so on. This mode is sequential, logical, easily understood and systemized.

During my days as a ski instructor in Kitzbuehel, Austria, I was forced to follow a behaviouristic learning model. Our teaching outline was clearly defined, specifying not only each developmental segment's goal, but also the process by which the goal had to be achieved, as well as how *long* this process was supposed to take. One week, I had a group of Americans who had never skied before. They were enthusiastic and reasonably athletic. We spent the first day on flat terrain getting accustomed to the skis. We walked and glided. At the end of the first day, we made a brief, but illegal, excursion into wedge turning; it was an instant success! The next day, wedges and wedge turning were on the agenda. We practiced not only until the turns were functional, but until they conformed to the aesthetic model imprinted in my head by the training I had received.

Our third day was devoted to side-slipping and traversing. I remember one of my students asking, "Why are we always skiing across the hill? Can't we go down?". My trained response was; "We are not just going across the hill *any* old way, we are 'traversing.' You must be angulated, bent sideways at the waist and facing downhill. Always keep your feet together!" I watched their performances intently, giving each student praise or criticism. "Now that's what I am looking for, George," or "No, Albert, that's not it, you've got to turn your shoulders downhill." I badgered the group into experts at traversing, diagonal side-slipping, vertical side-slipping and stairstep side-slipping. In retrospect, I'm surprised that this class stuck with me, but then again, I *was* the authority; they trusted me more than their own feelings. We spent the rest of the week perfecting necessary components of the stem christie. Toward the end, I caught one of my students skiing on the intermediate hill. I scolded him, "Jack, you can't ski here! We haven't finished our basic training. Now get right back down to the practice hill so that we can prepare for skiing this hill!" Jack nodded apologetically, pushed off with embarrassment and skied down to the designated area, making smooth, controlled stem christies. I realized the stupidity of what I had said. At that point I abandoned a lock-step progression and we spent the rest of the day skiing intermediate runs from the gondola. It was a delightful day of sunshine and smiles. We were filled with the spirit of skiing. As a group, we realized that skiing is more than a mastery of arbitrary techniques; it is freedom, joy and self-expression. The next day, I was fired for "neglecting to remain within the prescribed progression."

The humanistic alternative to behaviourism developed in the 1920's; it started with Gestalt (German for shape or form) theory. Gestalt learning focuses on cognitive ability. It holds that understanding is neither random nor accidental, but is based upon clearly perceived experiences. The individual approaches the task or situation as a whole. Learning is a continual process whereby experiences shape awareness.

Humanists feel that people learn from many different sources, in many ways and at various rates. They think that individuals respond differently to similar stimuli. Our learning patterns are more like a three-dimensional, geometric expansion, rather than a straight-lined, arithmetical progression.

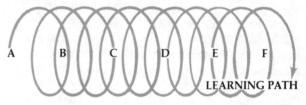

This means that people learn because each situation offers unique experiences, which, in turn, lead to personal revelations we are more likely to remember. People learn with greater ease and retain more of what they learn if they are guided toward self-discovery rather than being bombarded with concepts to which they personally cannot relate. Instructors are encouraged to teach less along the lines of mechanical analysis and shallow directives, and to work harder at creating on-the-hill experiences so discovery can take place.

Contemporary educational theory, influenced by brain hemisphere research, goes beyond the humanistic geometric model to incorporate concepts and experience.

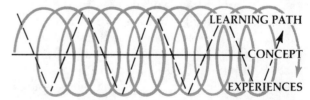

Behaviourist and humanist learning models demonstrate that learning is the product of a combination of experience *and* concept; the learning path is in constant vacillation between the two. By themselves, concepts are meaningless, just as experiences without any frame of reference have no value. Learning happens most efficiently when concepts and experiences go hand in hand.

A cognitive, humanistic learning theory applied to skiing puts the focus upon the student and the situation, rather than on the teacher or the task. Dialogue replaces monologue and awareness of what is actually happening overcomes concern about doing something "right" or "wrong." Such an approach promotes "exploration" over "memorization and rules." The learner develops autonomy, a sense of freedom from his instructor's judgement and advice. Too often teachers deliberately nurture dependence in order to feed their own feelings of self-worth, thereby denigrating their fundamental roles as educational facilitators. It is of primary importance for students to learn how to learn, not just to accomplish a particular maneuver in skiing. If a cognitive, humanistic learning theory is employed, coaches and teachers can escape the obsession of mechanical analysis and involve themselves in nurturing awareness within their pupils.

Many great athletes deliberately shield themselves from analyzing what "makes them great." The French ski team (once the world's best) lost prominence in the early seventies, due, in part, to the training staff's confusion about the role of technical analysis in coaching. The racers were overloaded with commentary and their performance promptly suffered. The value of mechanical examination by coaches or instructors cannot be disputed, but to effect a change in performance, the trainer must go beyond physiological analysis to reveal the necessity for changes to take place. The coach's challenge lies in his translation of analytical concepts into simple, effective requests for performance. However, it is vital to exercise awareness and caution when dispensing analytical information. For many years racers have been directed to "put their knees into the turn as soon as possible, to edge the skis and pressure the tips." Static demonstrations by coaches displayed the desired medial rotation of the bent leg, but the racers, during the pressure phases of a turn, generally kept their leg laterally extended, because the musculature required to sustain such articulation was under great stress and was far too feeble to accommodate that demand.

Another very prominent case of faulty analysis of cause and effect relationships in skiing is the issue of how to initiate a wedge turn. Teachers have always told their students to move the pressure to the outside ski of the upcoming turn in order to begin the turn. Electromyographic studies, coupled with slow-motion film, have provided evidence that *pivoting* the skis starts a turn, not *pressuring* them. There is further evidence that to start the pivot, pressure must temporarily be removed, not added!

Obviously, faulty analysis has provided students with equally faulty directives. Learners follow what they believed to be viable instructions. When results do not ensue, they may feel autonomous enough to attempt a trial and error process that deviates from their instructor's suggestions, not mentioning the experiment to their teacher at all. Consequently, their eventual success may not seem real or deserved. The resulting confusion is not rare in *any* sport or academic endeavor. Even the pros have the problem, as the subsequent story illustrates.

Joan Hanna, a U.S. olympic racer who now teaches skiing in Vail, Colorado, tells the story of her difficulty with Giant Slalom (one of her best events) in the Olympic Games in Innsbruch, Austria: "In the World Championship Giant Slalom the year before in Chamonix, I did very well, placing third, .19 of a second behind the winner. In 1964, the Olympic Games, it was a different story. Bob Beattie was the coach at the time and his emphasis then was the 'dyna turn,' a turning concept he had analyzed from the racing technique of Buddy Werner. Many directives and exercises were issued to the US team. Those of us who were farther from the mould were pushed harder to conform to the 'dyna turn' concept; but Jean Saubert was skiing very well and Beattie seemed to see little reason to alter her technique.

"Race day—the directive 'drive those knees' was dominating any other concern. Saubert won the silver medal in Giant Slalom; I was eight seconds behind! Upon returning to ski in the U.S. Nationals in Winter Park, Colorado, Beattie was not with us. Succumbing to a 'go for it' mood, I skied the way I was used to skiing. I came in third, .3 seconds behind Saubert, who was second behind Pia Riva, then an Italian team member."

The most effective coach trains so that each athlete can become "unconsciously competent," not preoccupied about what he is doing, but intuitively responding to the demands of each situation. Skiing ability has traditionally been the most important qualification for a ski coach or teacher, yet, performing well in a sport is *not* an essential condition for teaching it. This is most true at the highest levels of expertise where the coach cannot possibly fathom skiing as well as the athletes he is working with. At higher levels of performance, athletes no longer depend upon external models; these competitors create their own model in image and feeling. The coach working with beginning or intermediate athletes must proportionately hone himself as a model, until such time as the paragon he portrays must yield to the skill and kinesthetic awareness of his protege.

In some parts of the globe, there is still argument over the value of a mechanical knowledge of the sport being taught, but sound methodological directions can *only* come from someone who:

a) knows the sport from a standpoint of its mechanical makeup.

b) realizes factors influencing each individual's ability to learn and perform.

c) can perform the task and has had experiences that he can translate into kinesthetic associations *with* the sport.

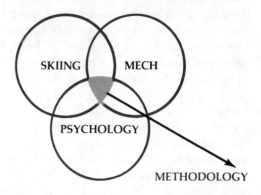

Sound coaching and teaching can only be the product of the joint elements of skiing experience, mechanical understanding of the sport and understanding how people learn and perform.

A teacher with no understanding of the catalytic elements of learning and performing is one who will use stereotypic methods that, because they are arbitrary, are meaningless. Realizing how people learn demands that the teacher understand the nature of fear, negative self-talk, anxiety and boredom, and consequently, promote methods to help students learn to cope with these conditions. A great portion of the instructor's time must be spent getting the participant into a learning/performing mode. While often a person doesn't need to be taught new skills, he wants help in allowing his existing talents to emerge.

In skiing (as in other activities), state of mind and level of readiness is dramatically expressed

---

"THE EFFECTIVE TEACHER"
CONSCIOUS COMPETENCE
"I am good at what I am doing, and I know why I am good."

"THE INEFFECTIVE BEGINNER"
CONSCIOUS INCOMPETENCE
"I know what I should do, but I cannot do it."

"THE INEFFECTIVE BEGINNER"
UNCONSCIOUS COMPETENCE
'I know nothing about it."

"THE EFFECTIVE ATHLETE"
UNCONSCIOUS COMPETENCE
"I am good at what I am doing, but I could not explain why I am good."

through posture and movement — or lack of! A stiff "outside-of-the-turn leg" is a sign of fear. Trying to correct the symptom — the rigidity (the mistake) itself — is rarely effective. Telling a frightened skier not to "lean into the hill" or even, as a more positive approach, to "lean away from the hill," is like a doctor telling a flu victim, "Well, just stop coughing." Most interaction between teacher and student deals with a specific technique of execution. Such instructions are generally of a technical or manipulative nature. Seldom do teachers attempt to regulate the energy level of the student through imaging or self-talk, but those methods yield incredible mechanical changes. Alterations of perception can be the route by which the learner achieves complex progress without ever being burdened with technical directives. Though the phrase "the body and muscles do not know English" is somewhat simplistic, it is an easy-to-remember slogan that hits an important issue squarely.

If a teacher chooses to teach a student with complexity and analysis, actual learning can never take place. The skilled teacher will use his wisdom to translate detailed observations and contemplations into simple, effective suggestions. This artful instructor simply creates situations through which certain desired responses will be inevitable.

Jean Claude Killy was one of the finest all-around competitors in alpine ski racing during the sixties and early seventies. In an interview with ABC Sports, when asked what he attributed his incredible success in skiing to, he responded: "While many of my competitors ski with great intelligence (pointing to his head) I ski with intelligent feet." This distinction between characteristic operating modes for coaches and teachers as opposed to learners and performers is an important realization to come to. At this time, I feel that few teachers and even fewer students comprehend the voluntary obstacles they build for themselves by ignoring the principle Killy refers to.

FUNCTIONAL TENSION

"The centipede was happy quite, until a toad in fun said, 'Pray, which leg after which?' That worked her mind to such a pitch, she lay distracted in the ditch, considering how to run."

Anonymous

Fear and anxiety in skiing can be sensible control factors, but can also cause a debilitating condition. Like the concept of error, fear is generally perceived as undesirable, as damaging. To facilitate effective learning, tension, timidity and anxiety are realities we must consider closely.

Challenge is essential to learning. Too much of it cripples the learner with fear but too little results in boredom. Between paralytic fear and lack of interest lies functional tension which, in turn, provokes motivation, interest and awareness. Optimal tension is the highest level of functional anxiety that permits the highest level

of performance. It is an alert, intense awareness. From this level of finely-tuned tension, an athlete can respond with the greatest speed and strength. Optimal tension allows a person to perform at his peak level of performance.

Coaches and instructors need to determine the functional tension necessary for each individual in a given task. They must also be equipped to help students and athletes reach that level of tension by employing techniques that either stimulate or reduce strain. Varying the intensity of breathing, certain exercises, tuning the intensity and/or speed of imaging and/or mental relaxation exercise can be used to help one attain

a level of functional tension.

Sometime in the late 1960's, an ABC sports commentary covering ski races focused briefly upon bright, fluorescent stickers on the helmets and fronts of skis of some competitors. These stickers had a white number "5" on the bright orange field of a circular sticker. The commentary explained that these stickers had the effect of reducing tension in a preconditioned manner. What preceded the display of the stickers was somewhat vague, but insinuated the following: each racer participating in the program was assessed as to whether he needed to be "revved up" or "calmed down" in preparation for a race. Individual conditioning was aimed at providing images, associations and feelings to assist the athlete in reaching an optimal level of readiness. The association of that mental state and the method of getting there became symbolically connected with the orange sticker and the number "5" on it. Before races, the skiers would see the stickers on the members of their own team while they waited to start. Their associations called up the necessary calming or stimulating reaction, thus helping them tune in to a more functional tention level for their own competition.

The athlete who catches himself in a state of mind that is not appropriate to the task at hand will benefit from processes through which he can make the desired adjustments. Coaching and teaching can make such mental reorientation a major target.

TENSION BAROMETER

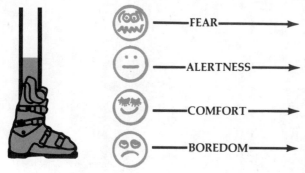

FEAR — Challenges are or are perceived to be too great. Stifling consequences result from too much tension.

ALERTNESS — Challenges require concentration, but are within the abilities of the athlete. A level of peak performance is aided by optimal tension.

COMFORT — The individual is at ease with himself and the challenges. He works within the range of functional tension.

BOREDOM — Mental and physical stimulation is lacking. Boredom is the predominant sensation of insufficient tension.

PRE-SKI CONDITIONING

BODY CONDITIONING

"My body is that part of the world my ideas can change."

G. C. Lichtenberg

The increasing popularity of Alpine and Nordic skiing since World War II has brought large numbers of people onto the slopes. Many of these novices lack sufficient conditioning to ski safely and, unaware of their physical limitations, take to the mountains largely unprepared. According to the National Ski Patrol, most injuries are fatigue-related and, therefore, avoidable. Proper overall conditioning can greatly reduce the chance of injury and make skiing more enjoyable.

Conditioning has traditionally implied a harsh regimen of rigorous exercise: sweat, pain, punishing running or cycling and pumping iron. While this training certainly has its proponents, the philosophy and activities of conditioning are changing. Modern conditioning programs draw from a number of different fields to optimize general well-being rather than focusing merely on developing strength. Holistic conditioning is especially important for skiing because of the variety of challenges encountered in the sport; physical and mental aspects of skiing are inseparable, so conditioning programs should reflect this same integration to be truly useful. An effective program of ski conditioning incorporates elements of nutrition, physical fitness and training in awareness and relaxation techniques. To be truly in shape, both the body and mind must be fit.

The following is a holistic program for ski conditioning. Not a rigid regimen, this program is a set of guidelines which you should adjust to your schedule, preferences and needs. For it to be effective, you should follow an exercise sequence at least three times a week but not more than five times. Conditioning ought to be an enjoyable part of your personal routine. If you don't look forward to it and have to drag yourself out each day, it's time to change something. Think about what is making you dissatisfied, then experiment with a variety of likely solutions.

The importance of proper equipment cannot be overemphasized. As injury protection (among other things) equipment is everything from supportive running shoes to a properly maintained bicycle. Clothes should be comfortable and appropriate. They should not only be compatible with the elements, but also should make you "feel athletic!" Seek an atmosphere that encourages you, choose music that entices you to move, places to run in pleasant surroundings and compatible partners to exercise with. Build yourself a positive addiction to your own physical program.

This particular training plan is specifically designed to prepare you for skiing, but the benefits will extend into all areas of your life. Total conditioning of mind and body will make you healthier, more energetic and better prepared to meet the challenges of each day. *(Note: Consult a physician before undertaking this, or any other, conditioning program.)*

AWARENESS: TUNE IN

Awareness is differential attention to what is going on around and inside you. Experimenting with awareness can open your mind, increase sensitivity and allow you to see and feel in a variety of new ways. Awareness practice should always accompany physical conditioning to monitor mental/physical effects, alert you to tension, rhythm, elation and "burn out."

Hard Focus/Soft Focus   Look at a common object closely, almost dissecting it into its parts — colors, textures, shapes, sizes. Now half-close your eyes and view the same object as if from a great distance. Notice its general shape; allow yourself to make associations. Finally, look at the whole object in relation to its surroundings.

Sensation Awareness   While stretching, focus on the muscles being extended; feel the stretch, the tension, the pulling, the elongation of the muscle. Then allow your focus to shift to other muscles. Are they involved? resisting? helping? hurting? relaxed?

Body Awareness   While walking, focus your mental attention on your feet. Feel the pressure change. Concentrate on the sensation in your toes, the balls of your feet, your heels, even your ankles. Slowly redirect that focus up through the legs to the knees, thighs and, finally, hips. Feel each part of you that moves when you take a step. As an additional experiment, try to consciously direct all the movements involved in walking (i.e.: flexing joints, spreading toes, lifting heels and muscle contractions/releases). See what happens.

NUTRITION: FUEL IT

In a conditioning program for skiing, good nutrition is knowing the body's needs and responding to them. The human body needs protein, fats, carbohydrates, vitamins and minerals, roughage and water for a well-balanced diet. The best way to meet these needs is by consuming 15% of your calories from protein sources, 30% from fats and 55% from carbohydrates. A proper combination of foods from the five major food groups (dairy products, meats and fish, vegetables, fruits and cereals and grains) will ensure your nutritional needs. Avoid processed, chemical-laden foods; not only do they lack nutrients, but they also require extra digestive energy to break down the ones they *do* contain. With a balanced intake of healthy foods, most people don't need supplements. However, special energy demands like stress/anxiety, pregnancy, illness and very high activity levels can deplete the body's resources, creating additional needs which must then be met by additional vitamins and minerals. *(Note: Consult a nutritionist to determine your individual needs before arbitrarily supplementing your diet.)*

Many people will, unthinkingly, grab a candy bar to rev themselves up during a hard day on the slopes, but it is wise to restrict your intake of refined sugar. Readily absorbed into the blood, sugar gives you an almost instantaneous "rush" of energy but this disrupts the body's blood/sugar balance, triggering the production of insulin. The sugar is burned up, but the insulin remains in the blood, again lowering the blood/sugar level. This makes you feel tired once more, so rather than elevating your energy level, in the long run refined sugar products lower it, in a process that is taxing to the body. Try a mixture of nuts and dried fruits instead of reaching for a Hershey bar.

Finally, remember to drink plenty of water to replace fluids lost through activity. When you're skiing, you may not feel thirsty but don't allow yourself to become dehydrated. Replenish the fluids you lose — keep your body functioning smoothly!

WARM UP: GET THE JUICES FLOWING

Begin with easy activities like walking, very slow running or "jelly-fish" jogging (jogging slowly in place with arms, shoulders and neck very loose) and continue until you start to breathe deeply (5-10 minutes). This will loosen you up, and raise your heart rate and body temperature. If the surrounding temperature is cold, continue this gentle activity for a longer period of time and be sure to keep yourself warmly dressed.

ANKLE ROTATION Sit with one leg crossed over the other. Stabilize crossed leg with one hand and gently pull the foot through a circular range of movement with the other hand. This stretches the ankle muscles.

LEG STRETCH Stand with legs crossed. Let torso and arms hang forward until you feel a gentle stretching in the calf of the back leg. Hold 20 seconds then cross legs the opposite way and stretch again.

THIGH STRETCH Leaning against a wall or tree for balance, grab hold of ankle, bend knee and pull leg up behind you to gently stretch the thigh muscle. Hold 20 seconds, then repeat on the other side.

SIDE STRETCH   Standing, spread legs shoulder width or a bit more. Extend arms high over head and gently bow sideways to stretch side muscles. Hold for 20 seconds, then repeat on the other side. Repeat several times on each side.

SHOULDER ROTATION   In the same stance as before, stretch arms out to the side; gently windmill both arms as per diagram.

Stretching should be an enjoyable limbering-up process, not a painful ordeal punctuated by grunts. Everyone's body is different, so work within your limits. Feel free to experiment with additional gentle stretches you feel you might need.

CARDIOVASCULAR FITNESS: REV IT UP

Cardiovascular workout, also referred to as aerobic training, is the most important type of exercise for skiing. It develops stamina and vitality by strengthening the heart and increasing the capacity of the respiratory system. You can choose any activity that raises the pulse rate to a recommended level* and keeps it there for at least 12 minutes. Running, jumping, cycling, vigorous hiking or aerobic dance are perfect aerobic practices. Cardiovascular exercise should be done at least three times a week and should always be accompanied by proper warm up and stretching. As you become accustomed to the activity you have chosen to improve cardiovascular fitness, the recommended heart rate can be maintained for longer and longer durations. Regular cardiovascular workouts will not only pay off with greater endurance on the slopes, but can become an essential part of your life, helping you to cope with daily stress and strain. *(*Note: When starting a cardiovascular exercise program, it is important to first check with your doctor for professional direction.)*

STRENGTH EXERCISES: MAKE IT BURN

In addition to cardiovascular fitness, skiing requires explosive strength, the kind that can be developed in soccer, tennis, squash, basketball, sprint running and some types of weight training. Activities like swimming and bicycling can develop explosive strength for skiing only if done in bursts of high energy rather than prolonged periods of low energy expenditure. Such "interval training" alternates periods of sprint-like exertion with short recovery periods to allow pulse and respiration rates to drop.

An interval program of running might include 10 sprints of 50 yards alternating with 50 yards of slow jogging or brisk walking. Start each run slowly, gradually accelerating to 60% of maximum output — hold this speed for 20 yards, then gradually slow down. In the next 5 runs, gradually increase output up to 80% of maximum expenditure. To increase the benefits as you progress, try uphill sprints, running in sand, and running in knee, ankle or waist-deep water.

Weight training is another way to develop explosive strength. Rather than slow lifts with very heavy weights, choose lighter weight loads which will finally produce exhaustion after 10-15 quick repetitions. Rest a few moments then perform another set. In successive workouts, gradually increase the number of sets up to a maximum of five.

If weight training is undesirable, try the following exercises. Adjust the number of repetitions per set to correspond with your own ability and strength. Do quick repetitions and stop each set when a burning sensation occurs in the muscle(s). Allow yourself a short rest to release the muscle tension, then begin another set.

LOW WALK   Keeping the hips as low to the ground as you can, walk around until the thighs start to burn. Repeat 2-5 sets with short breaks in between.

SQUAT JUMP   Jump up and down repeatedly from a deep squat until the muscles start to burn. Do 2-5 sets with short breaks in between.

BENT LEG SITUPS   Lie on your back, fold hands behind head, keep feet on the ground and bend the knees. Do repetitions of lifting the head and shoulders off the ground, trying to touch elbows to the opposite knees. Return to a position where the shoulder blades touch the ground and pull up again, working to a point of exhaustion, then rest. Do 2-5 sets of situps.

STRAIGHT LEG SITUPS   Lying on your back, lift heels off the ground and do skulling, frog or flutter-kick type movements until stomach muscles burn. Rest briefly and move on into 2-5 sets.

PUSHUPS   Do pushups from toes or knees depending upon the strength in your arms and torso. Another form of the pushup is the backward pushup. Instead of facing the floor, face the ceiling while raising and lowering your body. This requires greater arm strength, so try this once your muscles are more developed.

SKI JUMPER   Lightly bend knees and waist so that you are looking at the floor. Keeping the back level and arms at sides, straighten arms and raise them quickly behind you, pushing shoulder blades together. Do repetitions until you have muscle burn, then repeat as before for 2-5 sets.

DEEP STRETCHING: S-T-R-E-T-C-H

You have completed the warm up, easy stretching, aerobic and muscle strengthening parts of the fitness program; the final phase is deep stretching. The following deep stretches should be held for 20 seconds each, accompanied by consistent and relaxed deep breathing. This section of the training program allows the muscles to cool down in a relaxed state and thus is vital in the prevention of cramps and knots. Don't omit it!

4. Sit on the floor with legs spread and reach for your toes (if you can reach them, pull them toward you). Hold stretch. This works on the hamstrings (back thigh muscles). Be sure to keep the back straight and the head erect.

1. Position yourself beside a wall or stable object as though you are trying to push it away. The foot that is furthest away from the wall is flat on the ground, with the leg outstretched. Adjust your distance from the wall so you feel a thorough stretch in the calf musculature. Alternate legs.

2. Sit on heels and bend torso backward, feeling the stretch in the quadriceps (front thigh muscles).

5. Stand with legs spread, extending the arms above the head. Proceed to do large, slow revolutions making as big a circle as possible. Do 5 circles in each direction.

3. Spread the legs quite far, lunge with one knee as far as possible, stretching the inside of the leg and the groin. Alternate legs.

6. Stand with feet shoulder-width apart. Move outstretched arms in stiff forward circles. Do 10 circles, reverse and do 10 more in the opposite direction.

7. Stand tall. Put both hands behind your head and pull gently forward and down. Roll head to the side, stretching the neck.

Finish this stretching session off with a shaking down of arms, neck and shoulders, then legs.

Every conditioning program should include rest and relaxation in the general sense of of getting enough sleep and allowing sufficient "break" days, but also there is a more particular sense of practiced relaxation techniques. There are many methods and all relaxation techniques slow down physiological and neurological processes. The simplest relaxation practice is slow deep breathing. It's easy, brings immediate results and requires no special training. It produces a calmer mental state while reducing physical tension. More involved relaxation techniques include imaging, tension-release exercises, passive observation and focused concentration.

Imaging is concentration on a mental picture (the image) to effect relaxation. Tension relaxation exercises alter tightening and releasing a muscle or group of muscles; when the tension is released, the muscle gives way to a more relaxed state than it was in prior to being tensed. Passive observation and focused concentration center the attention on an object or sound to induce a state of relaxation.

Much as exercising for physical strength and conditioning, relaxation techniques can be practiced regularly to strengthen and condition the mental muscle. After you read through the exercises yourself, you may find it helpful to have someone read them to you in a slow soothing voice as you work through the program.

DEEP BREATHING TENSION SCAN Lie down and close your eyes. Begin focusing on your breathing. Rather than controlling it, merely be aware of it. Allow the exhaling to carry more and more of the tension out of you. Take time for this process — there is no hurry. Slowly scan your body to locate tension. Beginning with your left foot, gradually work your way up the left leg to your stomach, then do the same up your right leg. Whenever tension is encountered, permit your breathing to take that tension from you. Move on when the tension is gone. In this manner go on to the neck and face. When focusing on your head, sense tension in the temples, forehead and jaw. Let the eyeballs sink deep into their sockets. Allow your jaw to hang loose and alleviate tension-caused wrinkles. Feel the warmth and comfort that creeps into your body. Feel the weight of your limbs sagging against the floor. Anytime you feel that you are losing the "mood" let slow, unrestrained exhalation help you back into the flow.

IMAGING After your exercise program, slow your body down with some deep breathing. Closing your eyes (closing your eyes is not essential, but for novice practitioners is an effective way to prevent distraction), recall one segment of your previous workout. Imagine yourself in the work. Watch yourself move from the front, the side and the back. As you "see" yourself, stretch the movements out into slow motion. Feel the lightness, the easiness with which you move. Now speed up the movements to a fast motion, Charlie Chaplinesque series. Notice the effort and intensity, the abruptness of movement, the choppiness and lack of "flow." Adjust the image speed again until you hit *your* speed — the one that feels comfortable, the one that flows for you. Focus on how you feel, the muscles you are using, your breathing.

Interrupt to retrieve the present very gently, but retain the previous image. Begin to count slowly, concentrating on one part of your body and observe the image fading as your focus switches to the counting and then to the body part in the present. Continue to breathe deeply as you totally release the image and return to the present.

FOCUSED ATTENTION   Use of a mantra (repetition of a resonant, one-syllable sound such as "ummm") produces relaxation much as white sound has a calming effort. The mantra reduces thought activity because the brain is aware of only the slowed neurological processes which lead to a slowing of the physiological processes as well, giving the body a rest.

Use this ski conditioning program as a collection of suggestions. Play with it, change it, expand on it — make it work for you personally. You will ski with more energy and vitality, with less chance of injury or fatigue, with greater awareness of your body and better able to cope with fear and tension. Naturally, these benefits do not end with skiing. You may come to know yourself better, growing more and more aware of your limitations and potentials.

AEROBIC SKIING

For those who are fit and do not get enough exercise out of regular skiing activity, consider "aerobic skiing"—an endurance and strength-building activity that is a lot of fun!

Start off working towards nonstop runs. In smaller ski areas, this won't be much of a challenge; at larger areas, it certainly *can* be! Ski progressively longer segments of slope, until you can make nonstop descents. When this is no longer interesting, add extravagant movement and turning to your repertoire. Try the following embellishments:

- Bouncing turns, where everytime you turn, you lift the skis off the snow.
- Turn needlessly far from side to side, keeping your speed very slow.
- Exaggerate vertical action, making pronounced and superfluous bobbing movements when turning.
- Wedge-walk as far as you can go down a slope.
- Chase a friend, turn for turn. The leader must try to out-turn his follower, while the follower tries to match him.

Be inventive in creating different activities that get you winded and tired. Build your own collection of exercises and prolong the duration of each task. Keep tabs on your pulse and check the cardiovascular chart in the conditioning section of this book to monitor how much you should "push" yourself. Aerobic skiing is a fine way to add verve on a dull day, but it is also a great way for those who do not get enough exercise from regular skiing to stay in shape throughout the winter.

Work towards your recommended pulse rate* and plan your activity so you can maintain that load for 12 minutes at a time. If you lack the terrain, consider hiking uphill on skis or skating uphill in serpentines; both are viable alternatives to downhill aerobic skiing. Practice alone or with a friend and plan your exercises so you can dress for it. Ski aerobically at the end of the day so you can shower off your excess body heat right after you complete your training. Try it; you might like it! (*Note: Consult a physician prior to planning any aerobic exercise program.)

SAFETY IN SKIING

"Few are those who err on the side of self-restraint."

Confucius

The relative risk factor of skiing is higher than it is in tennis and lower than it is in mountain climbing. Though there is no inherent danger in the sport itself, negligent behavior or misjudgement on the part of skiers may give it a dangerous reputation. The following pages address a few issues which may help you act with sound judgement and thus make skiing safer for you.

COLD

Cold slows perceptual and response mechanisms. A person who is cold will be dominated by a feeling of discomfort which, in turn, monopolizes his awareness. At the same time, his stiff musculature is slower to respond to demands for action.

Warm up and/or stretch whenever you start feeling chilly, lazy or unattentive. While these suggestions are of great importance when the weather is arctic, even on seemingly temperate days, they should be part of your daily routine. The purpose of a warmup is to raise the body temperature, providing the musculature with nutrients, heat and flexibility. Stretching increases a muscle's range of motion to allow full and effective usage of the physique.

In order to get the body to functional temperature, consider a pace of exercise that is initially easy and light, very gradually intensifying both in load and tempo.

Here is an example of a warmup and stretching program that can be modified according to the temperature of the day, personal athletic abilities and/or age. All movements are to be done on skis.

- Shuffle your feet and skis.
- Increase the speed of the shuffle.

- Walk in place, lifting the knees high.
- Jog in place.
- Crouch low, then stretch as tall as you can.
- Hop skis off the ground.
- Hop and pivot skis to the left and right beneath you.
- Windmill your arms.
- Rapidly slap your hands on your thighs.

Continue the warmup until you breathe more quickly and deeply; develop an invigorating feeling that comes with increased circulation.

The following stretches should be executed with these thoughts in mind: hold the stretches 20 seconds or more, stretch to the point of feeling PULL but not PAIN and avoid bobbing movements. All exercises will be done with skis on.

- Extend one leg as far back as you can to feel a stretching in the calf muscle. Repeat on the other leg.
- Crouch and embrace your knees with both arms. Hold and repeat.
- Kick one ski forward on its heel; now pull your bellybutton towards the thigh of your raised leg. Repeat on both sides.
- Swing one ski tip out and backward until the ski tip rests in the snow behind you, with the ski tail tucked under your arm, bend the torso backward until you feel your thighs being stretched. Repeat on both sides.
- Crouch low, hands and arms inside the knees reaching for the toe section of your bindings. Now, push elbows apart until you feel a stretch in the groin.
- Lie back on your ski tails and push your bellybutton high so you arch up. Repeat several times.
- Stand up with hands on hips, then arch back as far as you can.
- Arms extended overhead, bend sideways one way, then the other.
- With arms extended to the sides, swing them around you to the left and right.
- Reach with your arms as high as you can while looking at your hands. Feel a stretch in the chest and shoulder region.
- Let your head hang forward, chin to chest; now, add the weight of your hands clasped behind your head to the forward pull. Pull sideways to the right and hold. Repeat to the left.
- Stand with your chin on your chest just a little longer. Let your arms hang loosely. Sense any tension within your body and let it leave you with long exhales of breath.

At the conclusion of the exercising and before pushing off for your first run, picture yourself making round, effortless, floating turns. Feel completely at ease with the image of this action. Draw your shoulders back as you inhale, open your eyes and begin to ski the types of turns you just imagined. With this physical and mental warmup, you will feel well prepared for your day on the slopes.

FATIGUE/TERRAIN

Tired skiers are more vulnerable to injury than refreshed skiers. Ski Patrol statistics give evidence that during the periods before noon and, again, just before ski lifts close, the incidence of accidents is greatest. Plan your day of skiing so you meet the physically stressful times while you feel warm, alert and fresh. Become sensitive to your body's signals; begin to recognize symptoms of deteriorating energy. Allow yourself to finish the day on a physical and mental "high"; avoid that last run that may catch you already "winding down." You will leave yourself less enthused and more exhausted when you could end a pleasant day anticipating your next shot at the slopes.

A popular measure of success in skiing is how steep a slope one can conquer. "Skiing the steep" has learning value if indulged in intermittently but to some skiers, such challenges become an obsession. Daring skiing can create defensive habits that may become a personal stereotype, characteristics which are difficult to shed later.

When building skills and confidence, ski terrain that looks inviting to you, select a slope where you can enjoy yourself, free to focus upon the elements of your performance. On these slopes you lay the groundwork for growth and change. Next time your friends invite you to join them on a run you know you will be uncomfortable on, politely decline and make your own choice as to where to ski. When you "ski the steep," you want to do so with eager confidence.

SNOW

Eskimos have many words for snow, and so do skiers. Descriptive names such as cement, bottomless, crud, mush, quicksand, wind slab, snag, marble, widowmaker and boiler plate tell tales of the nature of the snow we, at times, ski in. Whenever skiing a new area, inquire about snow conditions and local peculiarities. While mountain maps tell you about the layout of the slopes, they do not give evidence of the snow conditions.

A sun-exposed slope on a cold day is just the place to ski. On a warm day, direct sun exposure is a guarantee of wet snow and "mush." After a sub-zero night, this snow turns to glaze, crud and ice. Experienced skiers will travel a mountain as much by snow conditions as by traffic situations.

Wherever there might be a danger of avalanches, U.S. resorts' ski patrols will warn skiers of such conditions. Yet any great expanse of untracked snow in steep terrain ought to be viewed with suspicion. If you ski in open or out-of-bounds areas, it is prudent to ski with a local guide who has knowledge of the existing conditions. Electronic transmitters which allow rescuers to locate a person even under many feet of snow in the event of an avalanche are recommended.

SUN

In recent years, the pharmaceutical industry has launched a campaign to provide the market with better sun-screening products, as well as informing their customers of the inherent dangers of ultraviolet light to the skin. While many people associate a tan with health and well-being, dermatologists continue to tell us that tanning is no more than a symptom of irreversible damage that is inflicted upon the skin. And the sun's effects are strongest at higher altitudes and lower latitudes. Protection is vital!

Sun lotions and cremes are marked with numbers between 1 and 15. The lower the numerical value, the lesser the protective qualities of the product. Fair-skinned people should use the upper ranges *all* the time, while people with darker complexions can get away with lotions with lower protective qualities. When applying sun lotions, carefully cover *all* exposed skin. (Parents, take special care to protect your childrens' skin.) Though alcohol-based lotions sometimes sting when applied, this medium carries the protective ingredients directly into the skin so that it can't be wiped off or brushed off. The creamy lotions, though perhaps more pleasant to apply *do* wipe off;

remember to recoat with them periodically.

Eyes need consideration, as well. The bright, intense light experienced while skiing necessitates the use of sunglasses or goggles with dark lenses. These high-quality, filtering lenses prevent eye fatigue and symptomatic headaches, not to mention providing a comfortable light intensity and filtering out damaging ultraviolet wavelengths. Wear your eye gear where it is meant to be worn, not tucked sportively under the sweater while you get an even tan on your face. Enjoy the sunshine, but be aware of the harm it can cause if you are unprotected.

CLOTHING

When I started to ski, black was the only color a skier was expected to wear. I don't know the reasons black was magical at that time, but bright colors are the mode for skiwear today. Keeping the wet out while retaining body heat (but not causing sweat) and the possibility of regulating ventilation are the most important necessities of ski clothing. Absorbent materials like wool and cotton are best for underwear and socks. Flexible, loose, layered clothing is recommended over stiff, tight and single-layered garments. While fashion is not a must, function is.

For those of you bringing children to the sport of skiing, consider the following hints regarding their attire. Dress your child warmly and let the outer layer be a snowsuit with elastic cuffs to keep the snow out. Zippers are preferable to buttons, mittens are more useful than gloves, wool hats are better than caps, boots with leather insides are a must (plastic liners are cold and wet) to keep feet warm, and goggles are better than sunglasses. Equip your child with functional, warm gear rather than passing down equipment that does not fit.

SKI BOOTS

Over the last ten years, ski boot development has been considerable. More functional fit, superior materials and better adjustment potential characterize the boot evolution. It is important to find the type of boot that fits your particular foot shape best, so shop in a store with a large selection of brands and models.

Trying on boots takes time. Slip into a pair and

determine the general feel and fit of the boots. The focal areas of fit are: toes, balls of feet, heels, insteps, arches and calves. A well-fitting boot will give you a solid feeling of support without hard buckling. Voids or cavities that allow the foot to move inside the boot are not desirable. Cramping and numbness are the other extremes to avoid. Beginning and intermediate skiers should look for boots that allow movement of the ankle joint. Advanced skiers will gradually seek stiffer and stiffer boots, needing their greater support for higher speeds and impacts.

Once you have found the pair you like best (and it need not be a high-priced, high-performance boot), have the ski shop check your need for cants. Your ability to stand in your boots and keep the soles flat on the ground will have considerable influence over how you ski. Canting needs will be checked in every good specialty shop!

Bone spurs or prevailing aches in the feet while skiing may require the attention of a podiatrist. While such help is rather costly, boot inserts that correct anomalities can prevent a lot of pain and possible permanent damage.

BINDINGS

Modern ski bindings fulfill the paradoxical function of holding a skier's foot securely, yet releasing when stress forces become dangerous. Release bindings rely upon springs, cams, anti-friction devices and mechanism-shielding casings that allow the bindings to function in ice and snow, whether it is warm or cold.

Because of their simplicity and expediency, "step in" bindings are most popular. The old-style retention straps have given way to ski brakes, spring-loaded devices that bring the skis to a stop if skier and ski should part. There is one condition under which the conventional "strap" arrangement will be better: deep snow.

The bottom line of new technology is that skiing is safer — as long as the skier monitors the proper setting and maintenance of the binding. Vibration from a car or airplane in transit can alter settings on bindings; dirt and road grime can clog and coat components. Upon arrival at a ski area, have experts check the proper setting and function of your bindings. It takes only minutes — time well spent!

SKIS

Contemporary skis are quite sophisticated. They are well-adapted to the conditions the average skier will encounter. Most skis negotiate hard-packed, icy, powdery and bumpy slopes with a versatility that stems from the many hundreds of hours that engineers spent designing them. At this time, various ski manufacturers around the globe continue to experiment with new shapes and materials—the evolution of skis continues.

Beginning skis are not only short, to facilitate turning, but they are flexible and wide, for ease of handling; some skis for this level are designed to help a skier into carving (mid-ski waisted skis) while others are to be easily pivoted (mid-ski bubbles or pear-shaped toward the tails). Mid- and high-performance skis tend to be mostly "under-foot waisted" to enhance the skier's ability to employ them in shaping a turn.

It is recommended that beginning skiers rent skis, boots and poles when starting to ski. That way, an awareness towards certain characteristics of skis is developed; later, a specific choice can more rationally emerge. Rental shop attendants will assign beginners skis that are belly to chest-high. The agile and strong skier can afford to rent longer skis within a recommended range; more cautious, unconditioned skiers should try shorter ones. As important as the length of the skis is the condition of the running surface and of the edges of rental skis. Since renters obviously do not own the equipment, they tend to be rather careless about what they ski over. Running surfaces should be smoothly waxed and should have a shiny color, rather than looking like someone just ran a sandpaper over them. Edges should feel burrless and smooth. If conditions are icy, they should feel sharper than a formica counter edge, but perhaps not as sharp as a meat knife.

Once you decide to buy your own skis, let a specialty shop expert assist you. All manufacturers turn out good, indifferent *and* bad skis, the variation being the care with which they are finished. When selecting skis for their cosmetics, image or reputation, check them for how cleanly and evenly the edges meet the running surface material; check them for matching shape (hold them bottom to bottom, squeeze them so they are flat together, then run your fingers over the edges, to see if they match in shape) and, lastly, assess their flex (ideally when holding the ski vertical and applying pressure to the middle, they should show an even curve from tip to tail).

New skis inevitably need "tuning" or they will feel "hooky" or "snaggy." Ask for flat filing and edge prepping on your new skis. Have it done by experts in the field, since the skis' performance and lifelong speed will depend upon how they are initially prepared.

Give yourself some time when trying out your new skis. Ski easier terrain and exaggerate everything that contributes to turning. If you are tentative with new skis, they will have the better of you!

POLES

Racers seem to use their ski poles only to get out of the starting gate and to hit the snow in anger after a fall. Ski poles have subtle, but important functions! They work like whiskers for the skiers, helping them maintain and sense their position in relation to the snow surface. When turning at high speeds, the inside ski pole is almost always dragged for that reason.

The average recreational skier will use the ski poles in a dragging fashion also, though they will seldom be aware of it. Ski poles are mostly supposed to be "planted," the term for sticking one of them into the snow to define a turn. The rhythmic insertion of the poles in harmony with turning and the movements leading up to "pole plant" have much to do with efficient skiing. In order to encourage the versatile movements a skier performs with his poles, the poles should be the same length as the distance between the forearm held perpendicular to the body and a spot in the snow slightly ahead of the foot as you stand on your skis. Poles that are shorter than that will have a tendency to make you stoop and break at the waist; longer ski poles tend to make a skier so erect his torso/lower body movement becomes less flexible.

Ski pole handles come in a great variety of styles. Sabers (or "knuckle slips") are certainly the most convenient, since a skier can simply insert his hands and be off. Pole straps in form of loops that emerge at the handle top, are preferable, since they take into account the fact that poles are not held firmly, but are constantly "playing" in the skier's hands. The pivot point of the swinging movement is near the pole top. The loop allows, even supports, such movement; saber handles make it far more difficult and tend to make a skier cock his wrists outward. changing the arm and hand position in a way that is not as supportive to the skier's needs. Break-away loops are a must. This safety feature will detach loop and ski pole handle if the ski pole or ski pole basket should become tangled.

SKI SCHOOLS AND YOU

"Explain all that," said the Mock Turtle. "No, no! The adventures first," said the Gryphon in an impatient tone: "explanations take such a dreadful time."

Lewis Carroll

"I thought ski schools were only for beginners." "I already know how to ski." "No one has ever told me that I could become better." I've had this problem for years now; there is nothing I can do about it." "Go to the Buggaboos? Nah, I'm not good enough." "Racing is a little over my head—I'd like to do it, but I'm not good enough." These are typical comments I received from people when I asked them why they were not attending ski school.

The skilled intervention of a ski teacher can help you develop rudimentary skills to negotiate slopes; it can also hone specific abilities for coping with deep snow, bumps and high-speed skiing. Such help allows you to ski in a manner you never dreamed yourself capable of. It can get you "up" when you feel "down" and aid in new personal discoveries about how you relate to challenges and other

people. Skillful teachers help you to get the most out of a ski vacation, awakening you to rewards that go well beyond learning to ski. In this magical relationship, a good teacher is a coach one moment, a friend the next.

The question of "should I take a ski lesson or not" is, at the average price of a class, not as much a question of economics as one of planning it into your skiing experience. "Private lessons," arrangeable on a one-on-one or multiple-person basis, are somewhat expensive, but they are useful whenever you feel you have reached a plateau in performance you are unable to overcome. Individual attention received in a private lesson will permit you to make quick adjustments and corrections. Intensive feedback and shaping input can successfully hone or alter skills. During a short, private lesson (usually only an hour long), it is easy to effect changes, but difficult to learn for posterity. Unless followed up by appropriate homework and "check ups," such classes are a short-term investment.

Ski school classes vary in size from 5 to 10 people. In this setting, students learn much from one another and the social aspects contribute to a broader experience than that of a single-person lesson. There is less tension with more people sharing similar tasks, and a supportive atmosphere can do wonders to an individual's self-confidence. The one drawback of group lessons is that the teacher's attention must be shared among all students.

Another familiar question regarding lessons is, "How long should I take instruction?" When beginning to play the piano, a person may be contented to learn to play a scale; someone else may wish to continue to develop until he

plays a concert. Shorter ski lessons will be more "diagnostic," while longer ones allow performance to actually change. The more complex the "alterations" in performance, the longer it may take to make appropriate adjustments.

Learning does not take place by process of osmosis; neither does it happen simply because a student is taking a class. Learning happens only when a person is ready for changes to take place. Preparing a student to become a learner is often harder and more time-consuming than finally saying the right thing or doing the magical exercise that triggers the desired association and shapes a final result. One thing a student taking a lesson can do that will help the process is to be open-minded and to come with no expectations that interfere with the process.

LEARNING TO LEARN

"Children are born to act. Usually people grow up and out of it."

Joanne Woodward

In the first portion of this book, visual rehearsal, sensory feedback and relaxation and awareness introduced the reader to concepts that are useful in any learning situation. This second part deals with the evolutionary process of learning how to ski. In a symbolic fashion, we will deal with analytical and practical suggestions respectively. There will be certain thoughts for teachers and coaches, while suggesting actions and task designs that will elicit growth within the student himself.

VISUAL REHEARSAL

If you never have practiced "imaging," start at home before going to sleep. Close your eyes and picture something you like to think about. See the scene in detail; see it again in broader focus. Absorb the colors you see, the shades of light and shadow, the mood the image portrays and the movement that may be part of it. Look at the situation until you become aware of scents and nuances. Practice pre-sleep imaging until you become very good at it and you can hold an image vividly for some time, browsing through it with hard and soft focus.

On the slopes, observe someone you would like to ski like. Absorb the specific characteristics you admire. Rehearse this movement over and over again in your mind until it becomes part of you to the point where you can do what you are imaging flawlessly. Do not abandon this mental practice before you have done it several times "just right" and it feels good with you. When "playing the movie" in your mind, progress from viewing the film as a bystander to gradually picturing yourself following the image, catching up with it and finally becoming it.

Begin *feeling* what it is like to do what you are visualizing. Pick up the body movements and hear the sounds. The more complete the picture, the more powerful the learning aid. In addition to imaging, project moods into these "movies." Imagine yourself skiing a certain slope angrily, lightly or complacently; allow yourself to ski more daringly than you might think you are capable of skiing.

Visual rehearsal takes practice to be useful. With the initial discomfort and unfamiliarity of "viewing the movies" fading, the vividness and realistic association will grow, and with those associates come the benefits.

KINESTHETIC FEEDBACK

In an environment where movements are largely unconscious and seldom the focus of our attention, it may take some time to zero in on sensing what you are doing and to be able to distinguish intensity differences of movements. Since learning and changing are dependent upon awareness, it is important to develop movement in order to enhance your skiing.

Start off with a noncommittal exploration of your body to simply find parts you are most aware of. Sense the shape of a part without looking at it. "What is the foot like?" "How do my legs move when I walk?" "Which parts of the body touch most when sitting in a chair?" Through such explorations you gain a body awareness that will greatly benefit your skiing.

As you ski, scan yourself and isolate whatever it is that seems to be the focus of your attention. Do you find yourself looking ahead to pick out the path you are taking? Are you parking your attention upon a pair of ill-fitting boots? Are you thinking of the undone matters at your office? Are you aware of a mood that possesses you? An ache in the head?

Gradually allow your attention to move towards an aspect of performance that you would like to improve. If you would like to strengthen your turning, sense the amount of energy you invest in making turns; once you know what's going on, turn the "volume" of intensity up or down, however you like. If you continue to fall backwards when skiing, become aware of where you are standing on the ski. Mid-foot, forward, backward? Once you know where

you stand, experiment with the extreme possibilities. Sit back as far as you can while turning or lean way forward; then zero in to where you *want* to be.

The essence of kinesthetic awareness is that you need to "*feel*" it. In order to develop the desirable adjustment, sense also the alternatives you practice. Once you are aware of what's happening, you can make adjustments.

RELAXATION: AAAH . . .

Relaxing helps increase your awareness anytime non-productive tension dominates your mind or body. Relaxation clears the mind, releases the body and leaves both better prepared to accurately perceive and respond to the situation. Relaxation techniques were dealt with quite thoroughly in an earlier chapter. Practice the techniques you personally feel will be useful to your skiing.

Another issue is closely related to relaxation; I refer to it as "cleaning the slate." This process is intended to wipe assumptions, prejudices, biases and the like from the mind. By doing the odd thing on skis, by practicing silly moves and actions, by allowing the mind to roleplay itself into a "tin soldier" or a "Raggedy Ann," you can induce a playful, non-judgemental mode of performance. In this state, skiers demonstrate a spontaneity that allows them not only to break old, entrenched patterns, but also to build new talents with little or no resistance. Falling, looking odd and being silly is okay. In such a mood, risk-taking, falling, looking awkward, odd or silly is easily acceptable because there is no threat of potential failure. Play eliminates risk.

Sample activities for "cleaning the slate" in skiing are listed below. Select exercises according to ability level of the skiers:

- Make wedge turns backwards.
- How about some parallel turns backwards?
- Spin some 360's.
- Make turns in a "squatty body" position.
- Make turns on one ski.
- Make turns on the "wrong" (inside) ski.
- How about skiing a section of hill without using ski poles?
- Ski with a partner, holding hands while turning.
- Emulate someone's skiing in a caricature way. Have other people guess whom you are mimicking.
- Ski like an ape, a snake . . .

The success of this kind of activity rests (in part) in the willingness of the teachers to be silly WITH the class. The use of ridiculous images and crazy words will help in generating this "I don't care" attitude. Cleaning the slate is useful any time there is a break in thought or action; it's a great way to start a skiing day or to finish one.

H ere are ideas that have a tendency to get the best out in people:

- Use music in your skiing (sing, whistle or play a tape).
- Use rhythm and rhythmic shouting when skiing.
- Learn new things by way of analogies and existing experiences.
- Allow yourself to daydream and imagine things.
- Carry on a conversation where each person says only half a sentence, letting the other person finish it.
- Role-play yourself into different moods and modes of skiing.
- Explore nutty ideas: "What would it be like to fly down this mountain?"
- Disallow yourself any kind of judgement (no "good" or "bad").

- Ski to emotions such as anger, happiness . . .
- Ski to themes such as light, heavy, float, jam, hack, caress . . .
- Ski like someone you would like to ski like.
- Isolate a particular element from someone's skiing and emulate it, exaggerate it, ski it.
- Learn to attain functional levels of tension.
- Don't permit yourself any mechanical analysis while you are skiing (if you *must* analyze, do so before or after the day — and take an aspirin!)
- Feel what is happening and refine your sense so you can begin to distinguish fairly small variations in your movements.
- Listen to the sound your skis are making as they glide over the snow.
- Whenever you find yourself too serious or intense, put in a "cleaning the slate" session; feel yourself magically recharged.
- Practice skiing with "soft focus," seeing general moods of slopes, silhouettes of people. Avoid any attachment to detail, especially meaningless detail.
- Divorce yourself from the effort of "trying" and learn to "do."
- Learn to let go and develop a trusting relationship with yourself. Remember, you will ski as poorly or as smoothly and confidently as you allow yourself to ski.

THE ATM SYSTEM

AMERICAN TEACHING METHOD

"Simple style is like white light. It is complex but in its complexity is not obvious."
Anatole France

Ski teaching in the United States, as in the rest of the skiing world, has essentially been the imparting of a progression of mechanical maneuvers through technical directives. While the following segment of this book does not negate or change existing mechanical knowledge, it adds those elements that actually help a skier acquire the skills in a simple and lasting fashion. With the considerations that underlie "how people learn," students and teachers can achieve results that far exceed those usual through conventional methods. An important thought needs to be added: it is not enough to merely know about the various concepts/methods of ATM; it is essential to use these tools at the appropriate time, with the proper intensity and through interplay with other methods dealt with in this book.

Too often have we been told *how* to do something. We have had the movements described to us in the smallest detail, yet we find ourselves unable to do what it is that has been explained so thoroughly. Though we are physically capable, our nervous systems function and we have a perfect run-down on the task we wish to accomplish, we cannot perform it! ATM, the American Teaching Method, addresses these very issues; the approach combines our physical energies with our intellectual capabilities, making it easier for us to learn and perform. It blends the powers of each brain hemisphere and its respective function to facilitate learning through experience. Utilizing joint capabilities in this fashion, we can develop skills along with the necessary perceptions that are shaped by our attitudes about what we are doing.

Designed to complement already existing teaching methods, our approach is essential for any coach or ski teacher and useful to every skier and athlete, as well. By encouraging awareness of how we learn, we awaken the tools necessary to develop ourselves into quintessential skiers through an integral body/mind connection.

LEARNING TO SKI —TELEGRAM STYLE

**CLASS LEVEL
AND SKILL PROGRESSION**

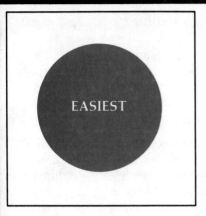

**CLASS A
MOVING ON THE LEVEL**

SLIDING ON A GRADE

**CLASS B
DIRECTION CHANGES**

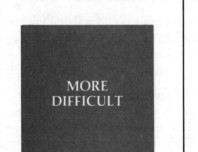

**CLASS C
SKIDDED TURNS**

**CLASS D
WIDETRACK TURNING**

**CLASS E
CARVED TURNING**

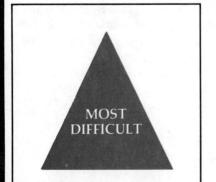

REBOUND TURNING

**CLASS F
ALL SNOW — ALL TERRAIN**

BEGINNING TO SKI: CLASS A

GOALS

- Developing balance on skis while walking and sliding about.
- Direction changes via stepping around.
- Climbing shallow inclines.
- Straight sliding.
- Wedging.

CHOICE OF TERRAIN AND SNOW

- Flat terrain with gentle inclines or rolls.
- Packed or soft-packed snow.

MECHANICAL DEVELOPMENT

- Learning to balance on slippery base of support.
- Acquiring mobility in stepping manner.
- Exploration of edging while climbing uphill and while wedging.

METHODOLOGICAL EMPHASIS

- Free exploring of mobility on level ground.
- Movement games.
- Much mileage, but carefully paced energy expenditure.
- Students' primary concern is "survival." Successes and encouragement will be helpful in generating necessary commitment.
- Self-paced learning should be an underlying thought at all times when teaching; a student must develop trust in his own capabilities. Allow learners to experience success. Choosing how high to climb on the first run, selecting which side to turn to, having the opportunity to say "I am scared," are liberties a teacher must allow the student.
- Movement is a formidable weapon against imbalance. Exercises that emulate certain ways of moving and tasks that elicit that physical response will be the best guards against developing asymmetry and/or instability.

- Emphasizing kinesthetic awareness works at all ability levels. Learning to sense (not see) what the extremities are doing, to be aware of the snow underfoot, to distinguish between intensity differences of movements and what they effect cannot be introduced early enough.
- Sound/action association is a powerful tool. The concept of synchronization, among other things, maintains that pendulum action of several clocks hanging next to each other will gradually move into harmony with one another. In skiing, the coordination of self-talk and action brings into harmony functions of complementing natures. Movement, in combat against imbalance, is effective, so explore different games and tasks while skiing (and sometimes standing) that deal with maintaining balance.
- Certain awareness exercises focus upon a skier's stance while he is standing still as well as when he is moving; awareness, as always, effects changes.
- Imaging equilibrium into reality requires practice to be effective for learners. Further information is presented in the chapter on *Visual Rehearsal*.
- Skis that are too short often cause people to lose balance backwards. If this is the cause, simply change ski lengths.
- Asymmetry is sometimes alleviated by encouraging a skier to stand taller on his skis. A beginner's buckled-up stance oftentimes leads to imbalance because novices tend to initiate turns from the torso.
- Crossing skis is often caused by unequal edging from ski to ski. Noticing how the skis are, or are not, edged will be a sure way to eliminate crossing them. The track a skier leaves behind can be a quick system of checking whether the skis are "cutting" or "brushing." If they cut, they are more likely to cross.

EXERCISES FOR WALKING AND SLIDING:

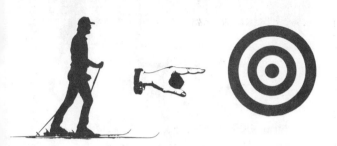

. . . Select a target in a flat area and move to it (a pole, a person, etc.) . . .

. . . Select another destination and walk there without using the ski poles . . .

. . . Now allow yourself to use the ski poles . . .

. . . Move backwards for some distance . . .

. . . Using your ski poles, push yourself into longer glides . . .

. . . Walk "tall," "small," "fast," "slow" . . .

. . . Have you ever skated? Skate to that tree . . .

. . . Turn 180 degrees . . .

. . . Now change direction in a stepping manner while pushing with the poles . . .

. . . Play "catch" within a confined area . . .

. . . Climb a shallow hill section with skis horizontal . . .

. . . See whether you can climb the hill without the help of ski poles . . .

. . . How about getting uphill, making a herringbone track in the snow . . .

EXERCISES FOR SLIDING DOWNHILL:

. . . Climb as high or as low on the hill as you like, then ski down . . .

. . . How many miles per hour do you think you are going? . . .

MPH?

. . . When you are skiing down, move your arms like a large bird . . .

. . . While skiing, step into a parallel track and then out again . . .

. . . Now slide downhill with the skis forming a letter A—tips close, tails a bit apart . . .

. . . Now alternate between pointing the skis straight, then pushing the tails out a little. Repeat this in a pulsating manner . . .

. . . Now push one ski tail out at a time—increase the intensity of the push . . .

. . . See how long you can balance on one leg, then the other . . .

. . . As you get towards the runout, make a slight turn by stepping first in one, then the other direction . . .

"aaaaa"

"AAAAA"

. . . While sliding, reach as high as you can, then as low as you dare—repeat this several times . . .

. . . Duck under an imaginary pole set at any height you decide on . . .

. . . Ski down varying the width of the A your skis are forming. As you make a narrow A, accompany it with a sound like "aaaaaaaaaaa." When making the A wider, turn up the volume to "AAAAAAAAAA." The vigor of the voice should correspond to the width of the wedge being executed . . .

"I CONTINUE TO LOSE BALANCE BACKWARDS WHILE SLIDING DOWNHILL"

. . . Practice more pole-pushing while sliding on level terrain . . .

. . . just kidding!

. . . Play "pushover" with a friend as you stand face-to-face on skis . . .

. . . When sliding downhill, place hands on thighs or knees . . .

. . . Teeter-totter as you stand in place, rocking from the balls of your feet to the heels. Register where you stand on your feet as you ski the next run . . .

. . . Attach your focus to a distant tree, house or person when sliding downhill . . .

. . . Before descending, imagine yourself sliding downhill just fine; review the movie until the image of you succeeding is solid, then push off and ski it . . .

. . . Check whether your skis are too short. Heavier and taller people need slightly longer skis than lighter, smaller skiers do . . .

"MY SKIS SEEM TO CROSS QUITE OFTEN"

. . . Stand tall while sliding downhill . . .

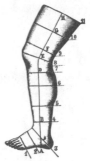

. . . Focus your attention on your feet. Where is most of the pressure—forward, aft, inside, outside? . . .

. . . Now that you know where you stand, choose to stand "flat-footed" and in the center . . .

. . . Look at your tracks. Are they telling you that you are digging in one ski but not the other? If this is so, try to leave a smooth, "flat" track behind you . . .

THE MECHANICS

In the following segment of this book, I will be focusing upon the characteristic development phases when learning to ski. In the first part of each chapter I shall provide examples of exercises and series thereof to demonstrate how a multisensory approach for learning to ski can be composed. This segment will help teachers as a model for lesson plan development, and it will help the student by characterizing the type of activities and emphases that are significant for the process of learning.

The second part of each development chapter will serve to look behind the scene, discussing mechanical, methodological and tactical issues as they relate to growth at that time. I recommend that the person reading this book for the purpose of learning to learn not linger with the segments of text concerned with mechanical analyses, but ingest tactical suggestions as well as allowing picture series to become thoroughly absorbed in memory.

During my years as a teacher I have met and have spoken to thousands of people wishing to be placed into ski classes. When focusing upon skiers on the starting level, I cannot displace the images of people's faces and body postures inevitably displaying a mixture of anxiety, self doubt, embarrassment or premature surrender to an activity they have not even tried yet. I am saying this to illustrate how fragile most people at that stage are, and I am saying this to emphasize the need to direct only the most skilled and sensitive teachers to interact with beginning skiers. In the most challenging phase of learning to ski, students will be in need of skillful guidance and very sensitive support. Beginning skiers are inundated with new experiences and knowledge, and while this learning phase can be fun-filled and exciting, it can also be exhausting and demeaning.

Stiff boots and "long feet" reduce most beginning skiers to stages of paralysis at first. Skillful teaching that emphasizes playful modes of learning, making tasks as nonmechanical as possible, will quickly help learners to levels of comfort or tolerance.

Learning now, or any other time, must be understood to include "lateral" learning or even digressing as far as performance is concerned. The student, feeling that learning is a linear expansion, and the teacher, assuming the same, set themselves up for frustration and unnecessarily prolonged setbacks fueled by such emotions.

Nonproductive levels of tension are generally enhanced by being judgemental about oneself or others, while play, relaxation techniques and diversion from the actual task at hand, reduce debilitating stiffness and tension.

The first five to ten minutes of being on skis are best spent in free exploration in a safe environment.

Poor instruction will come in the form of directives such as "When starting to walk, advance your right foot and leg while swinging your left arm forward." It is characterized by needless mechanical advice, which confuses and reduces the learning potential.

Effective instruction may come in the form of this kind of advice: "Hey Tigers; let's all shuffle over to this tree over here. Don't worry about getting there first, everyone is a winner, I can just feel it." While students follow this advice there may be a student who has difficulty with the task. "Watch me for a bit. Look where I place my ski poles in order to push with them, this, in contrast, is where I see you put them. Ahh, look how much better you can move now. Great, John!" Such advice is task oriented (rather than being mechanical) and engages in exploratory activity, at times deliberately doing the "wrong." Task changes such as "Let's move as quickly as we can, as slowly as we can . . ." are intensity variations that will expand the experience of the learner. Performance choices for the learner are beginning to emerge.

From past experience I must say that I feel beginning skiers are rushed too quickly to "tilted" terrain. It has been my feeling that the longer I stay with my students in flat or gently undulating terrain, the stronger and more rapid will their development be thereafter. Even strong and talented skiers will not mind staying on the flat, if the content of the program is skillfully conducted. I have had excellent results when spending the first morning of an alpine skiing class on cross country equipment.

PACING

Because of the relative inefficiency with which beginning skiers move, their energy expenditure and body heat generated will be high. It is very advisable to periodically interrupt regular skiing activities and break for a drink of water, walk about without skis on, listen to some stories about the surrounding mountains or the area, or spend time getting to know each other by exchanging anecdotes.

When speaking of pacing, I am not only addressing the considerate pacing of the student energy levels. I am also referring to the intensity and length of practice sessions, the adhering to one or the other thought or focus, the duration of time any skill is pursued. Learning theory tells us that the more complex a task, the more intermittent should the practice for skill acquisition be. Intensive pursuit of complex tasks tends to develop frustration and a "stuck-up-ness" that needs to be avoided by careful dosing of exposure to the challenge.

SLIDING DOWNHILL

Even smallest inclines become challenging "cliffs" to people who have never done it before. Having spent ample time in the flat, gliding on skis by pushing and striding long before it becomes a gravity-powered activity will do much to smooth the transition from "active" to "passive" sliding on skis.

Ideally the first slope the skier negotiates is long and gentle, with ample flat outrun and enough width to accommodate possible veering of the descending skier. Since people come with different levels of aggression toward skiing, it is useful to set up a practice environment where anyone can choose to go when they feel like it. The "line up" and "it's your turn now" organization not only intimidates many learners, but also deprives people of the right to exercise according to their own needs and wants.

I cannot help but stop and enjoy groups of students who, through the skilled intervention of their teacher, or because of the special qualities of a student, become a laughing, enjoying and supportive unit. Such atmosphere brings out the best in people, and in the absence of pressure and undue seriousness, learners develop the magical association with skiing that leads to enjoyment and keen perception. Contrast this picture with the somber, pearl-on-a-string-like groups that forever retain their "gray" and unenthused feeling. Such a gray learning environment will inevitably produce "gray" performance. If you see the situation to be too somber, do something about it: sing, joke, imagine something silly and ski to it, play a game, applaud each other, support each other and CHOOSE to have a good time.

First attempts at skiing downhill at times become a clear barometer of how people feel about themselves and the task. The frightened skier will double over at the waist and "hug the ground." The confident skier will stand tall and effortlessly on the skis.

It is useful to explore what it is like to go downhill in a "squatty body" position, then in a "tin soldier" position, thus experiencing the extremes, then choosing the functional, personal in between.

Functional standing on skis can be most easily developed by challenging learning skiers into movement. "Throw a snowball at the other students as you ski"—"touch the snow with your fingertips, then scrape the sky," etc. Movement enhances breathing; breathing fosters relaxation. Functional ways of moving shall not be described, but shall come about by practicing a variety of different stance possibilities.

Buckminster Fuller's statement, "Inherent in balance is motion; inherent in motion is balance," summarizes beautifully the point.

In summary of the first development phase, I would like to note that most methodological concepts referred to in the past chapter will find continued application in phases to come. When I am no longer making specific reference to them, it is not because I feel they no longer have any purpose. Store the ideas cumulatively, each time reflecting how past tactics or methods could find new application.

BEGINNING TO TURN: CLASS B

GOALS

- Developing direction changes from wedge basis.

- Gaining speed control through turning.

- Beginning to skid turn finishes.

CHOICE OF TERRAIN AND SNOW

- Shallow enough terrain so that a skier will not lose control even if going straight downhill.

- Packed snow.

MECHANICAL DEVELOPMENT

- Turning becomes a means of direction change and speed control.

- Turning results either from pivoting both feet with pressure on both skis or pivoting outside foot (of turn) in desired direction with a "stepping into the turn" movement.

- Skidding develops from increasing speed and from turning with a narrow wedge.

METHODOLOGICAL EMPHASIS

- Introduce turning with small and gradual direction change obligations.

- Narrow wedge basis for turning to avoid "snagging" the inside ski.

- In case mimicking does not work, suggestion of "pointing the feet (or toes)" is useful.

- Terrain choice is vital to maintain a "green light" attitude within the skier.

- Turning can be induced without much fanfare. Following a gently curving track in shallow terrain is within the capability of any beginner, provided that his stance is open and that his skis are slightly toe-in. Practicing turns without skis is merely one way for a person to get the feel of the movement with less pivotal resistance.

- By juxtaposing strong and mild turns, the skier becomes more aware of intensity differences and, thus, can broaden his inventory of turning experiences.

- Self-talk in the form of "counting through turns" establishes a personal checking system through which the learner can assess his own performance.

- Role-playing ("ski like . . .") is especially effective when the associations surpass mere image to include feelings and, if appropriate, sounds.

- The "number game," used here in conjunction with measuring the size of the wedge, can be useful in developing awareness towards many other features of skiing (the intensity of a pre-turn, the investment of energy in a segment of a run, etc.) .

- Most people are "sided" and do things better on one side than they do on the other. While there is no need to make a big issue of "sidedness," there are a series of exercises that will help to develop symmetry in stance and movement.

- Rhythmically linking turns is one method to help develop symmetry. Rhythm is a seeming "cure-all" for many problems in skiing; it works quite well in this situation, too.

- Imaging symmetrical performance is again powerful. The effectiveness of such practice (as previously stated) lies in spending ample time with the exercise, as long as it takes to "see" the desired, correct image several times.

- Many times certain errors will simply fade away, as long as no attention is called to them.

- Errors that are dealt with should only be the ones that have a detrimental effect on performance. Stylish or arbitrary deviations are not valid concerns.

- When dealing with fear, imperatives like "Relax," or "Don't be afraid" are as useful as balancing an aspirin on your forehead to combat a headache. Seek out the cause of the emotion and work on it. Distractive tactics — focusing on an object, a thought or a feeling — can prohibit fear from becoming the center of a person's attention.

EXERCISES TO INITIATE TURNING:

. . . Take your skis off and practice turning with just your boots on the snow . . .

. . . Still without skis, practice turning sharply, gently . . .

. . . Pivot skis off the toes, then the heels . . .

. . . Now ski downhill, making a gentle turn to one side . . . then try one to the other side . . .

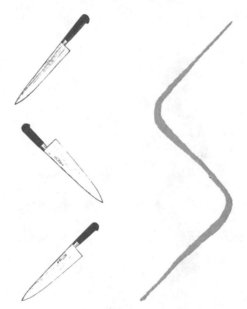

. . . Make a descent with "sharp" turns . . .

. . . Now do them the way you like them best . . .

. . . Follow another skier's track . . .

. . . Now make turns in sync with a skier in front of you . . .

. . . Obligate yourself to make gentle, infrequent turns by designing your own slalom course using gloves or something soft . . .

. . . Now weave through an imaginary course of equally imaginary markers . . .

. . . If you have trouble making turns with the previous processes, point the outside foot of the turn to where you wish to go . . .

. . . Make turns from as tall a position as you can turn from, then from as low a position as you can turn from . . .

. . . Swing your arms by your sides while turning . . .

. . . Bob up and down while turning . . .

"one, two"
"one, two, three"
"one, two, three, four"

. . . Make turns to the count of 2, then 3, then 4, each turn lasting as long as the count . . .

. . . What would it be like to turn like a butterfly, light and easy? . . .

. . . Now turn as heavy and strong as a Mack truck would turn . . .

. . . Most people *do* have a better side . . .

. . . While standing, step your skis into a narrow "A," and call this a number 1-A. Now move into as wide an "A" as you can and call this a number 5-A. Now estimate what a number 4-A, a number 3-A and a number 2-A would be like . . .

. . . Ski down and turn; when you turn, establish the size of the A, giving it a comparative number . . .

. . . See what makes you successful to your good side and begin transferring your findings to the other side . . .

. . . Whenever you can, choose to stop to your weaker side . . .

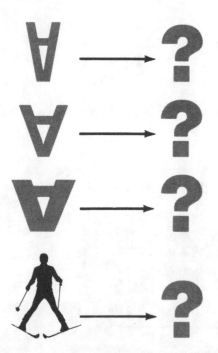

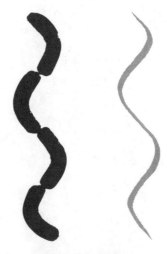

. . . Link turns rhythmically . . .

. . . Which "A" makes turning easiest? Which "A" makes it hardest? Which do you like to turn with best? . . .

. . . Now make several runs while turning with a number 1-A . . .

. . . Picture yourself making turns; gradually see yourself turning equally well to both sides . . .

. . . Don't feel that you have to eradicate asymmetry altogether before you move on . . .

"PEOPLE TELL ME I SKI WITH STIFF LEGS"

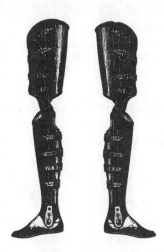

. . . Is this characteristic the cause of any problem? If you turn and stay in balance, ignore such comments—If you feel it hampers your ability to turn, consider skiing less challenging terrain or snow . . .

. . . Bounce up and down as you turn . . .

"I AM SCARED AND SHY AWAY FROM THE TURN"

. . . Select terrain you are comfortable on . . .

. . . Think through a turn and notice that when the ski tips point downhill, you will accelerate; when you turn the skis a bit farther, they slow down again. This realization will help you accept the initial acceleration . . .

. . . Listen to the sound your outside ski is making. Make it sound aggressive and in control . . .

THE MECHANICS

T hough the description of the development phases may seem like a back-to-back issue, it is understood to be at best a seamless joining and overlapping of progress and learning. A learning sequence therefore should appear to learners like a "flow," an inevitably linked chain of events; the connective "tissue" and characteristics of various maneuvers becoming as, if not more, important than the apparent maneuvers a skier learns to do.

The development of turning skills introduces the skier to changing direction as a need to avoid obstacles, or as a playful expression one feels good about.

Turning is best developed without much fanfare, by simply beginning to make straight descents gradually become slightly curved. Working on turning to both sides can be pursued by linking turns rhythmically from the start (if the terrain is shallow and long), or by alternating turning, first to one, then the other side (if the hill is steeper than desirable or too short). I have had great success with students learning to turn by having them simply making straight runs simulating the movements they see better skiers do. My own modeling inevitably will be one that overdoes all movements, thus leaving no doubt that movement is the secret to turning.

G radually the track that was until now straight will begin to curve and wiggle. Such spontaneity in learning to turn is by far more effective than developing turning as a product of "turning one or both feet, transferring weight, and steering the feet where you want to go."

Group dynamics can be helped by stimulating

peer instruction. People who turn easily can be encouraged to share their "secrets" with others. People who have a "chocolate side," but turn poorly the other way, can be made to analyze the reasons why they are successful to one side, then challenging them to apply such wisdom the other way.

It is always great fun to do exercises that are totally ridiculous (or at least are promoted to be that). Leaping like a mountain goat when heaving the skis from side to side is one of those practices that has never failed to elicit chuckles and laughter among students; slithering like a snake, bouncing like riding a pogo stick, flopping like a slinky are all metaphors and images that greatly promote looseness, a theatric exuberance most useful to learning "playfully."

As turning becomes a more consistent reality to learners, slalom poles or less threatening markers such as balloons, extra garments, or snow markers become exquisite learning aids. People love a challenge and as long as the markers are not as much a "barrier" as they are trigger symbols for turning, it will be a fun way to expand turning skills.

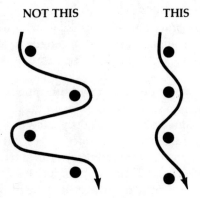

NOT THIS   **THIS**

The sharp turning obligations tend to develop defensive habits and torso turning and "leaning" habits. The well-spaced and invitingly "offset" markers on the right merely become triggers to the performer, leaving even nonturning to be a successful option. While the type of turning encouraged on the left develops rotation of the entire body, the model on the right will encourage the more useful action of turning with legs and feet.

A useful perception of how to turn is to associate pointing or turning the FEET (or foot) in the direction we want to turn. As much as physiologists may tell us (and rightfully so) that turning the feet is actually a rotating of the entire leg(s), the goal-specific encouragement of

turning the feet decisively brings the strongest results in learners.

The initial attempts of learning to turn may be characterized by insensitive and "hacking" movements, which may not please the aesthetic values of better skiers or teachers. It must be understood to be an almost inevitable development phase that will be followed by a gradual refining and dosing of movement intensity and range of motion. With practice, contributing movements to turning will become more efficient, smooth and effective. Progress needs to be seen in perspective. Increments of improvement shall be recognized and applauded.

The beginning skier, likewise, may not be very sensitive to kinesthetic experiencing; gradually though, feeling associations will become better and more sensitive. As part of the instructional or learning process, it is highly beneficial to spend time learning to sense, feeling one's extremities, sensing the pressure increases and decreases of the skis on the snow. Life today often deprives us of such practice, and it may take repeated focusing and practice to come into contact with one's physique and feelings. Take the time!

Most viable options of turning grow from a stance in which the skis are in a more or less converging relationship to one another — the ski tops point together.

A "Braking Wedge" (the more pronounced converging skis) serves to control speed by putting both skis at an angle to the direction of travel.

A "Gliding Wedge" facilitates a skier's intent to turn. Severe edging of the skis while opening the skis wide will slow the skier, yet it also makes turning the skis much harder.

The gliding wedge, on the other hand, provides speed control by the ability to turn from side to side, the lesser-edged skis providing enough push off support to turn from, but not interfering with the pivoting or turning efforts of the skier.

Aggressive learners may develop turning toward what are called SCHWUPPS or SPONTANEOUS turns. Such turning is characterized by turning both feet simultaneously from a more parallel ski relationship. The skier starts the turn with a guiding of the outer ski toward the turn, then, when sufficient turning momentum is generated, pivoting both feet. The dynamic SCHWUPPS phase is earlier in the turn picture when the skier

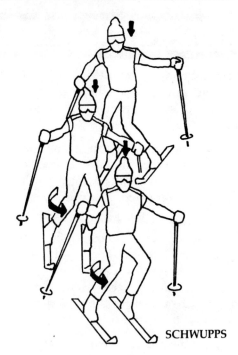

SCHWUPPS

is more skilled, and later at earlier stages of development.

SPONTANEOUS turning is the result of making gliding wedge turns at progessively higher speed, the skier's momentum contributing to a skidding of the skis from turn to turn. Spontaneous skidded turns need not, as the term suggests, be taught. By inviting skiers to ski aggressively on nonchallenging terrain, speed becomes the catalytic element that will automatically promote turning and skidding. Emphasizing *rhythmic* movement in concert with turning will amplify the already inevitable.

By now skiers are riding beginners' lifts, which allows them to accumulate much practice mileage. This prolonged practice opportunity without the debilitating effects of fatigue from climbing uphill will do much to accelerate learning.

Whenever there is a weaker student in a group, the helper or teacher can give physical assistance with ski poles (hooked up between teacher and student to brake speed) or cross-held slalom poles. All students thus can spend time on

the same hill, practicing similar skills, the temporarily weaker student catching up to others through the special attention received.

At this stage of development is it most useful for groups to work with a counseling system. The teacher designates a lift and a special route as the practice area. He places himself in an area that overlooks the slope, giving advice to people in his group as they pass by. Once a new proficiency level has been reached, this format should be abandoned and replaced by one that focuses upon a new chapter, with the group once more together.

The now-emerging skier will feel very much part of the "mountain activity." His ability to partake in skiing on a greater variety of slopes will not only boost his ego and self confidence, but also expose him to valuable images that will vastly accelerate his learning to ski.

Growing out of the nursery of the beginner's area is an exciting event. Careful planning of routes and snow conditions will determine whether the "high" of the emerging skier will remain a reality. Guidance shall be sensitive to not only the existing skill levels of skiers, but also their energy and endurance levels.

When leaving for a first "mountain experience" with a group of excited and red-faced beginning skiers, I carefully plan ahead. I choose a route that is easily within their ability range — I choose a route that will allow me to get to the bottom with ample time to make a couple or more runs on the beginner's hill they have just graduated from — I carefully plan my day so the learners leave with energy to spare, with a strong level of self confidence and a clear vista of where to go next. I find such precautions not only to be common sense, but to also enhance the chance of finding my group ready and eager to go the next morning.

Success and growth also depend upon the caring attitude of teacher and peers. Making sure that there is nurturing, ongoing communication between all people in the class will become the foundation of group rapport that is as much a reason to enjoy a learning experience as it is to have learned something.

IMPROVING YOUR TURNS: CLASS C

GOALS

- Improvement of skidding skills (adding more skid to turns).
- Linking of turns.

CHOICE OF TERRAIN AND SNOW

- Easiest terrain with a few steeper pitches (novice trails).
- Packed snow with some excursions into gentle bumps and shallow, soft snow.

MECHANICAL DEVELOPMENT

- "Walking into the turn" (turning with increasing movement from foot to foot) becomes the dominant way of starting turns.
- Increasingly the outside ski intensifies its grip to allow a rotary push-off from foot to foot moving from one turn to the next.
- While the wedging (or steering) phase to initiate the turn gets shorter, the skidding (or controlling) section gets longer.

METHODOLOGICAL EMPHASIS

- Rhythmic linking of turns.
- Stepping from ski to ski as a turn is started.
- Open ski relation enhances stance allowing more mobility and more stability.
- Techniques and methods we dealt with in past developmental phases retain their value at this time, as well.
- Practice the extremes of a movement. Practice the "error" to find the functional choice. Only from many choices will you be able to select what is most functional at any given time.
- Imaging and role-playing remain very effective tools to enhance learning and performing. As the skier becomes more skilled with them, the effects will come quicker and the results will be more intense. Remember that not only physical but also mental skills need practice.

- Sound associations may make people feel conspicuous at first; once the positive effects of such practice are felt, apprehensions are quickly overcome.
- Lack of commitment is often the real reason for lack of success, not an absence of physical skills. Loud and convincing self-talk can be of tremendous help in strengthening the level of involvement.
- Developing versatility, knowing how to accomplish one-and-the-same task in a variety of ways, and realizing one thing that leads to many different solutions all help to prepare a skier for the ever-changing situations he encounters.
- Changing snow and terrain conditions become increasingly important in solidifying skills.
- Mechanical misconceptions like "lean forward in skiing" are rather frequent. View any recommendation from well-meaning friends with some suspicion. Sense for yourself what *is* and what *is not* useful.
- Standing taller on skis has a tendency to flatten the skis, thus making skidding and turning easier.
- Take advantage of existing skills such as walking; this will allow progress to be swift and easy. Walking movements into turns are a viable way to make turning happen without constipating the learner with new and different directions.
- With increasing confidence fostered by inviting terrain and previous successes, the skier will increase his speed; with increased pace, momentum works in the skier's favor to make turning easier.
- Most skiers will initially start direction changes by turning the torso. Gradually the alternative of turning with the legs will emerge.
- Helper poles not only restrict certain movements, but also serve as an "umbilical cord" for those who do not yet have the confidence to ski certain slopes on their own.

EXERCISES TO IMPROVE YOUR TURNS:

. . . Select terrain you feel comfortable on and dare yourself to ski just a little bit faster . . .

. . . Alternately make two turns sharp, two turns easy and rounded . . .

. . . Ski rhythmically to a tune you like that matches your turning . . .

. . . Pick a skier who is slightly better than you. Watch him and ski like him . . .

. . . Next time, "catch a ride" with this skier when he comes by—Follow him for as long as you can . . .

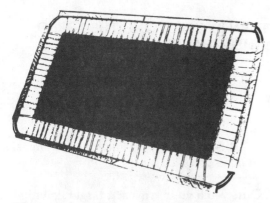

. . . Picture yourself on a trampoline. You are bouncing on the canvas with large, bobbing movements. Picture yourself doing this until you can "feel" yourself bounce. From this vivid picture, push off and ski with those feelings alive and vivid . . .

"SCHUMMM . . . SCHUMMM . . . SCHUMMM"

. . . As you link your turns together, sound out each turn with a noise like "SCHUMMM, SCHUMMM, SCHUMMM," thus making the turns sharply linked . . .

. . . Now slow the rhythm of your turning and produce a sound that matches this somewhat slower movement . . .

. . . Emphasize "WALKING" into your turns; step to the outside ski of the turn with greater and greater commitment. Feel turning become easier when the step is bouncy and strong; feel it be more reluctant when merely shuffling from foot to foot . . .

"TURN . . . TURN . . . TURN"

. . . Now vary the size of the turns. Turn to the word "turn." Say it curtly, then draw it out longer and longer: "tuuuuuurrrrrrnnnnnn"-"tuuuuuurrrrrrnnnnnn" . . .

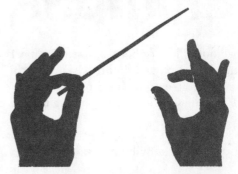

. . . Take several runs without your ski poles and allow your arms (like a conductor's baton) to signal the cadence of your turning. Become rather "lavish" in how demonstratively you move your arms—more is better . . .

"SWOOOSH?" "CREEWW?"

. . . Listen, again, to the sound your skis are making. Vocalize the sound you hear and amplify it. It may sound like: "SWOOOSH, SWOOOSH," or like "CREEEEWWWW, CREEEEWWWW"; what do your skis sound like? . . .

. . . Ski with a partner and play "Stop." One of the two of you intermittently call "stop," which signals the obligation to come to quick stops. Trade calling the signals and improve the speed of your stops . . .

. . . Expose yourself to easy and, at times, a little more challenging terrain. When making your choice gets a bit more difficult, *allow your eyes to do some fast traveling ahead of you* to select the spots where you wish to turn. Such tactical planning is an important skill to develop . . .

"uumph!"

. . . Seek out ankle- or boot-deep snow that is not wet and ski it. You will find that skiing such snow is much like skiing hard-packed snow, except you may have to "uumph" the turns a bit more . . .

. . . Also choose gently bumpy slopes to ski . . .

. . . On a smooth, gently pitched slope, skate between turns. If you dare, skate through direction changes . . .

"PEOPLE TELL ME I AM NOT LEANING FORWARD ENOUGH"

. . . Great, you don't need to do that anyway! Standing centered over your skis is just great . . .

"I STILL FIND IT HARD TO SKID THE TURN FINISHES"

. . . Stand taller on your skis when turning . . .

. . . Practice the different size wedges ("A's") when turning. Number 1 and 2 wedges will make turning easier . . .

. . . Check to see if the terrain is easy enough for you. If not, try gentler terrain where you will dare to go faster . . .

. . . Rather than trying to *control* speed, *enjoy it* when the situation seems safe to you . . .

. . . If the inside ski "snags" when skidding the turns, emphasize "walking" from foot to foot when turning . . .

NO  PUSH

. . . Actively push the skis around to finish your turns, rather than letting them "float" around . . .

"I TURN BY INVOLVING THE TORSO, RATHER THAN THE LEGS"

. . . Unless the torso involvement causes problems, allow yourself to use it to begin with . . .

. . . In order to activate legs in your turning, ski without ski poles . . .

. . . Outstretch your arms at a target downhill while continuing to turn. Keep your arms pointing at the target . . .

. . . Have a helper ski with a slalom pole held across to you. Hold onto the pole and link turns until you feel your legs doing the turning . . .

. . . As a further signal of success, continue to ski with pole assistance, but become more and more independent of it as you go . . .

THE MECHANICS

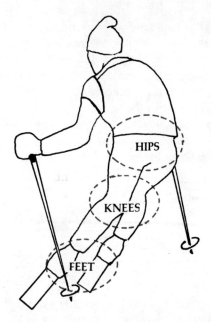

The focus of development at this time is better speed control, greater versatility of turning, and improved efficiency. The specific ski mechanical areas are:

    Sideslipping
    Uphill Christies
    Stem Christies
    Spontaneous Christies
    Widetrack Christies

SIDE SLIPPING

Conventional ski teaching emphasized the learning of parts, which were then put together, forming an entire maneuver. The sideslip was one of the fundamental parts for skidded turning. Contemporary thinking does not negate sideslipping as an element of turning, but does not necessarily demand that it be practiced before making skidded turns. With superior teaching methods, skidding may easily happen before sideslipping, yet any skier will benefit from practicing sideslipping in its many forms.

Learning to sideslip will give the skier greater sensitivity and control over the movements that determine the intensity of edge engagement. Sideslipping or skidding is controlled in any of the body regions identified in the above picture. Bending and extending in this manner is also referred to as "angulating." It ought to be understood as a movement rather than a position.

Angulating at the feet takes advantage of our primary sensors and the part of our body in which we make our most immediate corrective movements when balancing and recovering balance. Even inside our fairly rigid ski boots the feet are actively moving and articulating in a pronating and supinating fashion (see illustration). The emerging skier at this stage will

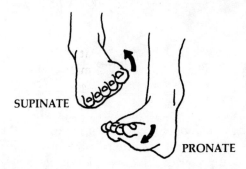

just be beginning to become aware of his movements and their effects upon the guidance of the skis. In sideslipping, when extraneous challenges are reduced, this sensitivity can be superbly developed.

Angulating the knees is essentially a "lateral" bending and extending in the knees, or so it seems. Medically trained people will be quick to tell us that the mobility factor in the knee joint itself is minimal. The majority of "knee angulating" is in effect a leg rotation that involves the entire leg from the hip joint down. The skier at class C level is usually still unsure of strong knee angulating movements, but will learn to do them cautiously.

Angulating in the hips allows the skier large

movements with which to control the edge angle. The skier at this time will favour movements closer to the skis, which do not move the center of gravity, over hip angulating motions. With growing aggressiveness and spontaneity skiers begin to increasingly involve movements that are more distant from the foot.

When practicing sideslipping, we will see combinations of angular movement rather than isolated motion in feet, legs, or hips.

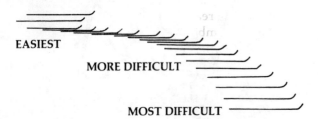

EASIEST

MORE DIFFICULT

MOST DIFFICULT

Sideslipping is easiest when the ski edges are released while traversing, slipping in a diagonal forward/sideways fashion. The steeper the angle, the harder it is to sideslip.

SUDDEN CROUCHING

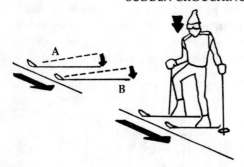

The skier generally will start to slip when the edge hold no longer is equal or greater than the skier's body weight wishing to move downhill. The skier can either "flatten" the skis on the snow (A) or overcome edging with a quick sequence of reducing pressure on the skis and then radically increasing the amount of pressure (B).

The learner should at first practice on short but steep hillsides, where gravity aids the exercise, then move to gradually shallower slopes. Sideslipping skills demanded are in inverse proportion to the steepness of the hill. Shifting the "action" of controlling the slippage from feet to knees, then hips and back, the student will soon develop the kind of sensitivity necessary for making turns with a more calculated radius and speed. Sideslip is an important exercise throughout all levels of skiing, although there is no need to develop it to any level of perfection.

UPHILL CHRISTIES

These movements can be viewed simply as the latter parts of any turn, intensifying the amount of turning toward the end to control speed and to set up for the coming turn.

Any time a skier balances where the binding places him, the skier/ski system will have a tendency to curve uphill. If the skier is in a slipping mode to start with, this tendency will be amplified.

The sequence of events contributing to uphill christies is similar to what I already described in the mechanics of sideslipping. The action can be invited through a release of the edge of the skis (flattening), thus allowing gravity and forward momentum to wed into a skidding of the skis. Yet most skiers will use the "power" method of overcoming the edge hold by pushing the skis' tails out and downward, thus thrusting them into a skid.

The initial attempt of making uphill christies will bring about short, harsh turning uphill, the still unrefined movements contributing to the roughness. Gradually the skier will better gauge the intensity of the movements involved.

Since pivoting and turning at this stage is not yet strongly developed, the skier may find uphill christies from shallower traverses easier than from steeper tracks. As confidence rises, pivoting and thrusting of the feet downhill and around will become bolder; increasing momentum will aid the uphill christy action. At this stage, practice christies with a deliberate "hard shove" and a progressively "softer push" of the feet. Center awareness around how the actions of the skier produce varying turning results.

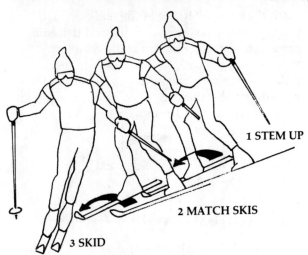

1 STEM UP

2 MATCH SKIS

3 SKID

STEP CHRISTIES

The above illustration shows an "UP-STEM CHRISTIE," which is a turn initiated by pushing the uphill ski's tail out, so that ski points in the direction you wish to go in. Gradual pressure, while continuing to "point" the ski (turn it) through the evolving arc of the turn, will deflect the skier in the direction of that pointed ski. Once the skier senses that the turn is sufficiently under way (turning momentum is felt), the inside ski of the turn is "matched" (brought alongside the dominant outside ski). The ensuing skid on corresponding edges is controlled by the amount of "steering" (turning), the amount of edging, and the intensity of pressure exerted onto the skis.

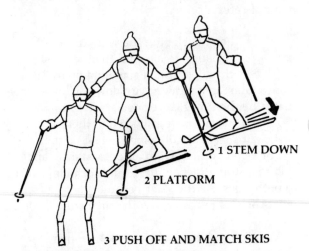

1 STEM DOWN

2 PLATFORM

3 PUSH OFF AND MATCH SKIS

This type of stem turn is referred to as a DOWNSTEM turn because the skier starts the turn after pushing the downhill ski's tail downward until its edges are dug in sufficiently to be used as a platform from which to push off. The nature of the pushoff will generate rotary

momentum, which is transferred to the outside ski of the turn and the skier's entire body. Once the downstem has outlasted its momentum it is matched to the outside ski, and both skis skid through the rest of the turn on corresponding edges. The skid is then controlled as described in the upstem christie.

The upstem christie is a more elementary maneuver at this stage. The skier entering an upstem turn allows himself the liberty of steering slowly or rapidly into the new turn, or aborting it altogether. The really cautious skier will even double stem, combining the elements of braking and steering in making a turn.

The more aggressive skier will reach for the downstem, deriving from it a sense of deliberateness, brought about by the platform feeling of the downstemmed ski from which the turn is positively, and without hesitation, initiated. Downstem turning will soon develop rhythmic linking of turns, which is the result of the commitment level a skier is at when using such turns.

Either downstem or upstem christies will promote movements from foot to foot. The one-two aspect honed at this time remains a most important element in skiing.

SPONTANEOUS CHRISTIES

Skiers descending with "narrow wedges" (skis are in a gently converging relationship) and turning in this fashion may experience skidding without any special effort. The narrow wedge places the skis on opposing edges, but in a minimal way. Once turning takes place at higher speeds, the accompanying inclination of the skier will change the inside ski's edge, thus allowing for a "breaking away" of the skis into a skid, momentum being the driving force.

The natural beauty of such turning is that the skier will have the wedge available during the actual beginnings of the direction changes, thus gaining the elements of control, balance, and turning; then, as the turn is under way, the "spontaneous" changing of the inside edges will free matters for skidding to take over, the skid being equally "spontaneously" brought about by the momentum of the skier. In surveying this type of turning, one can easily see how several things happen without direct, or conscious, labour by the skier. The magical ingredients come about by themselves, depending though upon the choice of terrain (choose a long, unchallenging hill that allows a skier to want to go fast), the image to follow (the instructor should show turns to be gentle, and flat bellied, rather than sharp and pronounced), and the quality of snow (the slope should be smooth and packed).

These type of turns also will be strongly supported by the emphasis of rhythm as it relates to the linking of turns. Continuous motion will foster such skiing, while standing still and stiff will thwart it.

"Sponters," as they are lovingly called by those who know the magic qualities of these turns, will soon develop more pronounced turn finishes, which in turn make the next turn easier and more positive. The more positive turn finishes will be the result of "down" (vertical movement) and "grip" (edging movements), which are encouraged any time the skier goes through the bobbing movements associated with rhythmic linking of turns. RHYTHM is the magical advice to the learner; any other detail discussed here is for the analytical person.

WIDE TRACK CHRISTIES

Some years ago, anyone would have been the subject of ridicule for suggesting that skiing with legs apart was an alternative in skiing. In those days considerations of function were superceded by the obligation to ski stylishly, and stylish skiing was skiing with the legs close together, no daylight being allowed between the stretchy cloth of ski pants. This bias has changed as function took precedence.

Skiing with the feet together is functional at high speeds, when skiing large radius turns, and when skiing "cruddy" snow conditions or certain kinds of deep powder. Yet even under such conditions reducing oneself to a "mono ped" should be avoided. Even when skiing the conditions described above, the very best and effective skiers will maintain the feeling of working both legs and feet independently.

The greater the obligation to make sharper turns, the more functional an open foot relationship. The open stance allows for the strong rotor muscles in and near the pelvic region to swiftly turn the legs and skis without the large counter-movements that may upset the skier's balance. The open stance also invites a greater edge sensitivity and utility, since the separated feet will also put the outside ski's edge closer to an

"active" angle, while the inside one can float, compensate, and correct. Edging and flattening the skis is also done more rapidly with feet somewhat separated, since not only is lateral mobility on one or the other leg ("knee joint") gained, but also the use of the medial and lateral muscles activating such movement.

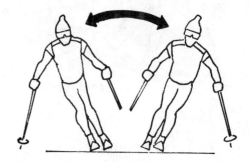

Look at the greater distance a skier needs to rearrange his body over the skis (or the skis beneath the body) when skiing with feet and skis together. Then compare the relatively shorter distance a skier moves skiing with an open foot and ski relationship. The leg adjustment is already closer to where it can be engaged, the body mass being favourably aligned to brace against the base of support in a balanced manner.

Although many ski publications have stated that the best open stance is one which places the skis about hipwidth apart, I feel that function (compensating for bow or knock knees, adjusting for speed, difference between male and female leg strength, etc.) makes that a general, but loose, point of reference.

When developing the wide track christies, it is useful to practice stop christies from a somewhat parallel stance. Start in a straight run downhill on a slope that is neither very flat nor so steep as to gain too much speed too quickly. When there is sufficient speed, rapidly pivot the skis either left or right, coming from an open stance, and skid to a stop. Practice these kinds of maneuvers to both sides. As the skier becomes more adept, pivot the skis more slowly; the turn should round out.

A typical widetrack christie looks somewhat like this: The general stance of the skier is a bit more crouched than normal, giving the "power triangle" (marked) optimal strength. In this crouched position, the skier turns by pivoting the feet, then pushing from the heel. The critical phase of any turn is when the skis are brought from a linear motion (or even a rotary motion in

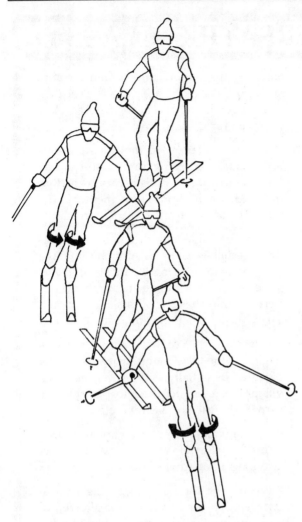

fashion. As a turn is pivoted through its finish, the skis will be pointing across the hill, while the skier's head and torso, in anticipation of the next turn, will continue to face downhill.

Generally, the stronger the twisting in the finish of one turn, the stronger the untwisting for the start of a new turn. Greater aggressiveness, and increased edging at the finish of a turn, will cause a more dynamic spring into the new turn. Though "rebound turning" generally does not become an issue until Class D and E, it is now that the elements of such action are born.

the opposite direction of the intended turn) toward the fall-line. This is when the need for torque is greatest.

When a skier initiates a turn from a traverse or sideslip in a widetrack position, he is likely to start turning either by steering the outside foot and ski until rotary momentum is established, then adding the more sudden movement of turning both legs simultaneously, or, if speed and/or strength is sufficient, the skier can immediately pivot. For the observer, it may be difficult or impossible to visually discriminate between the two mechanical versions.

The skier turning in a widetrack fashion, while rhythmically linking turns, will benefit increasingly from a mechanism referred to as "anticipation." The muscle-stretching and contracting mechanism involves the legs and pelvis, and the pelvis and torso. Picture someone holding a rubber ring that is twisted into a figure 8. When releasing the hold of either the upper or lower hand, the figure 8 will slowly unwind into a big O. A skier's body works in the same

S kiing widetrack turns with pressure on both feet and skis utilizes mechanics of turning similar to those described in conjunction with "wedge turns." The partly pressured inside ski becomes the fulcrum about which the outside ski is turned. Perhaps you remember some dance steps that also take advantage of such mechanics and require that both feet remain in contact with the ground.

Skiers favoring widetrack turns with a distinct shifting of pressure from foot to foot (as in walking) use a "pushoff" type of propulsion to enter turns. The outside ski of the last turn becomes the platform from which the skier bounds off onto the new outside ski, imparting rotary momentum to it. Regardless of how such turns are initiated, the remainder of the turns are controlled by the intensity of "steering," the amount of pressure placed upon the skis and the amount of edging performed.

Widetrack turning is the entry into a new and more dynamic chapter of skiing: with increasing speed, edging and interaction between body and ski mechanics, the skier becomes more efficient by increasingly using the skis' properties to turn.

BECOMING MORE VERSATILE: CLASS D

GOALS

- Increasing ability to vary radii and speed in turning.

- Gaining further access to different terrain and snow conditions.

CHOICE OF TERRAIN AND SNOW

- "Easy" and "intermediate" terrain, excursions into "difficult" realms.

- Gentle bumps and slightly deeper snow than before.

- Varying snow conditions with packed-snow base.

MECHANICAL DEVELOPMENT

- One-footed, steered entries into turns yield to turning feet and skis simultaneously.

- At this time it will be useful to explore stemming and stepping movements as alternatives.

- As turns become more rounded, emphasis should be placed on exploring edging and pressuring while turning.

- As turns are more and more rhythmically linked, the pole plant becomes very useful.

- Upper/lower body separation is beginning to develop while linking turns of shorter radius.

METHODOLOGICAL EMPHASIS

- Visualization of movement patterns is a great help. Learning to visualize may itself become an issue intrinsic to progress.

- Sensory awareness becomes the focus of the learning process.

- Pole action is taught in an intermittent fashion to avoid overload of what might be a complex issue.

- Rhythm remains a most important learning aid.

- At these higher levels of performance, the issue of further developing and refining skills consumes more time within the curriculum. Basic skills are always useful to review, but for all practical purposes, they are taken for granted by now.

- Developing nuances of movements, tempering skills, "turning the volume up or down" and exposing skills to varying terrain and snow conditions now become the dominant path for growth and versatility.

- VAK — Visual, Auditory and Kinesthetic-message delivery and task design remains a way to convey information most completely. Leaving any of those sensory media out merely diminishes the possible impact and clarity the instruction could bear.

- Synchronizing voice and action retains its magical value. Playing intensity variations triggered by equally varying vocalizations will prove, even to the most suspicious learner, the value of such practice.

- Realizing what a skier's functional tension is and how to attain and maintain it is now becoming a potential priority.

- Awareness is the key in learning to deal with fear. As long as a skier is allowed to entertain illusions that are the cause for his fear, the skeletons will remain in the closet. When fear and its motivations become the target of closer scrutiny, tension tends to diminish.

MAKING MORE ROUNDED TURNS:

Z ~~Z~~ ∿

. . . Make Z turns (the shape of the letter Z) indicative of rapid turning. Check your tracks to confirm . . .

S **S** ∫

. . . Make S turns (the shape of the letter S) indicating a rounder shape to those turns. Once again, check your tracks for telltales of the rounder turns . . .

"one,

two,

three,

four,

five

six"

. . . Make turns to the count or 5 or 6, turning as long as the count lasts . . .

. . . Make wedge turns with extremely gentle efforts, the turns "drifting" into their start rather than being "whipped" into . . .

DEVELOP GREATER CONTROL:

. . . Repeat the "Stop" game with a friend; choose steeper and steeper terrain while doing so . . .

. . . Play the "Stop" game at higher speeds . . .

. . . Practice side-slipping straight downhill and across the hill. Develop the ability to slip longer distances without stopping . . .

. . . Side-slip, deliberately regulating the speed of the slippage . . .

. . . Ski steeper terrain, linking turns and side-slipping: turn-slip-turn-slip . . .

"MORE!" "less"

. . . Link turns, focusing upon the amount of ski movement from one side to the other. Register greater turning movements with the word "more" and less movement with the word "less." If turning amplitude is the same, do not say anything . . .

. . . Ski in gentle terrain at a higher speed . . .

"crrrunch"

. . . Make your skis dig into the snow when finishing turns; the edges "crrrunch" . . .

SKIING MORE AGGRESSIVELY:

"NOW! . . . NOW! . . . NOW!"

. . . Ski to the rhythm of you saying "now," "now," "now." Make the sound of the word convincing and audible; pick up the rhythm and go with it . . .

. . . Ski slalom gates in *shallow* terrain, striving to gain speed . . .

. . . Go on a "mogul hunt"; on a groomed slope, find small bumps and jump off them. If you feel your maturity allows you to say "whoopie," say it every time you leap off a bump . . .

. . . While you ski, estimate how fast you are going . . .

. . . Role-play: imagine a racer booking through a course, sparkling with aggression. Now, *ski that way!* . . .

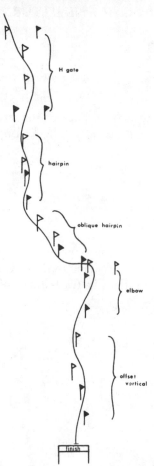

. . . Picture an imaginary race course and ski it . . .

. . . Ski that same race course but actually feel yourself brushing the slalom gates with your shoulders . . .

LEARNING TO DEAL WITH FEAR:

. . . How do you know you are afraid? . . .

. . . Where do you feel tension most? . . .

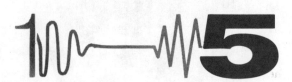

. . . The number 5 being very tense, 1 fairly relaxed, what do you judge your tension level to be? . . .

. . . Where else do you feel tense? Proceed with the same measuring! . . .

. . . Look at the hill you are afraid of and plot your run. Plan a segment of the descent in this way, then ski it; then map out the next section . . .

. . . Stand and close your eyes. Focus upon (but do not control) your breathing. Exude tension from your body with every exhale . . .

"TURN!"

. . . When skiing, say the word "turn" loudly and convincingly to yourself whenever you execute a turn . . .

. . . Ski the segment of hill in front of you in your mind. Ski it well that way before pushing off . . .

THE MECHANICS

When reading these chapters, realize that the different development phases melt into one another rather than sharply butting against one another. This FLOW is an important aspect of an effective progression, where elements are developed and honed throughout a larger spectrum, each time polishing another dimension of a seemingly already known mechanical aspect, thus gaining skill smoothly and confidently. In that sense will we continue dealing with widetrack, with anticipation, with weight transfer, with simultaneous leg rotation.

As we move into higher and higher realms of skiing, the mechanical complexity and versatility, and subtlety, becomes greater. The increasing chapter size of ski mechanics will be evidence of this development.

By now the skier has learned to turn, has acquired confidence in his ability to negotiate easy and some intermediate trails and is ready to diversify mechanically and mentally. He will be ready to explore "special conditions" such as moguls, running gates and deeper snow.

A specific selection of issues at this time are:
- Stem-Step Christies
- Widetrack Christies (continued)
- Skidding-carving
- Pole planting
- Deeper snow
- Tackling those bumps
- Running some gates

STEM CHRISTIES-STEP CHRISTIES

As the skier gains greater speed and confidence, "stem christies" will naturally evolve into "step christies." The development is one of subtlety and versatility. Stem christies are done in a fairly deliberate manner in which the skis at the time of turn initiation are brought into a converging relationship. "Step christies" bring about more versatility in the sense illustrated below.

STEM-STEP   PARALLEL-STEP   SCISSOR-STEP

While the learning skier may consciously practice one type of turn or another, the expert skier will intuitively reach for the appropriate maneuver that best achieves balance and the objective of the moment.

Step christies utilize the well-developed walking reflexes of moving from foot to foot. The skier uses the skis as a person on foot would use his feet and legs to move, direct and balance himself.

Stem-step turns are used by the skier wishing to enter turns quickly either to avoid an obstacle or to regain balance when the center of gravity is moving too much to the inside of the base of support. The feet have to be brought back into alignment with the balancing pressure vector of the skier's body. Stem-step turns engage the skis by moving the weight from the inside edge of one ski to the inside edge of the other ski. The weight-bearing ski is usually the dominant and guiding one. The ski with less or no pressure is usually the compensating one that the skier pushed off from; that leg also actively rotates in the direction of the turn, thus generating and storing further turning momentum. The angle of the stem-step decreases with increasing speed and the deflection comes from the added momentum instead of the severe angle.

While all step turns involve distinct weight transfers (shifting of pressure from foot to foot), the stem step tends to necessitate the least amount of shifting of the center of gravity, which must be immediately on the inside of the turn.

Stem-step turning starts with conventional stem christies, and is achieved with increasing quickness and nimbleness in moving from one ski to the other. With increasing efficiency, the stemmed ski becomes more quickly active once it is placed on the snow. Sensitive pressuring of the edged ski soon leads to better carving.

PARALLEL STEP CHRISTIES

It does not matter whether a skier steps convergingly, divergingly, or parallel, yet parallel stepping may introduce the skier to a level of finesse that will be helpful in the general development of skills.

Parallel stepping places the stepped ski onto the inside edge or the outside edge. In either case the skier will need to generate the turning impulse during the stepping movement; the ski placement itself does not contribute to the reorientation of the skier.

One of these mechanisms is the so-called "Hip Rotation" (A), a movement in which the skier during the pushoff phase rotates the pelvis in the direction of the intended turn, and when slowing or stopping this movement, transfers torque to the legs and skis. This movement is generally accompanied with an upward movement, which lightens the skis, making it easier to turn them.

Another popular and often-seen means to start the parallel-step turn is to "hip-project." This complicated-sounding term simply labels a forward and outward movement of the hips — a punching the paunch — which causes the skis to skid out sideways and thus gets the turn started (B).

Because of the relatively slower start of turning this way, the skier must develop much subtlety and patience to wait for the skis to come around and start actively carrying the skier into a turn. The resulting "floating" phase requires good timing, keen judgement and the level of finesse mentioned earlier.

The skier practicing "parallel-step christies" will discover that in order to better prepare for a more secure turn entry, a gentle down-check movement prior to the initiation of a turn will make the starting mechanics stronger.

The positive engagement of the edge of the displaced ski gives a firm base to start moving from and initiates the body mass moving toward the new turn center. When initiating the parallel-step turn, care must be taken that the extension, coupled with the hip movements described above, is directed toward the new turn center rather than in the direction in which the skis are pointing. If the latter were done, the "float phase" would be endless. The chance to get off into the new turn would be diminished, and a new effort to turn would be needed. A simple but fairly effective rule to avoid this is to stay facing downhill while turning; this will have a tendency to draw the torso in that direction.

SCISSOR-STEP CHRISTIES

When scissor turns were first observed, racers were using their inside ski's edge in an attempt to cut a closer line to slalom gates. This risky, but when done well, highly effective maneuver was referred to as "cramponage" (crampon climbing spikes). With evolving ski equipment, techniques changed somewhat, but the transfer of pressure to the inside ski to finish a turn has remained.

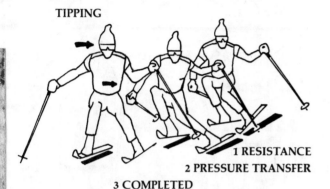

TIPPING

1 RESISTANCE
2 PRESSURE TRANSFER
3 COMPLETED

In its effective form, the scissor step happens in the following way: sensing the end of the turn by feeling the pressure accumulation getting near its peak, the skier subtly shifts pressure toward the inside ski; gradually letting it become the gripping ski, and the now-light ski merely coasts in a skating-like relationship. As the inside ski starts gripping, the skier's center of gravity will be accelerated toward the new turn center. The skier deliberately (or at least calculatingly) uses this tipping acceleration to move toward the new turn center. Had the skier at this time kept his grip on the outside ski, equilibrium would have been maintained between the centrifugal forces and the edging-resisting forces. The now freely moving outside ski contributes to the tipping acceleration, and once the tipping is under way, is brought alongside the now-dominant ski.

The fact that the skis are diverging accelerates the speed with which tipping is initiated, and the tipping in turn changes the edges. In coaching this movement, one needs to skillfully incorporate "anticipation" as the mechanism that pulls the skier into the turn; otherwise the skier will not realize the need for the base of support (feet and skis) to follow. The open attitude of torso and face is an easy and effective target of anticipation for the skier.

At this stage, few skiers will be able to perform a well-executed and functionally clean turn. One need not belabour this maneuver beyond developing a basic feeling for it by practicing skating in the flat and skating toward a turn initiation. The utility of scissor christies will rise sharply as speed of travel increases. The independent carriage of the legs helps maintain a functional alignment between the skier's body mass and the skis. It will be helpful for the skier to get repeated, dynamic images of well-done turns. A coach or teacher can thus lay the seed for this complex but natural-feeling maneuver to take hold.

WIDETRACK CHRISTIES

We started discussing "widetrack christies" already in the Class C description, assuming that skiers would at that level be able to begin linking turns in a rhythmic fashion. The utility of the open track is to provide the skier with strong pivoting strength, adding optimal freedom and mobility in the legs to edge and move from foot to foot when turning. With increasing speed, the open track will narrow, provided that the outside ski of turns becomes the pressure-dominant one. If this is so, the less-pressured inside ski will simply "drift" parallel to the outside ski, a result of centrifugal force.

With increasing roundness of turns, resulting from more controlled pivoting to start the turn and more effective edging and sensitive pressuring of the skis through the turn, CARVING will become a reality.

A skier must come to realize skiing is learning to let go of control. Control to the beginner is to be able to stop at any time, to feel balanced at every instant of the descent. The more experienced skier learns that surrendering in a calculated way to temporary "imbalance," judging speed and control as elements that are calculated in ever-increasing horizons and enjoying the sensation of "flight" on skis contribute much to the intoxicating qualities of the sport.

At this stage of development it will become important not only to discover these dimensions as an issue of thrill and euphoria but also to tap the dynamics of skiing without which the skier will stall at this level of development. The idea of "risking" imbalance is what brings a skater from a tentative shuffle to discovering the power of larger strides, is what pushes a bicyclist from struggling to maintain a straight line to powering through a curve, and is what promotes a skier from actively controlling every inch of movement to discovering the elating springiness of skis and snow.

"Judging" speed, rather than fearing it, going as fast on unchallenging terrain as you dare, using images of such as racecars, racers, airplanes in flight, and sensing speed by the flow of air on face and hair will all help raise the comfort level. When I speak of speed at this level, I do not picture speed with abandonment, reckless speed, but speed that may exceed the perhaps persisting "WHOA" attitude skiers may still harbour. An important point at this time is to ski mostly UNCHALLENGING TERRAIN fast, rather than gaining social merit points by surviving the steep. With that in mind, let us look at the evolving mechanics again.

To refine "widetrack christies," a solid dose of sideslipping will help. Linked "hockey slides" provide movement that hones pivoting, sensitive edging, and balancing adjustments fore and aft on the skis.

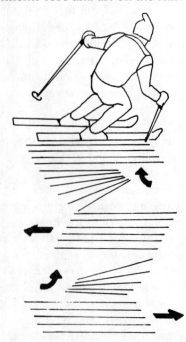

Start in a series of turns, making the skidding phase longer and longer. Stop the skid by planting the pole and pivoting the skis quickly, pressuring the heel. Now repeat, making the slipping aim more and more downhill, shortening the time it takes to pivot the skis. Throughout this action, the skier should be facing downhill, containing the movements for doing this to the lower body.

Further play with uphill christies will also help at this stage. Evolve from merely "kicking" the skid into existence and then sliding to a stop;

attempt to make uphill christies that create narrower tracks.

Another notable development takes place at this time: the beginning and early intermediate skier has a tendency to guide and direct the skis predominantly with movements of the upper body, but now will discover the benefits of turning with the lower body.

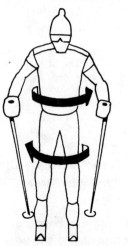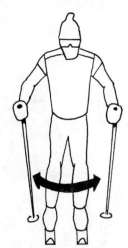

Lower body contributions to turning can be the result of turning upper and lower body simultaneously in opposite directions (taking advantage of Newton's discovery of "action and reaction") or rotating the legs from an open stance without involving the torso (what Georges Joubert refers to as "braquage").

Hopping in place, pivoting on top of gently rounded bumps, practicing quickly and more slowly linked short-radius turns become invaluable experiments to discover the interconnecting mechanics between upper and lower body.

By shifting the action of turning predominantly into the legs and feet, the skier will be quicker in turning and better balanced because he will be keeping the head and torso (and the center of mass) facing the direction of travel rather than having to twist and turn to generate the turning impulse.

Because of the maturing interdependence between upper and lower body and because of the increasing ability of the skier to turn the legs beneath the rest of the body, ANTICIPATION, a turn-assisting mechanism already mentioned, is now becoming a viable action.

The "windup-release" nature of anticipation becomes a stronger ingredient in turning as the skier uses the twisting relationship between torso and legs/feet at the end of any turn. With increasing edging skill, and the catalytic nature of increased pressure on edged skis, the skis will have an increasing tendency to finish turns. The upper body, being typically blocked by a pole plant and facing downhill, becomes the steady body mass against which the legs and feet do their "saber dance." The "bongo-board" experience of swaying, pumping legs beneath a quiet torso is a most harmonious and efficient manner of skiing, and most useful in short-radius turns, in bumps and in deep snow.

STRETCH ZONE

The readily identifiable muscle groups active in anticipation and release are of the lower back and abdomen, the ones tying torso and legs into the pelvis. A pole plant will certainly also involve the musculature of the shoulders and upper chest, thus closing a powerful linkage of muscles along the length of the body.

The skier at this stage has the following turning mechanism available to him: To start turns he can use a "rotary pushoff," a "lateral pushoff," rotating the entire body, use of the legs to turn, or use of anticipation or counter-rotation. The skier that knows about these alternatives and tries to select which one to use will be the one we will find wrapped around a tree, or we may locate him inebriated in the closest bar, still trying to find out the best way of turning. It is important to understand that the best way of learning about these options is by learning to resolve certain challenges in the most efficient way accessible to the skier at the time. The learner should focus upon feelings and sensations and should learn about skiing by sensing the connection between how he moved and what it caused. What we want to avoid at all costs is skiing remaining a conscious effort for any longer than the time necessary to hone a skill. The above analyses, therefore, are not for the learner, but for the person wishing to reflect upon the events AFTER they have been learned.

The teacher will need the analysis to clarify his perceptions and to guide what he offers to the learner.

✳ SKIDDING-CARVING

For those of you readers who know what the term "carving" stands for, isolate the track that most expresses carving to you. When you have found the best carving track, find the least carving track, and then gauge the rest.

Take a minute and contemplate how you would explain carving in a simple manner to a nonskier or a skier who does not know carving. Could your explanation sound something like: carving is turning with little or no skidding or slipping, changing direction by the ski that is bent into an arc scribing a circle, thus taking the skier with him? If your explanation included most of these characteristics, you did a great job.

What allows carving to happen is the waisted design of the skis, which you can see when looking at them from the top. A 2x4 board would not allow a skier to carve (if we allowed ourselves to imagine the ridiculous picture of a skier on 2x4 s). Carving is, in short, taking advantage of the design properties of the skis when turning.

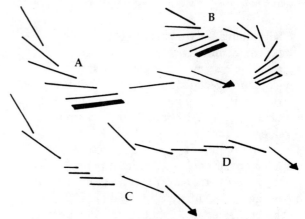

Now go back to the track pictures and juxtapose the most and least carving track. Picture what the skier is doing differently to leave either track behind. In (B) the skier obviously pivots the skis very strongly, while in (D) pivoting is virtually absent. A further question to the reader is: Do you suppose the skier in (B) used the design qualities of skis at all? Your answer is correct: "Not very much." The fact that you admitted, though, that ski design does enter whenever anyone turns any way but jump-hop, behooves us to look at the issue of carving and skidding in the following way.

With the publication of Warren Witherell's book "How The Racers Ski," skiers, coaches, and instructors contemplated the question: "Should we skid or carve?" Polarity opinions developed and harsh verbal fights established "clear" demarcation lines of who was your brother and who was your foe.

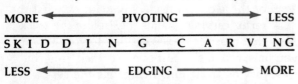

Upon closer scrutiny of the issues we quickly find only one issue. Looking at the graph as a reference, CARVING and SKIDDING share a large volume of mechanical ingredients and are differentiated only by the emphasis that is placed upon certain qualities.

Is the varsity kid playing on the basketball team a fine player? In comparison with backyard neophytes he is, yet in comparison with NBA players perhaps not. Is the skier developing from a strong skid to turning with less skid carving?

Any time we turn and have the skis on the snow we tend to pivot the skis and edge them. The intensity with which we play these ingredients will determine the amount of skidding and carving. With that in mind, we always skid — but we also always carve.

Skidding and carving are performance characteristics that can and should be rehearsed by skiers at many stages of development. Skidded turning not only brings greater utility to the beginning skier, but it is also easier to do; it is less complex and does not threaten balance.

Carving requires a more subtle and refined complement of skills that, at least temporarily, will require the tradeoff of "control" in lieu of a more aggressive attitude and line of skiing.

The best skier at World Cup level will have skidded and carved turns at his disposal, yet may be aiming to carve certain segments of turns in order to allow himself to descend as fast as possible from start to finish. The reason why I am saying, "He will carve certain portions of the turns," rather than indicating that carving should be done as much as possible, is no simple issue to explain: Carving tends to make turns round, which in turns leads the racer farther away from the fall-line. Deviating from the fall-line slows a skier. Contemporary fast lines are less rounded than they were some years ago; the quality and design of skis allow the racer to take straighter lines, still having the "umpf" in the skis to aid in the shortened and intensified phase during which turning takes place. Carving turns sets a certain predetermined radius to turning that, because of the speed and slipperiness of most race courses, is difficult to bring in concert with the rhythm of the poles' set. Carving the early part of turns may find the skier having to realize that the curve will fall short or wide of the intended line of descent; therefore he will have to add pivoting, or allow slippage for needed drift.

I am sharing these contemplations not to express my discontent with CARVING, but to put this viable mechanical action into perspective. As so often in a faddish sport, it has been taken too far. Check with the exercise segment of Class D for ways to work on carving.

✳ POLE PLANTING

As I am writing this section title, I realize how limiting the title is in relation to the functional use of poles. When we think of pole use we generally think of the savage stabbing of the ground we do when starting turns. Yet there are many more uses of ski poles that we seldom discuss or pay attention to.

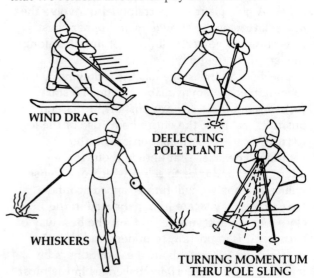

The ski poles serve as a "balancing bar" to the skier: the skier balances against their weight on either side. The wind drag of the poles also enhances balance; the resistance it offers is similar to our leaning against the table when tying our shoelaces.

Ski poles are very important balancing devices when they are dragged gently on the snow. The whisker effect is not appreciated until you deliberately not allow yourself to drag either pole on the snow. The most common use of ski poles is certainly the pole plant to start a turn. The deflecting impact from the pole plant will help turning considerably. If and when, during the precarious phase of starting a turn, things should go awry, the pole can help achieve a recovery.

Aside from these more or less obvious uses of the poles, someone will someday write a book about the less conventional uses of these tools: dragging your child uphill to ski class, picking up paper, inspecting a glistening object in the snow without embarrassing yourself in a lift line, getting your right of way by barring your neighbor's access to the alternating line, expressing your emotions to a fellow skier who just felled you like a tree, dragging between your feet to futilely attempt to slow yourself, pointing authoritatively into the surrounding, emphasizing your knowledge of people and mountains, retrieving your wallet from the drain joint in the restroom, drying your wet pants after skiing a steep run, etc.

Learning to plant the pole is a timing issue. The skier at this stage will have been amply exposed to seeing skiers plant their poles; he therefore probably needs little or no help in integrating this action into the rest of his skiing. The cerebral learner, though, will have much difficulty, just as he will have problems with the "step into the stroke" action in tennis. The best way to proceed is to ask the skier to watch a skier using his poles, emphasizing to watch the flow of motions, then emulate it. Most skiers who have lucked out and not been instructed in how to use the poles will succeed after a few observations and trials. If, at the question of how the skier sees the flow of the action, he responds "touch-turn," the coach or teacher will know that all is well. One should refrain from playing with relatively complex movements too long. A periodic visit to practicing, then focus upon something else, coming back to it, and so on, is the most effective way of dealing with it.

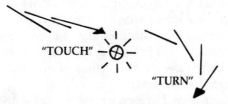

The learner exclaiming "touch" when the pole touches, "turn" when the skis start turning, will be a fabulous barometer of progress to any

teacher. It will be a fine "mirror" for the student as to how the action of pole plant and turning are interconnected. Initially poor timing is an important experience for the learner. The accompanying roughness provides ample motivation to seek a smoother linkage and timing connection. Another, but still rough, pole action and its effect will build the references a learner needs to hone.

I cannot begin to tell you the horror stories I observed in my many years of teaching, in which fellow teachers, helpful friends or self-teaching skiers moved through the labyrinth of coordinating pole action and skiing. I have seen instructors and students cursing themselves and each other, as well as students stomping off the slope in disgust, feeling forever clumsy and "not suited for skiing," just because a potentially complex issue was made even more difficult.

With the focus upon flow, with the method of learning being watching and doing by feeling, pole action is a cinch. Remember the intermittent learning pace as well, since going beyond the stage of observation and playing with the mechanics of pole plant brings about frustration that is merely being fueled by hard effort and "trying."

During this stage the skier is likely to discover that the pole aids the "kick" when starting a turn. The balancing effect when starting one turn and beginning another will give the skier a feeling of security, which in turn will make him more aggressive in starting turns actively and with commitment, rather than tentatively hoping it will happen through desire.

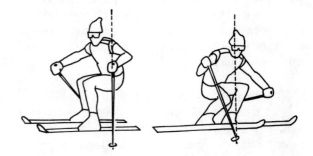

The pole action in the left picture is one of bracing and balancing; the one on the right is one of anchoring and deflecting. The more upright pole plant will take place when the skier starts turns of longer radius, or rotating starts; the one learning against the direction of travel is associated with shorter radius turns and turn initiations using anticipation or nothing but the deflection from a pole.

There are other forms of ski pole use. Descend without ski poles altogether, then use ski poles (holding them), but do not touch the snow. Thus the skier will begin to realize the kinds of assistance the ski poles provide the skier, and at the same time perhaps come to the realization that pole use may have corrupted the skier: he no longer balances well on the skis, or he uses the deflection from the pole too exclusively as the means to turn, allowing other mechanisms to deteriorate.

Experiment with different ski poles that offer different handle and basket weight distribution. The beginning skier may favour a very light ski pole, while the more advanced skier, wanting to ski fast, may favour a heavier ski pole. Good skiers often allow themselves the supportive luxury of having two types of ski poles, depending on the type of skiing they choose to pursue.

DEEPER SNOW

When we here in Vail think of "deep snow," we think of light, fluffy, bottomless "stuff" that is dry and light, and easy to maneuver in. I know that other people are blessed with equally fine "champagne" powder, while others again may have to have erotic dreams about such conditions.

The intermediate and early advanced skier will inevitably encounter slush or deeper, unpacked snow conditions. Some people dread the morning hours before the snowcats pack the snow after a storm, while others are nearly breaking down the lift maze gates to get to sample such conditions first. Some consider the snow an obstacle, others an exotic experience. What can one do to make this snow a pleasure? "Ski it."

The primary factor in learning to ski deeper snow (not knee-deep or more yet) is that you trust yourself to do it. Any skier having accumulated the skill level so far dealt with will be able to ski anything from a "trace to a foot," unless it is some ungodly "cement" that I have encountered in some nasty parts of this skiing world. Many skiers react to a fresh snow layer much in the same manner a mouse reacts to a snake. They freeze! Motionless, but with a defensive, sitting-back position, they wait for fate to strike — and it does, as it would were they to ski hardpacked snow in this fashion.

1   2   3

The mechanical difficulties are insignificant, and the slightly increased pivotal resistance is easily overcome by a slightly more aggressive "umpf" into a turn. In the depths of snow we are discussing right now there is no need to sit back or lean forward; as a matter of fact, doing either could either needlessly fatigue you or stall the turn midway, or could suddenly overturn the skis when leaning forward and finish the turn far sooner than desired (leaving you to inspect the situation from upside down).

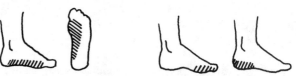

PRESSURE HERE RATHER THAN HERE OR HERE

The learner should be encouraged to start with a series of uphill christies in accommodating terrain, feeling out the situation. On a shallower stretch of slope, short-radius turns with strong pivoting movements (aided by liberal bounce) should become the overture for skiing "the deeeeep." Once under way, the skier should experiment with how much he may quiet the movements without losing the ability to turn. RHYTHMIC LINKING is the recommended fashion in which to make first turns, not one turn at a time.

The thus-successful skier should now try varying the rhythm to a faster and slower linking of turns, all the while skiing to a rhythm, and skiing shallow-enough terrain not to have to worry about speed control. Mileage will generate confidence. Once short-radius turns can be made with ease, longer turns should be explored. While the radius of turns changes, movements remain, though they slow perceptibly and commensurately with the flow of events. Stalling in movement will bring trouble. Keep moving, even if you have to "talk" yourself into and through the movements.

A skier reared in a progressive fashion to cope with deep snow will have no trouble skiing the deep, though it takes a predominantly hardpack skier a few minutes to warm up to "fluff." The skier who visits deeper snow rarely, being dragged along by friends, will develop a panicky attitude toward the white gold that will haunt them for a long time.

Bump skiing should merely provide an experience that combines familiar turning and feeling the undulation of the ground beneath you.

Enjoy yourself.

HOW ABOUT BUMPS?

In our effort toward diversification it is a must to become acquainted with the most common terrain form skiers are facing nowadays. Bumps are usually seeded by area operators in November, about the same time as winter wheat, and the harvest depends upon the frequency with which slopes are "massaged" by turning skiers. While moisture content of snow and temperature affect the growth of bumps, they seem to do best on slopes near or under ski lifts, where the warmth of people makes them pop up like mushrooms.

Start skiing gentle bumps that do not force their rhythm upon your skiing. Turn as you know how to, gradually feeling the shapes of the bumps and their affect upon your turns. The irregularity of bumps makes skis feel heavy, then light, then heavy again, then light. . . . The "light" phase is supportive of turning the skis; the "heavy" phase demands having the feet underneath so that the pressure can be dealt with. Begin identifying the part of the bump that tends to make you feel light, that which makes you feel heavy.

Once you are able to make turns through bumps, begin to harmonize your turns with the bumps, relying upon the experiences you have gathered from the "heavy/light" exploration. Remain in gentle bumps until you can ski them with confidence, then seek out larger ones, varying the speed with which you ski them.

I would strongly recommend that you stay away from bump runs where you will have to worry about speed control, line choice, etc. . . .

RUNNING GATES

Nonskiers will wonder what the phrase, "running gates," means. A skier has to dodge and weave through people when skiing; slalom poles stuck into the snow are an artificial way to mark a line of descent. The educational value of running gates is that skier learns to turn where he must, rather than where he cares to turn. Such discipline is not only great fun at learning levels, but is of course also the objective for racers to negotiate in the fastest possible way.

Gate running should follow the stage at which a skier has developed the ability to turn predictably left and right, but need not wait until a very advanced level. The attitude change a skier experiences when "attacking" a course brings about many mechanical changes that can be seen only while running gates, and they fade as quickly as Cinderella's carriage as soon as the skier passes the last gate. The reasons for such occurrences are easily explained: *not* thinking about how to ski, but focusing about where to ski, coupled with the possibly "animalistic" attitude toward self and the situation, are a winning combination. I am not mentioning animalism in a derogatory sense at all; on the contrary, I work very hard to elicit such a perception to help a skier into a new or rare performance level.

I would like to suggest you enroll in a slalom training program that is not really concerned with racing per se. My only hesitation with this suggestion is that I have seen too many poorly administered programs which did more harm than help. Carefully check around in your vicinity and seek out someone and a program you can trust, that has a good reputation in the sense that directives are simple, courses are well maintained, terrain is shallow, the general atmosphere is light, encouraging and spirited.

If you are guided well, you will probably start well outside the gates, reviewing your turning, honing edging, rhythm of movement, flow of motion. Having dealt with moguls will be valuable experience when beginning to run gates, since courses are rarely flat, but rather show "ruts" right where the skiers turn around the gates.

Your first runs will be made in openly set, single-pole courses, each pole placed in the snow where turns are encouraged. The rhythm will be simple left-right, tie gates being only gently offset, if at all, to facilitate success through easy interpretation. A coach is likely to "lay a line"

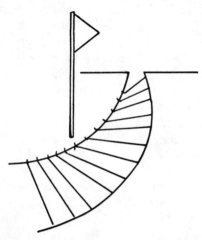

through such a course to make it even easier for you to follow an existing and visible line. The cadence at this level of expertise will be an easy, open sequence, neither so short as to challenge someone's ability to turn, nor so long as to make speed a likely threat. Careful surveillance of ability levels and equally careful design of the course to match the ability will be critical.

Make your first few descents with nothing else on your mind but turning where the poles tell you to. Left and right, left and right . . .pick up the gently swaying rhythm of the course and "dance" with it. Gritting teeth, making tough faces, getting "muscular" and low are gestures we'll leave to Hollywood. The turns will be as easy as you allow them to be, the added adrenaline flow triggered by the vincible challenge of turning around "gates" fueling your success. Many people find it helpful to breathe in

rhythm to the turns (don't make them toooo big, or you'll hyperventilate). Making the breathing audible will be better yet. Let the intensity of your audible exhalation indicate the power in your turn. This is by no means the only such methods help you ski.

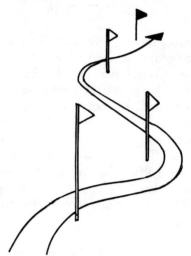

One fundamental, but always useful, mechanical element that will help you when skiing your first gate runs is that whenever turning itself seems to be difficult or inconsistent, concentrate on stepping to the outside ski of each turn. A skier's problems will vanish the more actively this suggestion is pursued. This mechanical focus will not only ensure the timely beginning of each turn, but also help maintain proper fore-aft balance (starting racers often "lose it" backwards).

Uncontrollable chattering on harder race course surfaces is a common occurrence. The beginning, but even the experienced, gate skier will get to know "chatter" as the eternal challenge to overcome. At first I would not worry about chatter, as priorities shift from simply "making the course" to doing so better, but it will be useful to learn about how to suppress chatter and direct skis smoothly through turns. "Chatter" is generally the result of too much pivoting when starting to turn. The skier's momentum will carry him sideways, and using the edges of the skis will be futile to stop the drift or change the direction of motion.

The answer to this problem is to ski rounder turns, give the gates a wider berth, and smooth the pivoting over a longer distance (A). Gradual turning of the skis allows direction changes of the skier's body mass to coincide with the redirecting of the skis.

Another reason for "soft chatter," which I'd

rather call "drifting," is that the skier simply does not edge the skis enough when turning. Like a sailing dinghy trying to turn without its centerboard down, the skier will drift sideways.

The solution to this problem is to practice sideslipping, hockey slips to edge setting, hockey stops, sideslip garlands, more uphill christies, etc. The focus of this process should center around the discovery of "carving" (B). A seemingly paradoxical reason for chatter is too much edging when the skier crosses already-existing "chatter

marks." To overcome this cause for chattering, the skier simply has to make the tactical decision to either avoid these chatter marks that so "rattle" his skiing, or to guide his skis at an angle to the existing chatter marks, thus avoiding their ripple effect. The lines (C) show the alternate solutions.

While I am providing all this "chatter" to avoid undesirable skidding, please do not chastise yourself for experiencing chatter. Even the best in the world will at best be trying to minimize chatter and drift, unable to totally control it or even wishing to control it for reasons mentioned earlier.

At this upper intermediate level it is important to keep in mind to keep things FUN. So if you find yourself getting grumpy, frustrated or short tempered with self or others, just make a cruising run, not thinking, striving, practicing, but merely enjoying yourself.

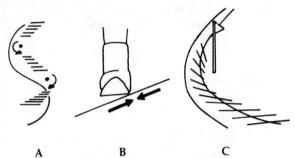

A   B   C

"DYNAMIC" TURNING: CLASS E

GOALS

- The skier develops a skilled manner in the employment of the skis as tools.

- All snow and terrain become a playground for the skier on this level.

- Versatility, in a technical sense, and increasing finesse are the trademarks of this skier.

CHOICE OF TERRAIN AND SNOW

- All terrain but extremes.

- All snow conditions but extremes.

- All speed ranges but extremes.

MECHANICAL DEVELOPMENT

- The skier is acquiring all sorts of techniques to start turns: upper body turn initiations, lower body turn initiations, coordinated turn initiations.

- Suppleness in dealing with the in- and decreases of pressure while skiing bumps and dynamic turn finishes is developed.

- Upper/lower body flexibility is honed.

- Linking of turns becomes smoother and more efficient.

- Pole action is now an integral part of skiing.

METHODOLOGICAL EMPHASIS

- While skiing varieties of terrain and snow, shift focus upon intensity of turning, edging and pressuring of the skis.

- Running slalom and grand slalom courses will greatly improve a skier's overall attitude during this dynamic phase of learning.

- The reason skiers at higher levels oftentimes find "mechanical advice" useful is because of their large inventory of experiences. Even so, past experiences should be directives that are of sensory value: feelings, sounds and images. Intellectual contemplations at this (or any other) level appeal to the analytical left brain, but do not help skiers as much as sensory input does.

- A wholistic approach at these complex mechanical levels is strongly advised. Dynamic entities are difficult to refine by working on them in segments; flow and cohesiveness suffer if a task is undertaken through its parts.

- Theme skiing is a great way to shape certain techniques. Skiing "light" - "heavy" - "up" - "down" - "stiff" - "slinky," etc. are contrasting experiences that loosen a skier up.

- These themes help in linking turns and improving their smoothness. A skier's rhythm and dynamics are enhanced at this stage of development.

- The theme of "tell yourself *what* to do, not *how* to do it" is still alive and well. Avoid movement directives whenever possible; rather, submit yourself to tasks that, by their nature, elicit certain responses.

- Images and analogies are now selected to depict dynamic characteristics — ski like a bull, treat your skis as if they were rubber bands you want to stretch and make bounce. The coach must draw heavily upon personal skills and experiences in the careful selection of imagery. Stereotypes are worthless at this level; images must be culled to suit the skier's need at that time.

- The use of slalom poles was, until now, only suggested; at this time, their employment is indispensable. The clever, premeditated setting of slalom courses can contribute much to the honing of skills and perception.

- Perceptive skills and decision making are high priorities at this time. Skiers learn to choose lines, vary rhythms, select pathways through bumps and changing snow. They deal with slalom courses with path selection a formalized limitation.

- The last series of exercises demonstrates creative use of slalom poles in tasks of shaping value; this type of exercise replaces the manipulative teaching manner which is far more cumbersome.

DEVELOPING REBOUND IN YOUR SKIING:

. . . While skiing easy terrain in an open ski relation, gently lean outside knee to inside calf when turning. Make large, well-rounded turns in that fashion, developing the feeling of the ski turning without much effort being put into it . . .

. . . Repeat the above but shorten the radius a bit . . .

 "CRRRUNCH"

. . . Now make such turns on steeper terrain with emphasis on the "crrrunch" of the edge-bite when you launch into a new turn . . .

. . . Make medium-radius turns. While doing so, feel the pressure on your skis increase throughout the turn. From a series of turns, determine at what point you feel heaviest in the turn . . .

. . . Make "J" type turns, where the end of the turn is a tightening of the radius. Feel pressure increase even more now . . .

. . . Think again of a trampoline jumper. The heaviest pressure is experienced before one bounces back. Transfer this feeling into skiing . . .

. . . As you feel the skis bounce back, compare the intensity of this bounce from turn to turn . . .

. . . Attempt severe bouncing, then smooth the bouncing out . . .

. . . Let the rebound help you to leap into the next turn. That game is called "skiing the leapers" . . .

. . . Now smooth out the rebound to the point of feeling light through the initiation phase of turns, but do not leave the ground. These turns are called the "floaters" . . .

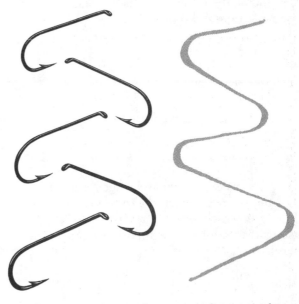

. . . Ski more terrain and snow conditions with "fish hook" turns . . .

. . . Develop the feeling that the finish of one turn helps start the next one. While this initially takes extra effort, eventually greater efficiency is developed . . .

IMPROVE YOUR ABILITY TO EDGE:

. . . Practice a series of stop christies . . .

. . . Skate through turns in shallow terrain . . .

. . . Make wedge turns at fairly high speed, sensitively, yet aggressively pressuring and edging the outside ski to carry you through the turns . . .

. . . Try the wedge wedel; while in a wedge, move from edged ski to edged ski. Allow increasingly less slippage while doing so . . .

. . . Step the outside ski into the turn. Step it far out and gently load it until you feel it carry you through the turn. Repeat again and again . . .

. . . Make a series of short swing turns, developing the feeling that the ski tails dig in to stop one turn and launch the next . . .

. . . Now make medium and longer radius turns; feel the entire ski length help you make the turn. Put your sensors into the ski, as if it is your elongated foot. Feel which portions of it are at work . . .

IMPROVE YOUR UPPER/LOWER BODY FLEXIBILITY:

. . . Ski with a partner. Have him ski straight downhill, while you ski behind attached to each other by your interlocked ski poles. Make turns and slow your partner down. Ski first in shallow terrain, then progress to steeper slopes . . .

. . . Make short swing turns side by side with a partner while you both hold onto a slalom pole as you turn . . .

. . . Make several descents without ski poles, concentrating upon short and medium radius turns . . .

. . . As you are linking turns, feel the twisting of the legs beneath a quiet upper body . . .

. . . Visualize a grandfather clock with a large pendulum. The clock body is your torso; the pendulum, your legs. While skiing, allow your legs to swing from side to side; the shorter the turns, the more severe the pendulum movement . . .

"PUSH . . . PUSH . . . PUSH"

. . . Ski a wedge with alternate lateral thrusts of your skis. Work on making the thrusting come mostly out of the legs. Accompany this action with the words "push," "push" . . .

. . . While making short-radius and medium-radius turns, aim the pole plant towards the center of the upcoming turn. Plant the pole so that your hand is palm (rather than knuckles) up . . .

IMPROVE YOUR ABILITY TO MOVE FROM SKI TO SKI:

. . . Walk through turns—this exercise is also called the "1000-steps" . . .

. . . Skate through your turns . . .

. . . Crab-walk: in shallow terrain, make a wedge walk from ski to ski . . .

. . . Ski a giant slalom course where, because of the offset gates, stepping up is necessary to make each subsequent gate . . .

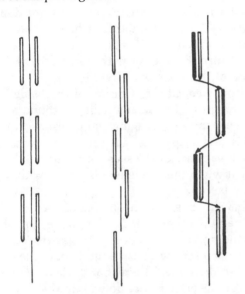

. . . Lay a line of slalom poles in the snow down the fall-line. Stand on one side of them and, as you slide, step to the other side, then back, then back again . . .

. . . Now leap from side to side of the pole string . . .

. . . Now make your steps as smooth as you can . . .

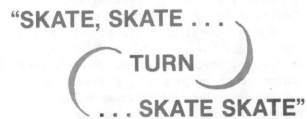

"SKATE, SKATE . . . TURN . . . SKATE SKATE"

. . . On an open slope skate into the hill and start your next turn from that movement. Repeat: skate, skate, turn, skate, skate, turn . . .

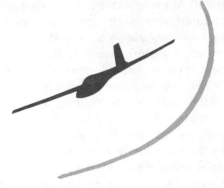

. . . When stepping into turns, explore moving forward with the stepping ski as well as to the side; in this way, develop the sense of "gliding" into the next turn . . .

THE MECHANICS

I find it very fulfilling to assist a beginner to "get his feet under him," I very much enjoy seeing an early intermediate develop mobility and "wings" to travel the mountain, I marvel when witnessing a skier develop the ability to rhythmically sway by linking turns, yet I find my role as a facilitator and teacher to be most critical and challenging during the stage of development we are dealing with in this section. Though it should have already started, this is the time to wean the skier from the input and guidance of the instructor; this is when the teacher should be concerned that the student can and will make sound decisions, that perceptions are clear, that styles does not prohibit further development. In that sense the nature of intervention is critical and is changing.

By now the skier is likely to have experienced all the fundamental mechanisms he will be utilizing while skiing. What now follows are refinement, improving consistency, seeking out the greater challenges and applying one's skills to them. Self image and clarity of perception will determine whether a skier can be brought to the threshold of excellence. At this level it is hard to distinguish beteen so-called Class E and F skiers, the characteristics of performance vacillating between degrees of inconsistency and the elating feeling of being unconquerable.

The conventional skier will expect at this stage to get further help of a mechanical nature (and he usually gets it — because the customer is always right); but while the truly catalytical events do incorporate ski mechanics, they also transcend it. At these stages I can achieve significant performance changes in learners by changing their perspective of what they are doing, by altering energy levels within the skier, by deepening sensory associations with what is going on, NOT by garbling movement flow with intellectualization. Metaphors, images that vividly demonstrate actions and feelings, role playing and games, as well as "super challenges" now become viable methods to rise from obscurity to being the skier others emulate.

I will be dealing with the mechanical aspects of skiing at this level, but I will also heavily interweave what I perceive to be significant perspectives as well. The fact that I will be discussing issues that we already touched upon is not an oversight, but rather a very deliberate action to nurture not only an idealistic picture of a maneuver or movement pattern, but also a feeling for the growth and maturation of skills along the way. With improving (changing) performance, focus will change too, though we essentially may deal with an already-known topic. Here are selected issues in the development phase of Classes E-F:

> Rebound turning
> Speed control
> Linking turns
> Polishing your skiing
> Powder skiing
> Skiing the bumps
> Ski racing
> Freestyle skiing

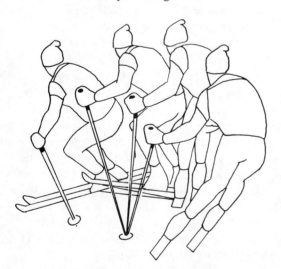

REBOUND TURNING

A rear view of the skier doing a rebound turn will give you a vivid picture of the nature of such turning. A braking turn

uphill puts the skis at an angle to the direction of travel, and the resulting slowdown sets the skier up to be bounded up and around, the intensity of the rebound depending upon the tightness of the braking turn. During the light phase that follows (caused by the rebound) the skier turns the skis. If the brake turn showed distinct displacement of the skis uphill, then the rebound will be easier, based on the principle of action and reaction (the trampoline effect). Once the skier has started the turn, continued steering will control the radius of the rest of the turn.

Introducing the rebound turn may be casual, but the dynamic significance of learning it is great. Overtures to this event already took place when practicing the "downstem," with the down-stemmed ski seeking and establishing an edge base from which the skier pushes off and starts into the turn. Further growth stages for the fruition of this maneuver were in the increasingly edged turn finishes of the "wide-track christies." The skier's ability to round out turns with increased edging and pressuring of the skis, and deepening edge sensiivity practiced through varieties of sideslips contribute to the fact that when this maneuver is played with, it will not be new.

Uphill christies, and the linking of such to one side, then the other, will develop the feeling of "rebounding." Just as dancers emphasize *pliez* (bend) when setting up for a jump, here the skier should so the same. The rebound will be stronger the more the skier settles down into the "brake turn"; the more strongly the skier feathers the skis' edges towards the edge set, the stronger the rebound. With feeble preparatory actions, the rebound will be such that it requires an active extending which is not really characteristic of the "rebound."

Timing and dosing of movement intensity will govern the success of rebound. The inter-dependence of the brake turning and the intensity of edging intensity capable of stopping this action and launching it into the opposite direction is clear. A skier can turn all he wishes, but as long as the stoppage is not there, no rebounding will result. If there is strong edging at the end of the brake turn, but the brake is not strong enough, no "bounding" will result either.

When discussing "interdependence," we also need to mention that the rebound must be directed so that the skis are propelled to the outside of the oncoming turn, while the skier's body is moving toward the new turn center. Developing these flow patterns will take time and practice. Reviewing the past two paragraphs, I shudder with the complexity of rebound turning, and I am convinced that anyone having to worry about such elements as a string of isolated mechanisms and concerns would never learn to do it. I am saying this not to devalue mechanical analysis, but to put it where it belongs: into the analytical corner frequented by coaches and teachers for the sake of having a clear understanding of what is going on. The learner should NOT be bothered with it!

Learners should rather work with mind pictures and feelings of trampoline jumping, doing fishhook-shaped turns, "ker boing" turns, kangaroo turns, and the many more exercises I recommend in the exercise section for learners.

The progressive track patterns supportive of developing rebound turning are like this.

This suggestion should be disgarded any time it is seen as a hindrance to someone learning rebounding. Yet in my experience, the majority of skiers at first do better doing medium-radius turns near the fall-line (generally skiing downhill). Such turns show a lot of skidding, the rebound benefitting from the fact that the brake turning and the subsequent turning are dramatic and fairly violent in nature, allowing the skier to experience rebound immediately.

From then on the general pattern of the skied track may be more carved in nature, increasing forward momentum, and the brake turn commensurately becoming less pronounced (speed makes up for the lesser tightness). The evolving track pattern looks increasingly like the shape of a fishhook.

Once the skier can consistently produce rebound in his turning, the rebound can be de-emphasized and become smoother. Initially the rebound was more "up and around" oriented, but it now is increasingly directed "out and forward." The resulting flowing fosters the general "punch" of such turning, turn beginnings increasingly being the product of sensitively finished turn endings. Once the above is

experienced by a skier, rebound will become the "oyster" of skiing, an experience that is revisited whenever possible, broadening in application and versatility.

This skier's movement trajectory is more vertically oriented, turning being very pronounced, the track being broad.

Here the skier's up-down movements flatten out, are more forward oriented, the direction change still a product of rebound to some extent, but gaining much from the carving deflection; carving reducing the need for massive "bounding."

I will be dealing with these elements in the sections on "speed control" and "linking turns" once more, but from a different viewpoint.

SPEED CONTROL

Speed is a relative quantity, yet every skier is concerned with speed control. To some skiers, control means being able to stop at any given point of the descent, while for others control is calculated planning to make acceleration and braking an issue that covers time and space.

I remember the time when I was skiing in Aspen, Colorado, on one of my rare days off, enjoying my runs, cruising at what I perceived to be moderate speeds, feeling good about myself and what I was doing. Suddenly the authoritative figure of a ski patrolman pulled up alongside me and motioned me over to the side of the trail. "You are a reckless skier, you are going way too fast; if I see you ski this way one more time, I'll pull your ticket." With that he was off, his bright parka and prominent white cross on his back driving home the message. What had I done wrong? I had not skied near another person, choosing my track carefully to avoid bumps and ruts. Why was I considered "reckless?" My trained eyes had for years been conditioned to pick out terrain, to judge people's movements, their direction and speed; I could accurately judge where people would move next, recognizing patterns that are characteristic of all skiers. What had I done wrong?

This little story is to illustrate how speed and control are issues of perception. While I was not angry at the white-crossed figure, his restraining me surely spoiled my day. I like to ski "fast," or as fast as the circumstances, the terrain, and the snow conditions will allow. To me such skiing epitomizes the harmony with conditions that good skiers need to develop, or should I say, that help skiers become good. Obviously I was not born with the ability to "fly," as a matter of fact, the stories about my childhood skiing rather tell a different story. I learned to go fast by knowing "where the brakes" were and developing the skills to use those brakes. Let's look at this issue a bit more closely.

Pointing the skis straight downhill will make us go the fastest; putting the skis at an angle to the fall-line will result in braking. Skiers have many mechanisms available to vary the braking while skiing downhill.

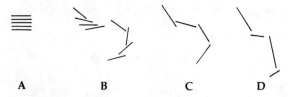

A   B   C   D

It is self apparent that the track on the left is the one offering most speed control. As you move right, characteristic tracks seek and offer less braking. Several successful world-class racers have broken the mold of making round turns (C), but are making harsher-looking, more strenuous, but faster turns that look somewhat like (D). A fairly straight approach line toward the next gate allows them to accumulate speed; the short and energetic "punching" of the edges elicits a rapid and violent reorientation.

While the majority of skiers will never start in an amateur or professional race, they will still benefit from the actions above, though their priority will mostly be one of going slow rather than at neck-breaking speeds. The actively turning skier will maintain a high level of control; the passively "floating" skier will not. The advanced skier will seek control by progressively decelerating, adding through successive turn finishes to braking rather than attempting to do it all in one turn. Looking ahead, planning the line with all its characteristic challenges and offerings become an important aspect of skiing at this time.

The better skier will use the terrain forms, the lay of the land, to help design the line of descent. Fluffy uphill sides of bumps become easy places to set edges and slow down, counterhills will do the same, sidehills become a good place to let the momentum evaporate on.

LINKING TERMS

This is not the first time we are emphasizing linking turns; I personally like to push the linking of turns from as early on as possible. I do so because I feel that a sense of skiing is not real until a flowing connectedness between turns is developed. Motions are immediately developed to cater to the dynamic relation of turns, rather than viewing one turn as an isolated maneuver. The "puppet on a string" appearance gives way to a smooth, gliding, snaking flow.

Some pages ago we spoke about rebound and the dynamic dimension this characteristic maneuver brings to skiing. The "bounding" can either be resisted, so it lifts the skier through a light phase, or it can be partially or totally absorbed, thus damping the recoil effects, giving the skier a chance to effectively reorient the rebound in a forward manner.

Smooth turn linkages are those where the finishing phase is not overpowering the edge hold, but rather "jets" the feet and skis smoothly forward just as the pressure phase of the last turn is felt. Yielding to those pressures is done in the legs, which are allowed to fold, thus giving the skis and feet the forward thrust that Georges Joubert coined "jetting."

A mechanical objective to improve turn linkages should be to ski medium- to medium-short radius turns, developing smoothness through early weight transfers. As the skier moves through the latter phase of a turn, the dominant ski is gradually abandoned, shifting pressure progressively toward what is still the inside ski of the turn. This will "procrastinate" any premature pivoting of the skis, therefore obliging the skier to ride a smooth turn connection. The weight transfer will also cause the skier to begin tipping toward the new turn center, a feature we already discussed.

Connecting turns takes spontaneity, much like dancing. Connecting turns takes a degree of abandonment, like running in the rain and not caring any more — running is easier and smoother. The entire flow of motion now becomes a coherent entity. Pole-planting movements melt into the angular movements of the body, while the vertical movements augment turning. Our bodies' exquisite sense of timing, when left alone, orchestrates skiing into a wonderful symphony.

PLAYING ENERGY GAMES

Often times I have heard from skiers that they are desperate about their inconsistency. One day or one run they do just fine, the next they feel lousy. I usually get to be with such people just at their low point, which is augmented by the fact that they have not admitted to having something wrong with themselves and are taking a lesson. I have found such students wanting less to be pulled out of their misery, as much as to be heard, pitied. So I let them go their course, shedding all their frustrating thoughts, taking some abuse in the course, and I look at them and their skiing. Generally advanced skiers suffering from a case of the "blahhhs" show a lack of motion, missing the punch they know so well because they have traded off doing with thinking and chastising. Coordination is lacking because our intellect is not capable of creating coordination, only our spontaneous self can. Further tell-tale indications of their state is that they sit back, are unable to keep up with their skis, miss turn finishes, then hack and fish themselves through the rest of the turn. The facial expression is usually hard, frowning, their eyes fixed in front of them.

Depending upon the severity of their feeling, I may choose to become the red cloth to a mad bull by getting them angry. Anger is an emotion I have seen people do far better with than frowning self pity. So I tell them to select a symbol of hatred, to think of someone they intensely dislike, and I tell

them that this person is right on their tail.

Generally they will start skiing faster, and, when I impersonate their target of hatred and ski right behind them, I pick out any shortcomings and tell them teasingly: "Why don't you ski a bit stiff-legged," "Why don't you ski like a tin soldier," etc. This comedy can be pursued as long or as short as it takes to get them out of their original mood. Once I have a student either panting from a teasing, non-stop run, or smiling in the realization of how self-defeating self-chastising is, then I can shift gears.

Other times I play a different energy game: I ask them to follow me, asking them to grunt with every turn finish as they hear me doing. I generally start with medium-radius turns (on a trail with little or no traffic), then gradually "hitting" the fall-line more and more, letting the grunts become more frequent as the turns do. The sound tends to tell me about a student's commitment level; if I do not hear much I will shout: "I can't hear you," or "can you shout this out more." While bystanders may consider such practice funny (not fun) because skiers generally are supposed to be suave, calm, tough, and composed, the transformation of mechanical nature I see in my students is tremendous. With sound comes motion, with motion we gain better balance, with better balance we feel better about ourselves, with that our turns become more positive, the turn finishes crisp up, the pole movements become more deliberate and timely. Had I chosen to discuss the technical elements of "what's wrong" with this customer type, I would have buried him in further frustration.

Energy-level increases are not always what you want. If a skier shows distinct signs of "muscling" his turns, it may be beneficial to mellow the technique a bit. Oftentimes I will ask such skiers to sound out the phases of greatest effort while skiing; in other words I ask them to produce a breathing tempo that equals that of their bodily tension while turning. The huffing and puffing will soon create a need to relax, a process I often encourage by TELLING the student to try to EXHALE after each turn is started and to find a turning rhythm that allows them to breathe easily and in a cadence that feels uncontrolled. This is an example where "Z" turns will smooth out to "S" turns, when sequencing one turn after another will soon slink them together.

POWDER SKIING

"Nothing can cure the soul but the senses, just as nothing can cure the senses but the soul."

Oscar Wilde

A non-skier considering powder skiing may well be impressed by the contradiction of skiers enjoying themselves in the cold, windy, precipitous environment, while armed only with two sharp poles, balanced on two thin laths, hurtling themselves down the mountainside. To make things worse, these wildmen are lifted uphill on little chairs high in the sky, bringing them back to what they seem to have barely survived just moments before. What the non-skier still might not know is that powder skiers often travel thousands of miles, spending hundreds of dollars on equipment, transportation and sustenance to return home broke rather than foregoing their powder experience.

What could possibly be so irresistible for these normal humans to behave so illogically? But then, how could a skier even come close to explaining the intoxicating qualities of packed-slope skiing to a non-skier, let alone convey the deep satisfaction and excitement of swooping down a powder slope, snow cascading over the head, wind in the face? How could we even attempt to transmit the euphoria that is complete and total therapy to those participating in this form of snow play? I consider it one of the healthiest addictions I can think of! On a sunny day watching skiers descend through untouched powder snow may well be an eloquent enough image to foster understanding! The mystique of grooving Rocky Mountain powder can be sensed, while admiring skiers swooshing through hip or chest-deep powder, rooster-tails of sparkling snow crystals marking their paths of descent. The skier's expression at such moments will be ample proof of the value such an experience has for him. Yet, as a person who has not loved always has difficulty understanding *that* particular state of mind; so the non-skier is unable to comprehend the ecstasy of powder.

You are invited to either learn to ski powder snow or to become more proficient at it. You can become a member of the wild-eyed, seemingly crazed crowd with the stake claimed on the back bowls of Vail Mountain (or wherever they have that same quality of snow). Yes, come and join us!

POWDER TECHNIQUE

Watching those first-to-take-off skiers float through untouched powder with ease and enthusiasm is somewhat deceptive, though deep snow skiing *can* be enjoyed at many levels of competence. What makes skiing the "deep" unique is not just the aesthetic beauty of it, but also the absence of "feelable," solid ground to use as a reference for one's movements and balancing efforts. Bottomless snow demands a *new* set of guidelines, a commitment to immersing oneself in a pliable, soft environment that requires considerably more refined sensitivity than hard-packed slopes do.

A typical modern-day deep powder turn may look something like this:

1. Through retraction, the skier brings the skis towards the surface.

2. In a pronounced articulated leg position, turning the skis is easy.

3. The skier turns the skis while retracting and now continues doing so while extending.

4. During the extension, the skier "submerges," building a platform as well as slowing the skis down.

For an intermediate (or better) skier, mastering deep snow is a matter of risking humiliation and falls, while honing inherent skills. Initially efforts will be somewhat mechanical and self-conscious but ultimately "skiing the deep" turns out to be a matter of letting go—the hilarious condition where it seems that nothing can go wrong and you feel like screaming and shouting! Even on the lift between runs, your legs twitch in anticipation of what is to come! However, before you can enjoy deep snow with graceful abandon, it's necessary to invest some effort and time toward developing certain physical skills and, of equal importance, a sensory association with the deep snow.

When comparing the sensory reference system developed on hard-packed slopes to the same in bottomless powder, an analogy may be helpful. When bouncing on solid ground, as soon as the feet touch, positive reference is established and the resistance and rebound are established right then and there. On the other hand, if you bounce on a trampoline, the feet hitting the canvas merely signals a stretching of the platform. The supporting surface is yielding! Gradually, pressure builds up underfoot and culminates in rebounding you upward again. The timing and nature of movements with either kind of base of support are distinctly different.

One of the first noticeable differences in powder is that all movements slow down and vertical action is an accordion-like compression of the legs, retracting and extending in smooth succession with the rhythmic cadence of linked turns. Harmonizing your interaction with the snow happens only by repeated exposure to powder conditions. Start off skiing a straight track, either down or across the hill (choose the track so you won't gain too much speed) merely bouncing up and down. Develop a feeling for the rhythm the snow encourages and the resistance it offers. The more sensitive a skier is to how he and the snow interact, the quicker his improvement will be! Gradually, use alternate pole touches as the baton for your rhythmic movements, integrating the body into one, lithe sequence. As vertical bouncing becomes second nature and pole planting is in sync, you will almost inevitably experience small directional changes with your skis. Take note of what causes them and amplify such movements, while maintaining rhythm in what you do.

In order to build up the necessary sensory inventory, start your powder work on shallower terrain; gradually choose steeper slopes as you see fit. If shallow terrain is not available, proceed in traverses, making little "half turns" more and more frequently across the fall-line; then link these turns together straight downhill. Initially, you should exaggerate whatever it is you feel is turning the skis in this kind of snow. Continue to overact it until you gain certainty that your turns are actually coming about. Amplify your vertical movement to start with, as well as putting much more steam behind turning your legs and feet from side to side. Gradually tone it down to what is actually needed to do the job! Think and ski in *series* of rhythmic turns and pick your descent line so your rhythm is not disrupted. Later, when skiing the deep is more comfortable, practice single, non-linked turns. Allow yourself the privilege of falling and don't trap yourself by equating your self-worth with how many times you fall. If that becomes the case, frustration and its resulting disruption of your concentration will interfere with your progress!

To sum up, select the difficulty of the slope and snow condition carefully at first. Sample short sections of this new snowy environment that allow you to "escape," to recuperate and review your experience; don't get stymied or fatigued in your first attempts. Stay clear of well-meaning, but perhaps unknowing, friends who invite you to ski over your head. Once you know how, you will enjoy their company, finding it most invigorating and complimentary.

It may help to hire a ski pro to ease you into this new challenge. Benefit from his shared experiences and guidance (and enjoy his helping hand when you fall in powder that often acts like quicksand). More likely than not such a teacher will lead you through some of the suggestions above, though there are many ways to learn to ski powder. An experienced ski teacher can prepare you for powder by beginning with some runs on hard-packed slopes, focusing you on the particular mechanical and mental issues you will be confronting before realistically testing them in the novel milieu. Then you'll be asked to deal with the increased resistance of turning in powder by amplifying everything in order to turn your skis. Directives to "turn the feet together" or to "settle your pelvis a bit further down to increase the bend in all joints and consequently, add power and stability to your system" may usher you into your first deep snow run. A conscientious teacher will introduce you to powder in a progressive way. Ankle-deep snow

gives way to knee-deep stuff. Hip-deep powder is the ultimate bottomless white environment; challenging it is much like kayaking through the Grand Canyon during the spring runoff, but at a fraction of the risk.

TYPICAL PROBLEMS WHILE SKIING DEEP POWDER

Fear, apprehension and lack of commitment are the most debilitating conditions a skier may suffer. They are the most frequent reasons a skier does not perform to his potential. Such mental blocks are not easy to eliminate, but here are some thoughts that may help.

Firstly, consider again some previous recommendations: build up your skills at an appropriate pace and with the support of a non-threatening environment (slope, snow, company . . .). Allow your confidence to mature as you experience success. Sudden appearances of self-doubt, fear or hesitation may have very real, worthy causes. If that's the case, you exercise good judgement by choosing less taxing conditions. If a block occurs in circumstances you know deep down that you are able to deal with (but there is this choking hesitation anyway) try one or more of the following tactics.

Reason with yourself; remember that the source of your fear is about as substantial as a ghost. We tend to fear most "what is not," rather than "what is." Consequently, you need a tool to bridge this reality gap.

Shouting out the word "turn" whenever you initiate a turn can be a most successful method of overcoming your fear of ski slope "ghosts." Let the rhythmic shouting fall into the cadence of your linked turns. The intensity of the shout can indicate your level of commitment to what you are doing. A hesitant, barely audible "turn" won't be enough to get one started—the turn stalls and you sit back and fall! On the other hand, a shout that comes from your gut, expressive of all your power, spirit and skill, will bring astonishing results! The expulsion of air has realistic physical/mental value. (Think of it—sound is an age-old method used by karate experts, fencers and weightlifters to increase their formidability.) The almost self-hypnotic effects of shouting must be experienced to be believed!

Another way of building up confidence and commitment is to begin thinking in terms of a series, rather than one turn at a time. Start by surveying the upcoming terrain; decide how many turns you need to link together, then ski down making them! Over time you will increase the number of turns in a series up to the point that numerical commitment is no longer needed. At that point you will be skiing endless, enjoyable snaking turns, with no underlying apprehension at all.

Mental rehearsal has been successful for some people in alleviating fear. With eyes closed (this way the imaging will probably be more intense) picture yourself skiing the slope. A tremendous advantage of imaging is that you can rehearse *perfect* runs, actively preparing yourself to ski that flawlessly. As usual, the intensity of the image will determine the benefits you derive. Allow yourself to feel the wind, the movement, the snow, while pre-visualizing your descent and make the image so real that you move your body in rhythm and sync with the movie you run in your mind. The benefits of this practice should be well known by now. Try it!

SITTING BACK

Many skiers refer to sitting back as a necessary ingredient for success in deep powder. Those of you who have attempted sitting back may remember the burning fatigue that quickly creeps into your thighs, debilitating you in more ways than one. The impression of sitting back as *the* powder technique stems from how we see a skier's silhouette in relation to the surface of the snow.

Because the binding is placed behind the middle of the ski, more weight is cast toward the tail section. The wider construction of the toe shovel further amplifies the pitched floating of the ski in the snow. These circumstances add up to the skis planing—much like waterskis—tips high, tails low. Balancing on skis oriented in this relation to the surface of the snow makes it seem the skier is leaning back or even sitting. While shifting pressure aft just a touch is, at times, beneficial, the pros in "deep" environment continue to suggest standing right over the skis. Will myth or reason prevail for you next time you ski powder?

If the reason you sit back is because you believe it is right to do it that way, merely try a few runs standing more directly over the center of the skis. Give the experiment enough time to become comfortable before dismissing it as a viable alternative. Habits are not changed very quickly!

If you have already incorporated the sit-back "armchair technique," it may take more time and effort to effect changes. Try a few of the following ideas.

Ski on easy terrain with your ski boots buckled loosely. This will rob you of the firm support of a tightly buckled boot, forcing you into a more centered stance. You may even wish to experiment on nordic equipment for a time; the relatively flexible running shoes and the non-fixed binding obligate you to be in a balanced position at all times.

A less dramatic way to evoke a balanced stance is to ski with a lot of vertical movement. Skiers "freeze" when out of balance, but mobility itself forces balance. Balance is inherent in movement! Movement is inherent in balance!

CROSSING SKIS

One of the most punishing kinds of mishaps is caused by crossing the skis and being catapulted face-first into deep snow. The suddenness of such a fall, along with the helplessness of being marooned upside down in soft snow makes it easily the most dreaded "error" of powder skiing. Crossing of skis can be caused by turning them with unequal intensity, pedaling them while turning in different snow depths/densities, hitting an object under the snow or articulating the legs (and, thus, the ski surfaces) unevenly.

To combat these problems, ski with your feet together, honing a solid, un-ski feeling. Though there are powder skiers who "dipsy doodle" (quasi-walking from turn to turn, shifting weight from outside ski to outside ski) in bottomless powder, it is safer to ski with your feet together. This in turn will also alleviate having to deal with the two skis in confronting different snow densities and, if an under-snow obstacle is hit, there is a better chance of pushing through it with both legs.

Be prepared to accept problems; ups and downs are a part of your evolution as a powder skier. Slowly you will automate the skills necessary for the condition and you will evolve the mental framework necessary to improve. Initial stiffness will yield to flexibility and large, excessive movement will give way to subtle motion. Your legs will take on more and

more of the responsibility, acting like a bellows that extends into the belly of the turn and retracts through the transition from one turn to the next. Initially the torso will be active (to begin with that's OK) but eventually this movement will quiet down. The floating sensation of powder skiing and a growing sense of security and confidence will be your portal to the euphoric experiences that await you in the "deep." The muffled sounds, the rhythm of movement, the gushing of the snow as you plunge from turn to turn will be yours to revel in. The total immersion in the snowy environment fosters feelings of intimacy, warmth and comfort unique to powder skiing. A perfect run, snow glistening, water melting on your face and a deep sense of accomplishment, makes powder skiing a metaphysical experience, a natural high! Come ski with us!

SKIING THE BUMPS

"You must never lose the excitement of life."

Jack Benny

Whether you like them or not, bumps are here to stay. They are inseparable from modern skiing. The softer the snow and the steeper the hill, the sharper and more densely arranged the bumps will be.

While some people disagree, it seems the difficulty of bump skiing is in the necessity to make rapid adjustments. You are required to "flow" with the terrain, rather than fighting it. The skills to ski moguls cannot be developed on the mogul slopes. These skills will have to be nurtured by skiing progressively more difficult bump slopes, realizing that it will take time to become fluid and confident on them. Wise skiers also realize that, while any bump can be skied, some of them may not be worth it!

In shallow terrain, bumps will be rounded and well-spaced. The room between them gives a skier the liberty to turn anywhere on top or between the moguls. Steeper terrain obligates a skier to make sharper turns, therefore creating sharper moguls that are more densely packed together. With less room between the bumps (that space may even become a single trough) the skier needs to accept the rhythm of the bumps totally, even conforming to the direction of the deep troughs.

Bump slopes with fresh snow evenly coating their corrugated surfaces are a delight to ski. The softness of riding the bumps cushioned by snow, coupled with the slowing effect that deeper snow has on your speed, demands less turning yet affords good control. However, fresh snow seldom comes without wind. Wind smooths over what is underneath the new snow, making for treacherous skiing. Not being able to see the ups and downs of the slope, having to guess where your skis will rise or fall, makes skiing snow-covered bumps very challenging. Such conditions should be left to people who are willing to accept the inherent risks.

MOGUL TECHNIQUES AND TACTICS

In order to become comfortable skiing bumps, allow yourself the confidence to become supple and flexible. Without this adaptation, you are forced to move the upper body downhill while manipulating the lower body and skis through ever-changing pitches; it is difficult to maintain your pace. To gain confidence, it is imperative that skills and slope challenges be carefully matched. "Surviving" a run on one's chest or derriere is not a constructive experience.

The typical mogul skier, while heading in a general direction (usually downhill) orients his upper body in that direction; the lower body will be pumping to turn and absorb the impact of the bumps.

A less experienced skier will not yet have developed the ability to separate upper and lower body in this functional way. Absorption skills may also be rudimentary. That skier gives the impression of rising and falling along with the shape of the bump slope. Each turn will, in essence, be skied as a single one; they won't be fluidly linked together. Skiers must allow themselves to feel a bit clumsy and stiff when starting to learn to ski moguls. With time, suppleness and flexibility become part of the repertoire.

When moguls are dense and choppy, aggressive, muscular skiers will choose to "stairstep" their descent, bouncing from one flat part of a mogul to the flat part of the next one in a manner reminiscent of descending a flight of stairs. The successive hard, short impacts make it necessary to have a finely-tuned sense of the center of the skis. Any lack of balance at "impact time" will cause a jackknifing or banana-peel effect on the body. Because turns in bumps are generally of shorter radius, a fairly upright upper body with arms held closer to the sides will be useful.

RHYTHM AND LINE

The following illustrations give examples of different ways bumps can be skied:

1. This illustrates another easy way of skiing a bump slope. Most bumps have developed in a patterned way; a continuous rhythm of linking turns created them to begin with and this same turning pattern can be maintained while you are skiing. For the most part, ski displacement makes the skier feel that he is confronting somewhat consistent terrain. 2. An optional pattern for the beginning bump skier who does not yet have the confidence to ski straight downhill is to link turns across the slope; this approach allows the skier to enjoy an environment he otherwise may not yet have seemed ready for. 3. Another way of skiing bumps is to "stairstep" the slope. The flat, uphill-facing parts of moguls become launching pads for the turns. Keen judgement and strength are necessary in this technique. 4. Skiing long-radius turns on bumps is a technique available to either the fool or the expert. Excellent judgement and ski handling ability are essential to this style. Advance planning and split-second decisions make this approach rather unusual. The challenge of this technique will only become apparent when turns are rounded (not zig-zagged) linking direction changes with traverses.

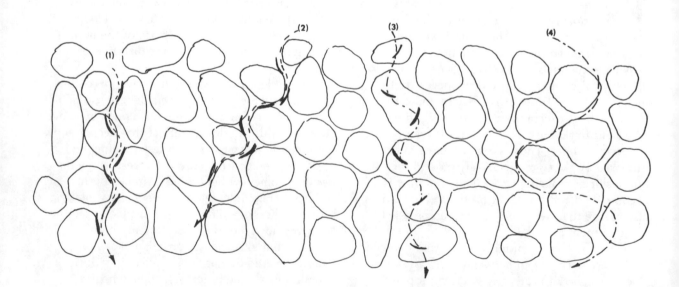

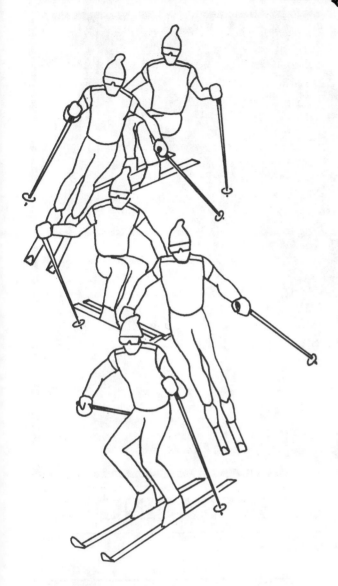

- When watching skiers (in your mind or in reality), glean general impressions, i.e.: flexibility, fluidity and harmony with the bumps. Forego specifics.

- If you are concerned with technical detail you are trying to ski bumps prematurely. Let yourself simply respond to the circumstances rather than tackling the slope in a calculated manner.

- Realizing that bump skiing is largely a matter of "commitment," develop a tactical plan whereby you select to ski a series of turns rather than a bunch of single ones. Look at the terrain and then decide to ski a "3'er," "4'er" (or however many turns you choose to). Ski whatever you have committed to, gradually increasing the number of turns in a series. Ultimately the diminishing strength in your legs (not lack of commitment) will be the determining factor of how long you persist before stopping.

- Another very helpful piece of advice for apprehensive bump skiers is to shout the word "turn" or "now" in rhythm with the turning. The more aggressively you shout the word, the more committed your turns will be. (Shyly whispered words will result in shyly executed turns.)

- Eventually come to the realization that there is nothing evil or dangerous in the bumps. What makes them seem that way is how they appear to you. If you see them as foes, they will probably trip you. If you view them as more or less rounded terrain shapes, you can develop a way to deal with them.

HINTS FOR THE ASPIRING BUMP SKIER

- Choose to develop control skills before indulging in bumps of any size.

- Graduate yourself to bumps that you know you can handle (regardless of where friends want to take you).

- Learn to be comfortable on one type of slope; foster an aggressive attitude towards its bumps before moving on to more challenging mogul runs.

- Since bump skiing requires a high degree of perceptual skills, practice bump skiing with your eyes (imagine yourself skiing a hill section) as you survey the terrain.

- Also use imaging to rehearse the motions of a good bump skier.

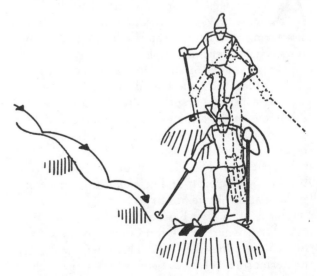

FUNDAMENTALS OF SKI RACING

"Racing and hunting excite man's heart to madness."

Lao Tse

As skiers improve, they search for new challenges. Competing with difficult snow, navigating through tough terrain or weaving through the bamboo jungle of a race course become enticing goals.

Skiers that have matured to the level of racing discover that there is less need to practice new physical skills; adapting their already acquired techniques to the demands of race courses will be more expedient. Running gates causes the skier to polish perceptual skills, to plan ahead and make split-second decisions about line and tactics. Another little-spoken-of, but important, aspect of learning at this stage has to do with commitment. A skier has no longer the option to make turns wherever he cares to turn—the course determines the turns. This skier, furthermore, is forced to turn as little as possible; speed is essential when skiing slalom courses.

Part of the addiction to racing gates is the vicarious feedback that is provided instantly and continuously. There is no need for a coach or teacher to comment about "how one did." The fact that a skier finishes a course and the speed in which he completes that task will provide him with an intoxicatingly clear picture of his performance and progress. Most successful coaches train equally successful athletes by setting courses that shape the athlete's talents. Physical challenges replace mechanical directives; suggested moods like "ski the course angry," "light & smooth," "float it" and "punch it," replace technical advice which, due to the skier's speed, cannot possibly be followed. Tactical advice ("cut the gates close and jam your turns" or "ski the course wide and round") is as much detail as can be usefully incorporated in training for gates.

HOW TO START

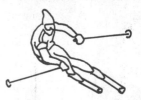

Races are won by fractions of seconds. Starting plays an important role in getting speed up as quickly as possible.

The majority of recreational racers start from a stand or a teeter-totter movement back and forth, in rhythm with the countdown. With ski poles anchored beyond the wand, the extended arms will be able to provide a strong acceleration when leaving the gate. Opening the wand slightly out of sync with the countdown will not disqualify you.

The jump starts of experienced racers require strength and training and are, for this reason, somewhat exclusive to seasoned racers. Although many racers mimick this movement, it, more often than not, is inefficient and causes the person to lose, rather than gain, time. Even a well-executed jump start saves only a small margin of time.

RACING TURNS

In short-radius turns, mechanics demonstrate the separation of upper and lower body. While the upper body takes the shortcut towards the next turn, legs and skis pivot beneath and brace against centrifugal force. The "hyperactivity" of the lower body allows the upper body to remain relatively quiet. Turns are mostly the result of leg action.

In long-radius turns, skis and skier follow a more unified path of descent; upper and lower body separations are subtle. In the longer control phases, the body inclines towards the inside of the turn without the characteristic break visible between short turns. Such turns are started with subtle upper body movement.

Medium-radius turns are skied mainly with a combination of the mechanisms described in both long and short turns. When linking medium-radius turns performed at high speeds, the nature of their mechanics is closer to that of shorter-radius turns; when not linking turns or when skiing turns beyond their "heavy" point, longer-radius techniques predominate.

Stepping elements in turn initiations are evident in short, medium and long-radius turns. Stepping serves the purpose of changing edges, of gaining laterally while lining up for a gate and, finally, of maintaining balance by relocating the base of support. In a dynamic sense, all of these functions melt into each other; the size and direction of the step express the motivation for the movement.

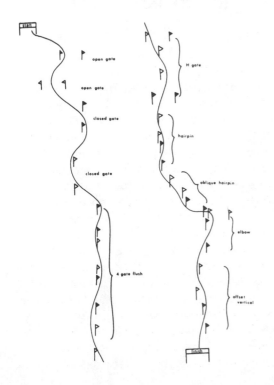

open gate

open gate

closed gate

closed gate

4 gate flush

H gate

hairpin

oblique hairpin

elbow

offset vertical

RUTS?!

Bumps on slopes are equivalent to ruts in race courses. After a few racers have participated, banana-shaped troughs will develop and become deeper as each subsequent skier makes his run. Bumps and ruts are caused by erosion. When skiing a rutted course, strive to enter the turn where the rut starts. Position yourself in a compact, but flexible, crouch and allow your skis to run right through the length of the rut. Your outside hand should aim toward the next pole plant. A lateral step may be helpful if the ruts run low toward the next gate. If the rut is deep with a kick finish, absorb this effect in the way you deal with moguls. Unless you have a specific reason for doing otherwise, avoid trying to squeeze between the rut and the pole. More often than not, you will slip off the narrow shoulder because you cannot edge through; the closeness of the gate prevents you from inclining. Once you slip, the skis will "catch" the rut, suddenly accelerate and leave you sitting back— you experience the "banana peel effect," a frequent bane to inexperienced rut racers! In preparation for this rather unforgiving course condition, you can rehearse by skiing bumps and aggressive "J" type turns; their challenges are similar to those of the ruts.

HOW TO FINISH A RACE

Finishing techniques, like starting techniques, have changed over the years with the advent of electronic timing devices. The most common finishing technique is to thrust the skis forward just as you approach the finish line. While the forward thrusting of the feet will reduce the total running time by a small margin, it also poses a hazard to tired racers trying to maintain balance. Upon leaving the last gate of the course, some racers will tuck into an aerodynamic position; others prefer to skate through the finish. What the skier does is ultimately determined by the nature of the terrain of the finish. If it is steep, stepping out of the last gate and tucking will be very effective. If the slope is flat, skating may be called for, provided that the racer has the stamina to do so actively, rather than being so spent that the skating action causes him to wipe out.

FREESTYLE SKIING

"Everything is sweetened by risk."

Alexander Smith

Largely a product of the independent sixties, freestyle skiing escapes the stylization associated with traditional Alpine events. It incorporates movements borrowed from such sports as figure-skating, gymnastics, ballet, skateboarding and high-diving. The three disciplines (ballet, aerial and mogul skiing) are constantly evolving as individual participants devise more complex and exciting tricks.

Stunt skiing began in America in the early twentieth century. In 1929, Dr. Fritz Reuel simultaneously authored *New Possibilities In Skiing*, a book recognizing the applicability of figure-skating to free-form skiing, and the famous Reuel (now bastardized to Royal) Christie which is a popular ballet skiing movement even today. In the fifties came the flashy somersaults of Stein Erikson; in the sixties Hermann Goeliner added a twist to come up with the Moebius Flip. The first organized freestyle competition was held in 1971 in Waterville Valley, Vermont, but it wasn't until 1973, after some terrible accidents suffered in the sport, that the International Freestyle Skiers Association was formed. The I.F.S.A. established rules of competition and determined more effective safety controls for the sport. However, due to the sheer dare-devilry of some competitors, insurance rates have today made authorized freestyle competitions unfeasible. No longer are mogul slopes and jumps conscientiously cultivated; many freestyle clinics may suffer a decline—but a creative skier will always have his own "free-style!"

BALLET

Each of the classic types of freestyle is characterized by its own tones. Individually selected music and fluidic movement performed on short, flexible skis over a smooth and gentle terrain comprise ballet skiing. Think

of Suzi Chaffee—a dancer on snow. In ballet, the value is placed on skill, innovation and a flawless performance. Any skier with a good sense of balance and an artistic spirit can perform ballet on skis.

AERIALS

Aerial skiing is basically freestyle jumping. This is the discipline that develops its moves from high-diving; in fact, many aerial competitors practice their latest tricks off the end of a diving board—water is a bit softer when a trick doesn't "happen." Upright jumps like spread eagles and double daffies, the twist of helicopters, and inverted flips demand "air sense" which in turn creates the thrilling aerial style.

MOGULS

The ultimate in kamikaze skiing is mogul freestyle—"skiing the bumps!" In this competition, the skier utilizes music to ski by in much the same way as the ballet freestylist does, to enhance and "choreograph" the performance. Of course, to ski the moguls, you don't listen to *Swan Lake*! The competitor takes as many turns and jumps as he can; the aim is to ski the bumps as fast, as flamboyant and as flashy as possible, while maintaining complete control at all times. A good motorcross rider may come the closest to experiencing this incredible sensation.

The acme of aesthetic beauty and physical limits of skiing is captured by the three disciplines of freestyle. Hot-doggers "catch a wave and they're sittin' on top of the world!"

STAR TEST

GO FOR THE GOLD

"The length of things is vanity, only their height is joy."

George Santayana

How do you rate yourself as a skier? Novice? Intermediate? Advanced intermediate? Expert? Better-than-average-but-not-that-great? When you are sitting around the fire in the lodge and someone asks you if you are a good skier, does your reply resemble one of the following:

Evasive: "Oh, I make it down the mountain in one piece most of the time."

Humble: "I'm just learning." (Aren't we all.)

Totally honest and out front: "I can make wide-track parallel turns but only to the left and not in powder or later than three o'clock in the afternoon. My right-hand turns are a kind of modified stem turn with a lot of up-unweighting and blah blah blah . . ."

Inverted modest: "You're asking me? I'm really a complete klutz on skis. You should have seen me etc., etc., etc. . . . ."

Brazen: "Well I wouldn't say I'm great, but just this afternoon up on Prima, I was . . ."

Pedantic: "Am I a good skier? That's an interesting question. But before we begin, how do you define 'good skier'?"

Actually, the pedant is probably giving the best answer. How *do* you define what makes a good skier? By the level of ski school classes achieved? By the number of "Most Difficult" slopes skied in a single day? By the length of skis used?

The Professional Ski Instructors of America (PSIA) has the answer to this question in its STAR Test International. Patterned after a similar testing system (called Test International) that has been in use in Europe for some time, and more recently in Japan and Canada, the STAR (for "Standard Rating") Test is designed to tell you exactly where you stand in terms of skiing proficiency.

The system works like this: You decide which of three tests you'd like to take, either novice (bronze), intermediate (silver), or advanced/expert (gold); pay a fee; and go with a specifically trained instructor/tester to a particular trail that has been designated the official STAR Test trail for that level. Once there, the instructor has you perform five basic maneuvers.

In the novice test, for example, the maneuvers include a diagonal run brought to a stop by angled stepping, traversing with minimum slippage, and five linked, skidded turns. In the intermediate test, the skier is required, among other things, to skate on the flat without poles, traverse over gentle bumps, and link long-radius turns on a smooth slope. Those going for the gold will be required, among other things, to link medium-radius turns in varying snow conditions, link a series of medium-radius turns through a mogul field, and perform linked "One-thousand Steps turns" on a smooth slope—a very difficult maneuver. The tester will rate each maneuver from 1 to 5. For the gold, a passing score is 15 points or better.

If you receive a passing score in four out of five maneuvers, you receive a pin in the appropriate color—bronze, silver, or gold. You also receive a STAR Test passport signed by the tester, verifying your results, and you receive a scorecard with the tester's comments.

According to Mike Doland of the PSIA, the bronze test will be "easy," the silver "moderately difficult," and the gold "very, very difficult, the highest standard." Doland says that only about 50 skiers a year will obtain the gold pin, making it a very prestigious award.

Paul ("P.J.") Jones, PSIA's marketing vice-president and a six-year veteran of the elite PSIA Ski Team, is the program administrator. He spent an entire fall flying around to the ski areas participating in the program, training the testers and choosing the slopes that will be used for each test. At Snowbird, UT, for example, the bronze test will be given on Big Emma, the silver on Harper's Ferry, and the gold on Regulator Johnson. At Mammoth Mountain, CA, Lower Mambo will be used for the bronze test, St. Anton for the silver, and the Upper Gondola run for the gold. By picking slopes of similar difficulty and making sure the testers have identical training for the job, P.J. is working to ensure that this Standard Rating test stays standard throughout the country.

BY BILL GROUT

BRONZE TEST DESCRIPTION

Slope: 7 to 10°. Packed snow with no bumps, constant fall line.

Sample Bronze test slopes are:

Lower Mambo . . . . Mammoth Mtn.
College . . . . Sun Valley
Big Emma . . . . Snowbird

1.) The candidate must perform the skill proficiency events to the standards set by the PSIA STAR Test International accredited instructor.

2.) The technique used must be in harmony with good sound skiing technique even though it may differ from the technique taught by PSIA.
  Ski length is optional.

3.) To succeed, the skier must show a certain consistency in technique, along with a good basic stance and show of balance.

4.) Scoring for Bronze is: A minimum score of at least 3 on four of five events. Therefore a minimum passing Bronze score is 13.

$$4 @ 3 = 12$$
$$1 @ 1 = \underline{1}$$
$$13$$

5 excellent
4 very good   PASS
Scale   3 satisfactory-good
. . . .
2 unsatisfactory-fair
1 poor   FAIL

If a candidate fails on his first try, he will get another chance at each event. This is at the Bronze level only.

PERSONAL TEST RECORD

DATE	TEST #1	TEST #2	TEST #3	TEST #4	TEST #5	TOTAL POINTS

BRONZE PROFICIENCY TEST #1

Eight linked skidded turns; on a groomed
slope with the last turn leading to a stop.
Your score is determined by how well you
skid both skis, how fluid your movements are,
how consistent your turning radii are and how
well you control your speed.

BRONZE PROFICIENCY TEST #2

Traverse; across a groomed slope with no lateral slippage. Your score will be determined by how well you maintain balance and how effectively you use your edges.

BRONZE PROFICIENCY TEST #3

E ight rhythmically linked wedge turns; on a groomed slope with the last turn leading to a stop. Your score will be determined by how fluid your movements are, how consistent your turning radii are; and how well you control your speed.

BRONZE PROFICIENCY TEST #4

S ideslip to both sides; on a groomed slope, is started from a traverse position by pushing yourself downhill with both ski poles. Your score is determined by how well you maintain your sideslip and your balance.

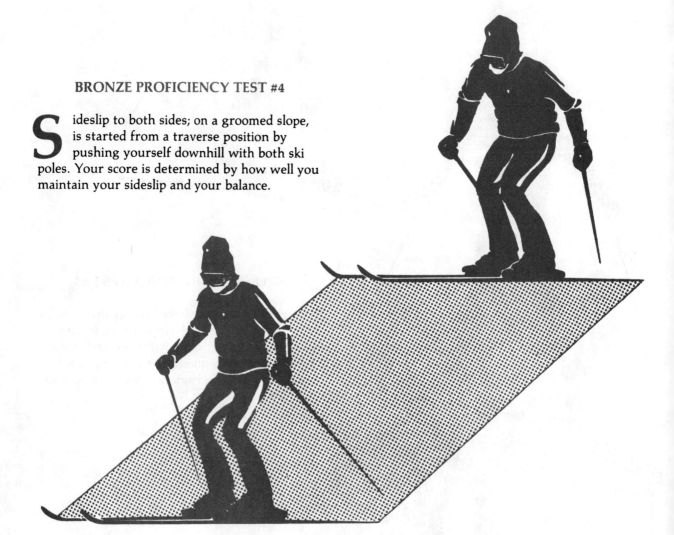

BRONZE PROFICIENCY TEST #5

Angle steps to a stop; begins with a traverse across a groomed slope; stop is made by angled steps up-hill. Your score will be determined by how fluid your movements are, how solid your balance is, and how well you hold the traverse on edged skis.

SILVER TEST DESCRIPTION

Slope: 15 to 20°. Semi-packed snow, gentle bumps or round easy bumps.

Sample Silver test slopes are:

St. Anton . . . . Mammoth Mtn.
Flying Squirrel . . . . Sun Valley
Harper's Ferry . . . . Snowbird

1.) The candidate must perform the skill proficiency events to the standards set by the PSIA STAR Test International accredited instructor.

2.) The technique used must be in harmony with good sound skiing technique even though it may differ from the technique taught by PSIA.
  Ski length is optional.

3.) To succeed, the candidate must show stability and consistent control over the length of the run.

4.) Scoring for Silver is: a minimum of at least 3 on four of five events. Therefore a minimum passing Silver score is 13.

$$
\begin{array}{l}
4 @ 3 = 12 \\
1 @ 1 = \underline{1} \\
13
\end{array}
$$

Scale

5 excellent
4 very good   **PASS**
3 satisfactory-good
. . . .
2 unsatisfactory-fair
1 poor   **FAIL**

On the Silver Test, the skier *does not* get a second try on any event except under special circumstances.

PERSONAL TEST RECORD

DATE	TEST #1	TEST #2	TEST #3	TEST #4	TEST #5	TOTAL POINTS

SILVER PROFICIENCY TEST #1

T raverse in both directions across varying terrain with no lateral slippage. Your score will be determined by how well you maintained your balance, how effectively you adjusted to the terrain and how effectively you used your edges.

SILVER PROFICIENCY TEST #2

Ten long radius turns; on a relatively smooth slope with the last turn leading into a stop. Your score will be determined by how well you perform long radius turns; how fluid your movements are; how consistent your turn radii are, and how well you control your downhill speed.

SILVER PROFICIENCY TEST #3

Twelve skating steps; on *level* and groomed terrain; is started with an angle step and push off to either side. Your score will be determined by how fluid your movements are; how solid your balance is; how well you use your edges and project through the skating steps.

SILVER PROFICIENCY TEST #4

Safety stop to both sides; on a groomed slope, is started from a steep traverse then skid both skis to a stop. Your score will be determined by how well you maintain your balance; how fluid your movements are and how well you control the skid to a stop.

SILVER PROFICIENCY TEST #5

Twenty linked short radius turns; on a relatively smooth slope with the last turn leading into a stop. Your score will be determined by how well you perform short radius turns; how fluid your movements are, how consistent your turn radii are; and how well you control your speed.

GOLD TEST DESCRIPTION

The gold is the standard of success to this program. Therefore it must be worthwhile and made to be very prestigious.

Slope: 20 to 25°, except for "thousand steps" which should be on 15 to 20° slope. Varied snow conditions and terrain and the mark of the Gold Test.

Sample Gold test slopes are:

Upper Gondola .... Mammoth Mtn.
East or Little Easter Bowl .... Sun Valley
Regulator Johnson .... Snowbird

1.) The candidate must perform the skill proficiency events to the standards set by the PSIA STAR Test International accredited instructor.

2.) The technique used must be correct and efficient, in harmony with the techniques of the best skiers today. One does not simply get a Gold. He/she must be an expert and earn the Gold.
    Ski length is optional.

3.) To succeed, the candidate must be aggressive, show skiing know-how and good skiing judgment relative to speed, terrain, and snow conditions, as well as consistent control throughout the length of the run.

4.) Scoring for the Gold is: A minimum of at least 3 *on all five events.* Therefore a minimum passing score on the Gold is 15.

5 @ 3 = 15

Scale

5 excellent
4 very good PASS
3 satisfactory-good
....
2 unsatisfactory-fair
1 poor FAIL

PERSONAL TEST RECORD

DATE	TEST #1	TEST #2	TEST #3	TEST #4	TEST #5	TOTAL POINTS

GOLD PROFICIENCY TEST #1

Fifteen Linked Step Turns; these are done on a relatively smooth slope with the last turn leading to a stop. Your score will be determined by how well you perform step turns; how fluid your movements are; how consistent your turn radii are; how well you control your speed; and how dynamic and crisp you perform these turns.

GOLD PROFICIENCY TEST #2

Six Linked Thousand Steps; done on approximately a 15 degree slope which is groomed. Thousand Steps is a leg independence maneuver and balance exercise. Your score will be determined by how well you perform Thousand Steps; how fluid your movements are; how well you use your edges; how well you maintain your balance; how consistent your turn radii are; and how well you control your speed.

GOLD PROFICIENCY TEST #3

Twenty-five Linked Short Radius Turns; on relatively smooth slope with the last turn leading into a stop. Your score will be determined by how well you perform short radius turns that are crisp, dynamic and fluid; how consistent your turn radii are; and how well you control your speed.

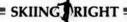

GOLD PROFICIENCY TEST #4

Twenty Linked Medium Radius Turns; on a moguled slope. Your score will be determined by how well you perform these medium radius turns on a moguled slope; how fluid your movements are; how consistent your turn radii are; how well you control your speed. These turns, as all Gold maneuvers, should show good ski know-how, and be very dynamic and crisp.

GOLD PROFICIENCY TEST #5

Twenty Linked Medium Radius Turns; in varying snow conditions with the last turn leading into a stop. Your score will be determined by how well you adjust to the varying conditions; how well you control your speed; and how consistent your turn radii are. These turns should show good ski know-how and be very crisp, dynamic and fluid.

SKIING TERMINOLOGY

IN TERMS OF SKIING

"Snowflakes, like people, are all different and beautiful, but they can seem a nuisance when they lose their identity in a mob."

Bill Vaughn

"**W**ill putting Weinsteins on my Howards improve my Parallel Oslos next time I snowshoe Powder Meadows?"

If the laws of ski nomenclature followed the laws of logic, we would all be talking like that. The above query, for example, means: "Will putting Burt bindings on my Head skis improve my parallel Christies next time I ski Vail?" Ski terminology—even the name of the sport itself —has been shaped by the forces of history, egotism and sheer caprice.

Remember John A. "Snowshoe" Thompson, the legendary postman who skied a 90-mile route to deliver mail through the Sierra snows, from Carson Valley, Nev. to Placerville, Calif.? Well, he wasn't known as "Ski" Thompson. Back in his heyday—1865—the word "snowshoe" meant a long, upward curving board used for snow travel. Thompson, born in Telemark, Norway, referred to them in English as his "gliding shoes." Thompson

not only delivered the mail but delivered the message that "gliding shoe" races were a good way to pass the long winter.

Our most basic term of all—ski—actually comes from the Old Norse, *skith,* meaning snowshoe. In Norwegian and other Germanic tongues, "ski" is pronounced "she." Most modern languages use the word ski or local adaptations.

As recently as the 1930's, the *Fresno Bee's* ski editor Bill Berry (no relation to SKI's I. William Berry) tried to flush out oldtime Sierra skiers. He got nowhere, until he started asking about "snowshoers." Perhaps it is just as well that we have abandoned the terminology of Thomson's time; back then, wax was made of beeswax and sperm whale oil and referred to as "dope."

The Telemark, that graceful kneeling turn cross-country skiers love to flaunt, was aptly named by being developed in the region of Telemark, Norway, in the early 1800's.

But for the grace of journalists writing about Norway's first ski jumping rules committee, the cross-country buffs would be doing Morgedals instead, for that was the particular Telemark village where Telemark-turn creator Sondre Norheim lived. Instead, the pioneer sports bureaucrats down south in Norway's capital decided to honor a well-known district instead of an insignificant hamlet.

If you were going to name a ski term after a town, they thought, it should be a big town—like a nation's capital. Thus the journalists named the parallel turn for the city of its invention, Christiana ("Christie"). In 1924, when the modern nation of Norway shaped up, the locals changed the name of their capital to Oslo, but it was too late to change the name of the turn.

By the 1920's, technique development had slipped into the hands of the Alpine countries (notably Austria), and that self-appointed honorary Alpine nation, Great Britain. That is when Hannes Schneider, who lived in Austria's Arlberg region, began to perfect the technical innovations of his countrymen (notably Mathias Zdarsky, who lived close to Vienna). Since Schneider was the master teacher and popularizer, the technique for stemming, snowplowing and rotating became known—not as the Greater Vienna technique—but as the Arlberg technique.

By this era, skiing *down* a hill was called skiing. Skiing across a flat soon became known as *langlauf* (long running) in German, *ski de fond* (skiing at the bottom) in French, and cross-country in English. The Scandinavian countries called it skiing; they called cross-country travel skiing to distinguish it from slalom, which, to them, had nothing to do with a race between gates. To this day, Scandinavians will still use the word slalom to mean skiing performed at any speed.

Slalom was chosen to be the name of a race by the man who invented that form of competition. Arnold Lunn, later Sir Arnold Lunn, a Britisher who spent much time in Mürren, Switzerland. In 1928, Sir Arnold figured we could increase the challenge of racing while decreasing the risk if we required racers to snake through control gates. To find a name for his invention, he turned to Norway where the Telemark's skiing lexographer, Sondre Norheim, had used regional dialect to come up with the term "slalom" from *sla* (slope) and *lom* (track). In a book written just before his death in 1974, Sir Arnold noted, "Modern slalom as created by me has nothing to

do with the Norwegian slalom. Had I known that the Norwegians intended to make use of their slalom history to appear as pioneers, I (would have) never used the modern word of slalom. I should have invented something quite different." He did not say what.

Nor has Burt Weinstein told us why he called his retractable binding the Burt, not the Weinstein. After all, Dr. Richard Spademan did not call his binding the Doc.

Howard Head opted to call his metal skis Heads (not Howards), whereas Hart Holmberg did the reverse, passing up the chance to call his product Holmbergs instead of Harts. Head says he probably wouldn't have named his skis after himself at all if he had a name with less **pow**, like Bartholemew or Holmberg.

K2 was the designation applied by a British surveying party to a peak in the Karakorum which turned out to be the second highest mountain in the world. Bill Kirschner, who founded the K2 ski company in the mid-sixties, chose the name for its mountaineering connotations and because it could as easily refer to his brother and himself — the two K's.

"Rossignol" happens to mean "nightingale" in French, but when Abel Rossignol and his brother began making skis back in 1907, they didn't name the company after a bird. Lange boots are named after Bob Lange; Caber boots after the Caberlotto family; Daleboots after Mel Dalebout; Salomon bindings after Pepe Salomon . . . You get the picture—the ski business is a sort of family portrait.

As for resort names, the dream mountain that the Tenth Mountain Division veterans were building just over Vail Pass was supposed to have a jazzy, marketable monicker—Powder Meadows. But during its development everyone took to calling it after the highway-construction hamlet that had developed while a Colorado engineer paved a highway over the pass. His name was Charlie Vail, ergo Vail Pass, Vail hamlet, and goodbye Powder Meadows.

But let us return to the slope-track. The Norwegians did not get to name every-thing. Why do we call a bump a mogul? I met a Tenth Mountain veteran named Mogul who claimed to have been the worst skier in the division, and that bumps became moguls because of him. "I used to fall down a lot, and get buried under the snow, and whoever would see me would holler, 'Careful. Don't ski over Mogul.' " Perhaps. But more likely the real reason we call it a mogul is that mogul is Austrian dialect for "little hill." And the reason wiggling down a slope, knees riveted together, is called wedel is that wedel is Austrian slang for "tail-wagging." Schussing (to go fast) is the plain old German word for "shoot" and the sitz-mark, meaning exactly what it sounds like, was first noted by those speaking German.

By the time the French became important enough to decree terminology in skiing, all the good phenomena had been taken. Their chief linguistic contribution is *avalement* (A-val-MON) meaning swallowing, as in absorbing terrain.

It would be nice to blame foreign lands and tongues for such dubious terms as angulate, up-unweight or non-simultaneous foot action and give America credit only for crystal-clear terms like wedge turn and inner skiing. Unfortunately, the urge to obfuscate is international, as prevalent in Nordheim's Telemark as in Snowshoe Thompson's California.

BY ABBEY RAND

TERMS

Knowing and understanding ski terminology will not make you a better skier. It will give you the ability to understand specific verbiage. As any other profession or sport, skiing has developed its own unique verbal symbols for complex mechanics and methodology. While the beginning skier may find little use for this section, the more advanced and curious will discover that a clear picture of dynamic complexes of skiing will aid their progress. Abstractions of these issues should be reserved for coaches and ski teachers.

ANGULATING: Lateral movements in which one part of the body forms an angle with another part of the body. Such movements influence the degree that the skis are edged, how much or how little pressure is exerted and how a skier maintains balance.

ALPINE COMBINED: A scoring system in alpine skiing that adds the combined times and points accumulated in all three alpine disciplines—Slalom, Giant Slalom and Downhill—to determine the overall winner of a combined race. In contrast, some racers enter events as specialists in one or the other event, not competing in all three disciplines.

ANTICIPATING: Anticipating is a mental atti-

tude and/or a physical movement in preparation for a turn. On a mental level, "anticipating" is to allow the mind to become involved with an event that has not quite started yet. Physically, it is to twist the torso in relation to the lower body; the release of this coiling movement starts the next turn.

ATM: The "American Teaching Method" is the synthesis of mechanical, biomechanical and psychological principles of ski instruction. ATM is drawn from a constantly expanding inventory of the factors which influence skiing and instruction.

BALANCE: An automatic response to maintain equilibrium. Human balance centers are located in the inner ear and in muscle spindles assisted by visual references (horizon, etc.). Although the sensory system usually cannot be improved, physical reactions to imbalance can, through strength, agility and coordination, be developed.

CARVING: Pure carving utilizes the mechanics of the ski design to turn with a minimum of skidding. A novice skier also uses ski design in his/her turning, but to a lesser degree. With increasing skill, sensitivity and subtleness, a skier is able to exploit the design more and more.

CHECKING: An abrupt displacement of one or both skis followed by a quick cessation of such a movement. Checking is used to reduce speed and/or set up for a new turn. The most common form of checking involves a shortening of radius at the end of the turn, resulting in a rebound into the next turn.

COUNTER-ROTATION: Twisting the upper and lower body in opposite directions to turn the skis. Such twisting is most effective *when unweighting* using a *hopping or extending movement.*

EDGING: A integral aspect of all skiing, edging is the adjustment of the angle between the running surface of the ski and the slope. In a turn, edging allows the skier to resist centrifugal force; generally, the greater the edge-angle of the ski in relation to the snow, the greater the holding ability of the skis.

EDGE CHANGE: Movement from one edge of the ski to the other. In some turns, the edge change will happen on both skis simultaneously; in others, it happens on only one ski at a time. Generally, parallel turns will show a simultaneous changing of edges while in stem turns, edge change happens with one ski at a time.

FALL-LINE: The imaginary line from any point on the hill following the greatest angle of the slope to the bottom.

FREESTYLE: Freestyle skiing is composed of ballet skiing (an expressive "dance" on skis); aerials (acrobatic jumping) and bump skiing, a creative, aggressive attack of mogul slopes. The term was coined to contrast this style with the highly-disciplined and regimented mode of traditional skiing. The term connotes an expressive form—a skier explores the outer limits of mobility.

FUNCTIONAL SKIING: An approach toward skiing that confronts the demands of each specific situation. In the past, certain skiing techniques were pursued arbitrarily, regardless of their appropriateness. Modern ski instruction generates an awareness of numerous factors affecting skiing, then develops the necessary versatility and flexibility to deal effectively with them.

GLM: The "Graduated Length Method," a program of ski instruction in which the beginner starts on very short skis and then, as skills develop, progresses to longer ones. The general use of shorter, learning-length skis in modern ski schools has made learning much easier.

INCLINING: Leaning into a turn allows the skier to balance/compensate/offset the effects of centrifugal force. Picture a motorcycle rider gunning through a curve to get a vivid picture of inclining.

JETTING: Accelerating the skis, feet and legs in relation to the rest of the body when finishing one turn and starting the next. As the pressure builds up at the end of one turn, the thigh and abdominal muscles relax, resulting in a "squirting" advancement of the skis.

MAMBO: Starting a turn by rotating arms and torso into the turn, then finishing the turn by counter-rotating this. It was, at one time, a playful form of skiing that is not popular anymore.

MOGULS: German for bump. Moguls are the result of slope erosion.

NASTAR: "National Standard Race," a recreational racing circuit where any skier can measure him/herself against the best in the nation. Annual, early-season Nastar handicap races establish the hierarchy of handicaps among the pacesetters in the nation (zero is the fastest handicap). Bronze, Silver and Gold medals are awarded.

OPEN STANCE: Standing on skis with feet apart. An open foot relation provides the skier with greater stability, speed with which skis and feet can be turned and a wider range of lateral leg movement to play the edge-angle of the skis. Historically, a "foot together" stance was the goal of every aspiring skier. In contemporary skiing, an opener, more independent leg and foot relationship is favoured, especially in shorter radius turns.

PARALLEL SKIING: Turning the skis while maintaining equal distance between the skis throughout.

PIVOTING: Turning the skis about an axis perpendicular to the running surface of the skis. Practically all turns are initiated by pivoting, yet at higher speeds and greater levels of sophistication, the skier uses less and less pivoting, replacing it with more carving.

POLE PLANT: A temporary anchoring of the ski pole in the snow. It is generally done to start a turn, to help deflect into the new turn and to make the skis lighter for the turn. The constant dragging of one or both poles (mostly the inside one of a turn) helps the skier orient himself in space (the analogy of a cat's whiskers comes to mind as an image when contemplating this concept of pole use).

PRESSURE CONTROL: Actively adjusting the pressure between skis and snow. This includes the mechanism of moving from one ski to the other, raising or lowering the center of gravity, or shifting the pressure fore/aft on the ski.

REBOUNDING: The recoil or spring-back effect following a compression of the skier's body and skis on the snow. The skier will not experience rebound until he skis with greater speed and edging at advanced levels. At that time, he/she begins to gain a sense of connecting turns dynamically. One turn emerges from the last one much as one good trampoline jump deserves another.

ROTATION: A ski technique of turning whereby the momentum of the skier's body, in the direction of the planned turn, causes the turn to take place. Emile Allais, a French racer and teacher, promoted the "rouade"; Hannes Schneider, an Austrian colleague, introduced the Arlberg technique. The former was a rotation with a down movement, the latter a rotation with an up movement. Since then, rotation had been labeled obsolete, only to reemerge in modern-day skiing as a viable mechanism once more.

SHORT SWING: Linked, short-radius turns in rhythmic succession.

SKI MOVEMENT:
SLIDING
SLIPPING
SKIDDING

SLALOM: An alpine race characterized by obligating male racers to ski between 55 and 75 gates (paired flags) while female racers have between 45 and 60 gates. The altitude differential in this race for men is approximately 200 meters; for women it is 170 meters.

SCHUSS: German word meaning shot. The word relates to skiing straight, without turning.

SIDESLIP: See "ski movement"—slipping.

SNOWPLOW: An alpine skiing technique in

which the skier controls speed by angling just the ski tips toward one another while pushing the ski tails apart. The intensity of braking is determined by the wedge the skis are placed in, in relation to the direction of travel.

STEERING: Guiding the skis with subtle movements through a turn or portions thereof. Steering is a form of "pivoting," the differentiating characteristic being the intensity of the movements involved.

STEP TURNING: A type of turn where the skier steps from ski to ski to effect the direction change. Stem turns in earlier stages of development lead to step turns. Stepping can lead to a converging, parallel or diverging ski relationship when starting the turn.

TERRAIN GARDEN: A manmade practice slope complete with selected snow shapes that provide a learning environment. Bumps, rolls, snaking bobsled tracks, gates to duck under, etc. challenge the skier and provide valuable learning experiences.

TELEMARK TURNING: A turn in which the skier advances one ski from the other, gradually angling the tip of the leading ski in the direction of the intended turn. Such turns are predominantly done by skiers with nordic equipment, where hinge bindings allow stride movements to be performed.

TORLAUF: German word for slalom—see slalom.

TRAVERSING: Crossing the slope in a somewhat perpendicular path to the fall-line.

TURNING: The act of changing direction.

WEDGE: An A-shaped configuration (previously called the snowplow) in which the tips of the skis point together, while the tails of the skis are spread apart. When the angle is severe, it will have a braking effect upon the skier's speed. A narrow displacement of the skis will greatly facilitate directional changes, which, in case of a severe angle, is not the case.

SKIING DIRECTORY

GAZETTEER

I n skiing, as in the appreciation of fine wine, there is something for every palate. Wherever there are inclines (unless you like to cruise out on cross country treks) and snow (although Southern Californians have been known to resort to sand, at times) people ski. From backyard to remotest mountaintop accessible only by helicopter, afficionados can quench their lust on a vast array of skiing opportunities. The gazetteer that follows provides in-depth information and referral phone numbers for the major ski areas on the North American continent. Peruse and dream — there's someplace wonderful for every skier.

The white areas indicate parts of the world where skiing has become popular. These areas are constantly changing due to world political and economic pressures and the continuing growth in the popularity of skiing.

CANADA

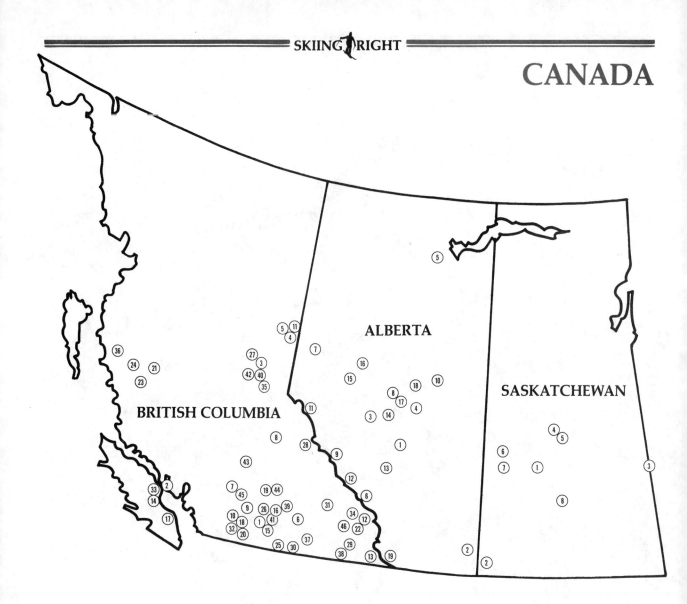

BRITISH COLUMBIA

NAME OF AREA	LOCATION	TELEPHONE #	VERTICAL DROP	NUMBER OF SLOPES	% BEGINNER	% INTERMEDIATE	% EXPERT	LONGEST RUN'	ANNUAL SNOWFALL"
1. **Apex Alpine,** Penticton, BC		(604)493-3200	1800	33	15	46	39	7500	
2. **Arrowsmith Mountain,** Port Alberni, BC		(604)723-7512	1300	25				7920	
3. **Azu Ski Village,** Mackenzie, BC		(604)665-8466	1100					7920	
4. **Bear Mountain,** Dawson Creek, BC		(604)782-4988	410	5				3000	
5. **Big Bam,** Fort St. John, BC		(604)785-6977	700	6				2700	
6. **Big White,** Kelowna, BC		(604)765-4111	1900	48	6	85	9	15840	420
7. **Blackcomb Mountain,** Whistler, BC		(604)932-3141	4000		20	50	30	36960	400
8. **Blue River,** Blue River, BC			300					900	
9. **Botanie Bump,** Lytton, BC			200		90			1200	
10. **Cypress Provincial Park,** Vancouver, BC		(604)929-8171	1181	8				6900	
11. **Dawson Creek Ski Club,** Dawson Creek, BC		(604)782-4988	410	4				3500	
12. **Fairmont Hot Springs Resort,** Fairmont Hot Spgs, BC		(604)345-6311	1000	12	25	60	15	7000	90
13. **Fernie Snow Valley,** Fernie, BC		(604)423-6041	2100	25	25	40	35	15840	250
14. **Forbidden Plateau,** Courtenay, BC		(604)334-4744	1150		25	65	10	7920	300
15. **Gibson Pass,** Manning Parc, BC			1388		30	50	20		250
16. **Grandview,** Kamloops, BC		(604)374-6070	580					5280	
17. **Green Mountain,** Nanaimo, BC			700					7920	
18. **Grouse Mountain,** Vancouver, BC		(604)984-0661	1200	13	20	40	40	5280	122

continued . . .

NAME OF AREA / LOCATION	TELEPHONE #	VERTICAL DROP	NUMBER OF SLOPES	% BEGINNER	% INTERMEDIATE	% EXPERT	LONGEST RUN	ANNUAL SNOWFALL
19. Harper Mountain, Kamloops, BC	(604)573-5115	1400		25	50	25	13200	418
20. Hemlock Valley, Harrison Mills, BC	(604)731-7711	1200	20	22	65	13	5450	600
21. Hudson Bay Mountain, Smithers, BC	(604)847-2058	1750	14				7920	
22. Kimberley, Kimberley, BC	(604)427-4881	2300	35	15	60	25	21120	108
23. Kitimat Alpine Ski Club, Kitimat, BC	(604)632-2892	250	1	100			900	
24. Kitsumkalum Ski Hill, Terence, BC	(604)638-1616	1400	15				5595	
25. Last Mountain, Westbank, BC	(604)768-5189	700	14				6000	
26. Le Jeune Lodge, Kamloops, BC	(604)374-2165	800					4500	
27. Little Mac, Mackenzie, BC	(604)997-3221		2					
28. Mica Creek, Mica Creek, BC	(604)834-7430	240					2500	
29. Morning Mountain, Nelson, BC	(604)352-9969	400	6				2300	
30. Mount Baldy, Osoyoos, BC		1400					11880	
31. Mt. McKenzie, Revelstoke, BC	(604)837-2526	1025	6				6000	
32. Mt. Seymour Provincial Park, Vancouver, BC	(604)929-5212	615					4970	
33. Mt. Washington, Campbell River, BC	(604)287-8912	1600	25				13200	
34. Panorama Mountain, Invermere, BC	(604)342-3224	3200	15	22	63	15	1300	105
35. Purden Ski Village, Prince George, BC	(604)559-2876	1100	5				10560	
36. Rainbow Lake, Prince Rupert, BC	(604)624-6263	550					2700	
37. Red Mountain, Rossland, BC	(604)362-7384	2700	25	20	40	40	23760	120
38. Salmo, Salmo, BC	(604)357-2232	1100	4				4200	
39. Ski Loos, McBride, BC		260	4				2200	
40. Silver Star Vernon, Vernon, BC	(604)542-0224	1600	35	35	50	15	10000	200
41. Snowpatch, Princeton, BC	(604)295-7248	500					2640	
42. Tabor Mountain, Prince George, BC	(604)963-7542	800					10560	
43. Timberland, Williams Lake, BC		800	11				10560	
44. Tod Mountain, Kamloops, BC	(604)578-7151	3100	27	25	25	50	27460	100
45. Whistler Mountain, Whistler, BC	(604)932-3434	4280	59	38	47	15	36960	450
46. Whitewater, Nelson, BC	(604)352-7669	1300	19	20	30	50	5300	220

ALBERTA

NAME OF AREA / LOCATION	TELEPHONE #	VERTICAL DROP	NUMBER OF SLOPES	% BEGINNER	% INTERMEDIATE	% EXPERT	LONGEST RUN	ANNUAL SNOWFALL
1. Canyon, Red Deer, AL	(403)346-5588	500	9	40	50	10	1800	45
2. Cypress, Elkwater, AL	(403)893-3961	520	4				2740	
3. Drayton Valley, Drayton Valley, AL	(403)542-2837	275					1000	
4. Edmonton Ski Club, Edmonton, AL	(403)469-4369	110	8				600	
5. Fairview Ski Club, Fairview, AL		297					2391	
6. Fortress Mountain, Calgary, AL	(403)264-4626	1100	27	30	40	30	5280	200
7. Grande Prairie, Grande Prairie, AL	(403)532-6796	460					6150	
8. Lake Eden, Edmonton, AL	(403)963-3262	200	10				810	
9. Lake Louise, Lake Louise, AL	(403)522-3222	3250	36	20	45	35	21120	185
10. Long Lake, Newbrook, AL	(403)576-9905	200	9				2640	
11. Marmot Basin, Jasper, AL	(403)852-3816	2300	25	35	35	30	18400	225
12. Mt. Norquay, Banff, AL	(403)762-4421	1350	14	35	15	50	8245	140
13. Paskapoo, Calgary, AL	(403)288-4112	300	7				2200	
14. Rabbit Hill, Edmonton, AL	(403)955-2121	300		40	40	20	2900	21
15. Silver Summit, Edson, AL	(403)435-6243	1000	11				4000	
16. Swan Ridge, Swan Hills, AL	(403)333-4337	560	3				1200	
17. Sunshine Valley, Banff, AL	(403)762-3383	3514		20	60	20	11880	295
18. Swiss Valley, Edmonton, AL	(403)469-0279	230					1800	
19. Tawatinaw Valley, Westlock, AL	(403)698-2212	215	18				1922	
20. Westcastle Park, Pincher Creek, AL	(403)627-5101	1700	11	17	35	48	7920	200

SASKATCHEWAN

NAME OF AREA / LOCATION	TELEPHONE #	VERTICAL DROP	NUMBER OF SLOPES	% BEGINNER	% INTERMEDIATE	% EXPERT	LONGEST RUN	ANNUAL SNOWFALL "
1. **Blackstrap,** Saskatoon, SA	(306)492-2276	390	12				1200	
2. **Cypress Hills,** Maple Creek, SA	(306)667-2981	411	6				3300	
3. **Duck Mountain Regional Park,** Kamsack, SA	(306)542-4111	325	9					
4. **Little Red River Park,** Prince Albert, SA	(306)764-5464	102	5				452	
5. **Minatinas,** Domremy, SA	(306)423-6222	230	12				3000	
6. **Table Mountain,** North Battleford, SA	(306)937-2920	400	6				3600	
7. **Twin Towers,** Stranraer, SA	(306)337-2033	300					2500	
8. **White Track,** Moose Jaw, SA	(306)692-8114	300	4				2600	

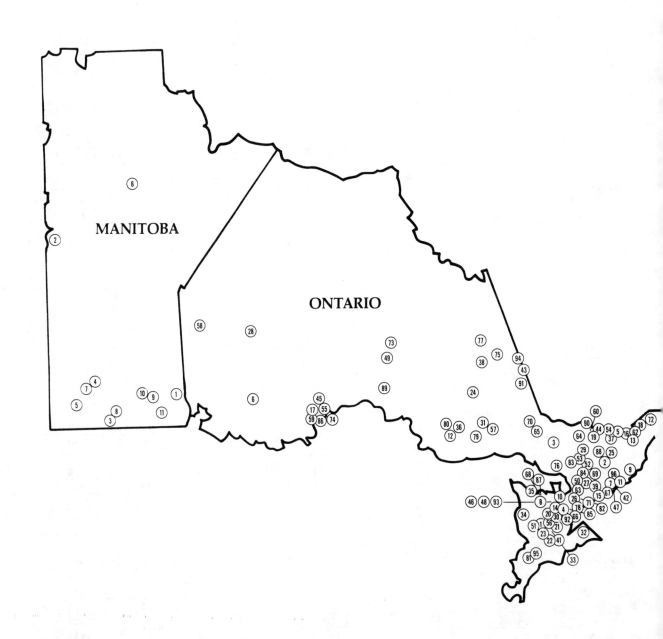

MANITOBA

NAME OF AREA / LOCATION	TELEPHONE #	VERTICAL DROP	NUMBER OF SLOPES	% BEGINNER	% INTERMEDIATE	% EXPERT	LONGEST RUN	ANNUAL SNOWFALL
1. Falcon, Whiteshell Provincial Park, Falcon Lake, MN	(204)349-2201	141	4				1121	
2. Flin Flon, Flin Flon, MN	(204)687-3446	200	2				500	
3. Holiday Mountain, La Riviere, MN	(204)242-2172	300	8				2000	
4. Mt. Agassiz, McCreary, MN	(204)835-2246	505	8	20	50	30		65
5. Mt. Glenorkey, Brandon, MN	(204)728-1950	180	5				1200	
6. Mystery Mountain, Thompson, MN		230	9				2000	
7. Ski Valley, Minnedosa, MN	(204)867-3509	248	5				1600	
8. Snow Valley Resort, Roseisle, MN	(204)828-3362	200	12				1800	
9. Spring Hill, Winnipeg, MN	(204)284-5618	125	2				1200	
10. Stony Mountain, Winter Park, Winnipeg, MN	(204)344-5977	125	5				400	
11. Winnipeg Ski Club, Winnipeg, MN	(204)284-2852	100	4	100			200	

ONTARIO

NAME OF AREA / LOCATION	TELEPHONE #	VERTICAL DROP	NUMBER OF SLOPES	% BEGINNER	% INTERMEDIATE	% EXPERT	LONGEST RUN	ANNUAL SNOWFALL
1. Aberfoyle, Puslinch, ON	(519)822-5764	180					2500	
2. Abitibi, Iroquois Falls, ON	(705)232-5331	150					1400	
3. Adnac, Sudbury, ON	(705)566-9911	200	2				1500	
4. Albion Hills, Palgrave, ON	(416)661-6600	125	2				700	
5. Alice Hill Park, Pembroke, ON	(613)732-2770	210	3				4000	
6. Atikokan, Atikokan, ON	(807)597-6594	247	5				2000	
7. Batawa, Batawa, ON	(613)398-6568	180					1800	
8. Beaver Valley, Kimberley, ON	(519)986-2520	505	27	20	50	30	4620	130
9. Big Ben, Cornwall, ON	(613)933-6377	165					2400	
10. Blue Mountain, Collingwood, ON	(705)445-0231	800	45	27	56	17	3960	110
11. Brockville "Y" Ski Centre, Brockville, ON	(613)342-7961	200	1				600	
12. Buttermilk, Goulais Bay, ON	(705)649-2061	180	5					
13. Calabogie Peaks, Calabogie, ON	(613)752-2720	760		25	35	40	9000	80
14. Caledon, Caledon, ON	(519)927-5221	260					1400	
15. Camborne Village, Cobourg, ON	(416)342-5323	170	4				1500	
16. Candiac Skiways, Dacre, ON	(613)432-5305	600	7				9504	
17. Candy Mountain, Thunder Bay, ON	(807)939-6033	734	10				9240	
18. Carlington Park, Ottawa, ON	(613)729-8102	70	1	100			700	
19. Caswell Resort, Sundridge, ON	(705)384-5371	175					1800	
20. Cedar Highlands, Orangeville, ON	(519)941-1262	300	5				1200	
21. Centennial Park, Toronto, ON	(416)621-3702	130					700	
22. Chedome, Hamilton, ON	(416)528-1613	340					1800	
23. Chicopee, Kitchener, ON	(519)724-5844	200	13				2000	
24. Chapleau, Chapleau, ON	(705)864-1028	100					1000	
25. Curlew, Huntsville, ON	(705)789-9998	200	10				3500	
26. Dagmar, Claremont, ON	(416)649-2002	200	15				2000	
27. Devil's Elbow, Bethany, ON	(705)277-2012	350	9				3000	
28. Dryden, Dryden, ON	(807)223-6345	170					1000	
29. Echo Ridge, Kearney, ON		350					3800	
30. Edelweiss, Bolton, ON	(416)857-3120	150					2000	
31. Espanola, Espanola, ON	(705)869-9934	200					1300	
32. Fonthill Ski Centre, St. Catharines, ON	(416)934-2682	125	4				800	
33. Glen Eden, Milton, ON	(416)878-4131	240	13				2000	
34. Happy Valley, Walkerton, ON	(519)881-1590	175	8				1800	
35. Harrison Park, Owen Sound, ON	(519)376-0265	80					2500	
36. Heyden Ski Hill, Sault Ste. Marie, ON	(705)777-2082	200	4				2000	
37. Hidden Valley Highlands, Huntsville, ON	(705)789-5942	330	12	30	50	20	1800	125

continued . . .

NAME OF AREA / LOCATION	TELEPHONE #	VERTICAL DROP	NUMBER OF SLOPES	% BEGINNER	% INTERMEDIATE	% EXPERT	LONGEST RUN	ANNUAL SNOWFALL
38. Kamiskotia Ski Resort, Timmins, ON	(705)264-8114	350	14				3000	
39. Kawartha, Peterborough, ON	(705)277-2311	360	14				2500	
40. Kiwissa Ski Club, Manitouwadge, ON	(807)826-3870	330	6				2600	
41. King's Forest Winter Park, Hamilton, ON	(416)547-9042	240	2				3000	
42. Kingston Ski Hills, Kingston, ON	(613)542-7166	125	7				800	
43. Larder Ski Club, Larder Lake, ON	(705)643-2523	175	7				850	
44. Laurentian, North Bay, ON	(705)474-9950	310	8				2000	
45. Loch Lomond, Thunder Bay, ON	(807)577-5787	800	14	25	40	35	6000	200
46. Loretto Ski Resort, Loretto, ON	(416)277-8230	185	6				1500	
47. Macauley Mountain, Picton, ON	(613)476-8943	200					1500	
48. Mansfield Skiways, Mansfield, ON	(705)435-5302	400	12	30	60	10	2640	70
49. Marathon, Marathon, ON	(807)229-0397	200					2600	
50. Medonte Mountain, Barrie, ON	(705)835-2001	400	20				4000	
51. Minto Glen Sports Centre, Harriston, ON	(519)338-5250	180	8	25	75		1500	
52. Mountain View, Midland, ON	(705)526-8149	150	7				1300	
53. Moonstone, Coldwater, ON	(705)835-2018	450	12	20	60	20	5000	60
54. Mount Antoine-Mattawa, Mattawa, ON	(705)474-9950	630	9				10000	
55. Mt. Baldy, Thunder Bay, ON	(807)683-8441	650	12				6500	
56. Mt. Chinguacousy, Brampton, ON	(416)791-6510	100	3				700	
57. Mount Dufour, Elliot Lake, ON	(705)848-6655	315	3	33	33	33	2000	
58. Mt. Evergreen, Kenora, ON	(807)548-5100	250	9		80		2100	
59. Mt. McKay, Thunder Bay, ON	(807)623-6822	625					6000	
60. Mount Madawaska, Barry's Bay, ON	(613)756-2931	450	7				5000	
61. Mount Martin, Deep River, ON	(613)687-2516	150					700	
62. Mount Pakenham, Pakenham, ON	(613)624-5290	280	7	50	25	25	3000	90
63. Mount St. Louis, Barrie, ON	(416)368-6578	500	18				4000	
64. Nipissing Ridge, Callander, ON	(705)472-2827	405	4				4500	
65. Nordic Hills, Sudbury, ON	(705)522-6663	255					2400	
66. North York, Downsview, ON	(416)638-5315	130	4				1000	
67. Northumberland Forest, Cobourg, ON	(418)349-2779	260					1600	
68. Old Smokey, Kimberley, ON	(519)599-5433	600					4000	
69. Omemee, Omemee, ON	(705)799-6734	260					3500	
70. Onaping Ski Hills, Onaping, ON	(705)966-3939	320	8				2400	
71. Oshawa-Kirby Ski Club, Oshawa, ON	(416)983-5983	300	14				2500	
72. Ottawa YM/YMCA, South March, ON	(613)832-1234	100					1000	
73. Otter Slide, Longlac, ON	(807)876-2740	150					600	
74. Pine Top, Thunder Bay, ON	(807)683-8061	550	4				3000	
75. Raven Mountain, Kirkland Lake, ON	(705)567-3738	520					4000	
76. Rainbow Ridge, Bracebridge, ON	(705)645-5266	180					2000	
77. Remi Lake Winter Recreation Area, Moonbeam, ON	(705)267-2442	145	2				1640	
78. Rouge Valley, Toronto, ON	(416)284-0249	130	4				800	
79. (The) Sault, Sault Ste. Marie, ON		160					1300	
80. Searchmont Valley, Searchmont, ON	(705)253-4179	700	12				6000	
81. Skee-Hi, Thamesford, ON	(519)461-1720	150			100		1500	
82. Ski Dagmar, Ashburn, ON	(416)649-2002	200	15				2000	
83. Sir Sams's, Haliburton, ON	(705)754-2798	330	8				4000	
84. Snow Valley Resort, Barrie, ON	(705)728-9541	325	11				3200	
85. Summit, Richmond Hill, ON	(416)884-8101	80					300	
86. Sundance N.W., Thunder Bay, ON	(807)577-8813	750	15				7000	
87. Talisman Resort, Kimberley, ON	(519)599-2520	600	8	10	85	5	4000	105
88. Tally-Ho Winter Park, Huntsville, ON	(705)635-2720	208	5	50	50		1800	
89. Terrace Bay, Terrace Bay, ON	(807)825-3502	170					1000	
90. Thorne Ski Resort, Thorne, ON	(819)627-3529	670	11				5000	
91. Tri-Town Ski Village, New Liskeard, ON	(705)647-4050	320	7				2500	
92. Uplands Ski Hole, Thornhill, ON	(416)889-9405	110	5				1200	

continued . . .

NAME OF AREA	LOCATION	TELEPHONE #	VERTICAL DROP	NUMBER OF SLOPES	% BEGINNER	% INTERMEDIATE	% EXPERT	LONGEST RUN	ANNUAL SNOWFALL
93. **Valley Schuss,** Orangeville, ON		(519)941-8751	380	14				7800	
94. **Windsor Valley,** Kirkland Lake, ON		(705)567-7065	120	6				1300	
95. **Woodstock Ski Club,** Woodstock, ON		(519)462-2625	110					1600	
96. **"Y" Ski Center,** Athens, ON		(613)342-7961	125					600	

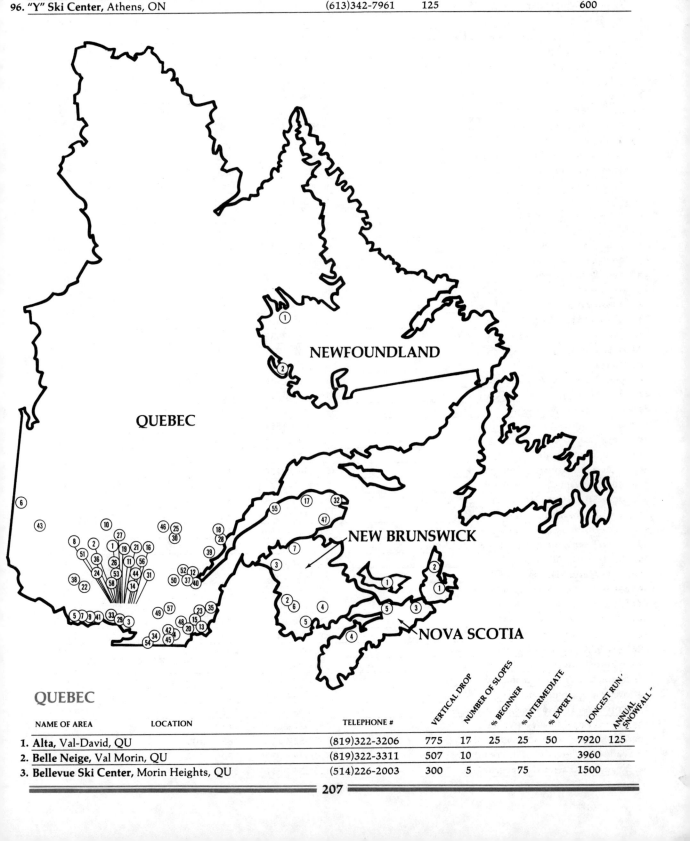

QUEBEC

NAME OF AREA	LOCATION	TELEPHONE #	VERTICAL DROP	NUMBER OF SLOPES	% BEGINNER	% INTERMEDIATE	% EXPERT	LONGEST RUN	ANNUAL SNOWFALL
1. **Alta,** Val-David, QU		(819)322-3206	775	17	25	25	50	7920	125
2. **Belle Neige,** Val Morin, QU		(819)322-3311	507	10				3960	
3. **Bellevue Ski Center,** Morin Heights, QU		(514)226-2003	300	5		75		1500	

continued . . .

NAME OF AREA, LOCATION	TELEPHONE #	VERTICAL DROP	NUMBER OF SLOPES	% BEGINNER	% INTERMEDIATE	% EXPERT	LONGEST RUN	ANNUAL SNOWFALL
4. Bromont Ski Center, Bromont, QU	(514)534-2200	1300	15	33	53	12	13200	
5. Camp Fortune, Old Chelsea, QU	(819)827-1717	620	17				3600	
6. Chalet Suisse, La Sarre, QU	(819)333-6727	54	3				90	
7. Edelweiss Valley, Wakefield, QU	(819)459-2859	625	15	30	40	30	5000	225
8. Gray Rocks, St.-Jovite, Mt. Tremblant, QU	(819)425-2771	610	18	33	29	38	5280	170
9. Lac De L'Argile, Notre Dame De La Salette, QU	(819)766-2341	600	3				2000	
10. La Tuque, La Tuque, QU	(819)523-2204	430	11				5240	
11. L'Avalanche, Saint-Adolphe-D'Howard, QU	(819)327-2411	410	7				3260	
12. Le Relais, Lac Beauport, QU	(418)849-3073	650	7				4300	
13. Mont Adstock, Thetford Mines, QU	(418)487-2242	720	8				5300	
14. Mont Alouette, Ste. Adele, QU	(514)229-2717	509					4800	
15. Mont Apic, Saint-Pierre-Baptiste, QU	(819)362-2109	300	6				4960	
16. Mont Avila, Piedmont, QU	(514)861-6578	600	8				4960	
17. Mont Bellevue, Monts Gaspe-N, QU	(418)763-5511	350					2500	
18. Mont Belu, Port Alfred, QU	(418)544-5044	550	5				5280	
19. Mont Blanc, Saint-Faustin, QU	(819)688-2444	600	9				5450	
20. Mont Carmel, Mont Carmel, QU	(819)374-4534	495	11	50	50		3150	
21. Mont Christie, Christieville, QU	(514)226-2412	560	12		75		4000	
22. Mont Comi, St. Donat, QU	(418)739-4066	997	13				6000	
23. Mont Elan, East Angus, QU	(819)832-9011	325	6	50	10	40	2600	
24. Mont-Faustin, Saint-Jovite, QU	(819)425-2461	700	9				7920	
25. Mont Fortin, Jonquire, QU	(418)542-5711	150	7				1000	
26. Mont-Gabriel, Mont Gabriel, QU	(514)229-3547	750	18	10	50	40	5000	
27. Mont Grand Fonds, La Malbaie, QU	(418)665-2334	1200	8				7500	
28. Mont Garceau, Saint-Donat, QU		275	9					180
29. Mont Habitant, St. Sauveur-des-Monts, QU	(514)227-2637	550	7	30	40	30		130
30. Mont Jacob, Jonquiere, QU	(418)542-5711	120	3				1500	
31. Mont La Reserve, St. Donat, QU	(819)424-2377	1150	8				5280	
32. Mont Miller, Murdochville, QU	(418)784-2908	700	6				5490	
33. Mont Olympia, Piedmont, QU	(514)866-0747	800	11					
34. Mont Orford, Magog, QU	(819)843-6548	1650	15	40	33	27	13200	200
35. Mont Orignal, Lac-Etchemin, QU	(418)625-1551	850	6				6500	
36. Mont Plante, Val-David, QU		450	11				5280	
37. Mont Sainte-Anne, Beaupre', QU	(418)827-4561	1875	27	22	41	37	14500	
38. Mont Saint-Sauveur, Saint-Sauveur, QU	(514)866-7190	700	16				4600	
39. Mont Sauvage, Val-Morin, QU	(819)322-2337	600	9				5280	
40. Mont St-Castom Des Neiges, Lac-Beauport, QU	(418)849-6776	550	6				2740	
41. Mont Ste-Marie, Lac Ste-Marie, QU	(819)467-5200	1250	19	23	67	10	12950	100
42. Mont-Sutton, Sutton, QU	(514)866-5156	1550	25	30	40	30	11880	211
43. Mont Tremblant, Mont Tremblant, QU	(819)425-2711	2131	25	16	56	28	18480	165
44. Mont-Video, Abitibi, QU	(819)734-2193	350	5				4000	
45. Owl's Head, Mansonville, QU	(514)292-5592	1770		20	60	20	12000	180
46. Saguenay-Lac St. Jean, Alma, QU	(418)662-2901	175	3				1200	
47. Saint-Edgar, New Richmond, QU	(418)392-4684	300	6				3400	
48. Saint-Georges, Saint-Georges, QU	(418)228-8151	246	6				2106	
49. Saint-Gerard, St. Mathieu, Lac Bellemare, QU	(819)539-5451	400	15	50	30	20	3900	
50. Ski Montcalm, Rawdon, QU	(514)834-3139	400	12				3000	
51. Ski Morin Heights, Morin Heights, QU	(514)226-3231	700	21				5280	
52. St-Raymond, St-Raymond, QU	(418)337-2866	350	6	40	60		2000	
53. Stoneham, Stoneham, QU	(418)848-2411	1250	13	60		40	10500	
54. Universite De Montreal, Montreal, QU	(514)343-6150	175	1	100			950	
55. Val D'Irene, Matapedia Valley, QU	(418)629-3040	940	10				10560	
56. Vallee Bleue, Val-David, QU	(819)322-3427	365	10				3000	
57. Vallee Du Parc, Grand' Mere, QU	(819)538-1639	550	14				4800	170
58. Yvan Coutu, Saint-Marguerite, QU	(514)228-2511	550	14				1840	

NEW BRUNSWICK

NAME OF AREA LOCATION	TELEPHONE #	VERTICAL DROP	NUMBER OF SLOPES	% BEGINNER	% INTERMEDIATE	% EXPERT	LONGEST RUN	ANNUAL SNOWFALL
1. **Brookvale Prov. Pk.,** Charlottetown, Prince Ed. Island	(902)892-7411	180	6				1400	
2. **Crabbe Mtn. Winter Park,** Millville York Co., NB	(506)463-2686	850	9				7920	
3. **Mont Farlagne,** Edmundston, NB	(506)735-6557	589	9				5280	
4. **Poley Mountain,** Waterford, NB	(506)433-2201	750	8				5280	
5. **Rockwood Park Ski Hills,** Saint John, NB	(506)658-2844	150					1350	
6. **Silverwood Winter Park,** Fredericton, NB	(506)454-3151	305					2600	
7. **Sugarloaf Provincial Park,** Atholville, NB	(506)753-6258	150	7					

NEWFOUNDLAND

NAME OF AREA LOCATION	TELEPHONE #	VERTICAL DROP	NUMBER OF SLOPES	% BEGINNER	% INTERMEDIATE	% EXPERT	LONGEST RUN	ANNUAL SNOWFALL
1. **Churchill Falls,** Churchill Falls, Newfoundland	(709)924-3311	690	4				1450	
2. **Smokey Mountain,** Labrador, Newfoundland	(709)944-3505	910					5000	

NOVA SCOTIA

NAME OF AREA LOCATION	TELEPHONE #	VERTICAL DROP	NUMBER OF SLOPES	% BEGINNER	% INTERMEDIATE	% EXPERT	LONGEST RUN	ANNUAL SNOWFALL
1. **Ben Eoin Recreation Centre,** Sydney, NS	(902)828-2222	470					2700	
2. **Keltic's Cape Smokey,** Ingonish Beach, NS	(902)285-2880	1000					6600	
3. **Keppoch Mountain,** Antigonish, NS	(902)863-1764	465	5				4000	
4. **Martock II,** Windsor, NS	(902)798-4728	610	12				6600	
5. **Ski Wentworth,** Wentworth, NS	(902)548-2089	700					9240	

UNITED STATES

ALASKA

WASHINGTON

OREGON

IDAHO

MONTANA

ALASKA

NAME OF AREA / LOCATION	TELEPHONE #	VERTICAL DROP	NUMBER OF SLOPES	% BEGINNER	% INTERMEDIATE	% EXPERT	LONGEST RUN	ANNUAL SNOWFALL
1. Alyeska, Girdwood, AK	(907)783-6000	2800					10560	
2. Arctic Valley, Anchorage, AK	(907)272-7767	1400		20	65	15		
3. Cleary Summit, Fairbanks, AK	(907)456-5520	1200		20	65	15	6000	
4. Eaglecrest, Juneau, AK	(907)586-3300	1400	20	30	40	30	10560	250
5. Mt. Eyak, Cordova, AK	(907)424-7455	900	3					
6. Viking, Petersburg, AK	(907)772-3508	500	4	50	25	25	1800	

WASHINGTON

NAME OF AREA / LOCATION	TELEPHONE #	VERTICAL DROP	NUMBER OF SLOPES	% BEGINNER	% INTERMEDIATE	% EXPERT	LONGEST RUN	ANNUAL SNOWFALL
1. Alpental, Snoqualmie Pass, WA 98068	(206)434-6112	2200	15	20	40	40		160
2. Badger Mountain, Waterville, WA 98858	(509)745-2703	1500						
3. Bluewood, Dayton, WA 99328	(509)525-8410	1200	8				11880	
4. Crystal Mountain, Crystal Mountain, WA 98022	(206)663-2265	3102	33	10	20	40	18480	204
5. 49° North, Chewelah, WA 99109	(509)935-6649	1845	17	30	40	30	16896	120
6. Hurricane Ridge, Port Angeles, WA 98362	(206)452-4501	695	3				695	
7. Loup Loup, Twisp, WA 98856	(509)826-0537	1200						
8. Mission Ridge, Wenatchee, WA 98801	(509)663-6543	2140	30	30	50	20	26400	60
9. Mt. Baker, Bellingham, WA 98225	(206)734-6771	1500	25	15	60	25	6500	500
10. Mt. Spokane, Spokane, WA 99208	(509)484-3908	1514	23	20	50	30	7920	192
11. Sitzmark, Tonasket, WA 98855	(509)485-3323	630						
12. Ski Acres/Snoqualmie Summit, Snoqualmie, WA 98068	(206)434-6161	900	4	20	45	35	6600	170
13. Squilchuck, Wenatchee, WA 98801	(206)663-1303	200						
14. Stevens Pass, Leavenworth, WA 98826	(206)973-2441	1800		14	39	47	6047	120
15. White Pass Village, White Pass, WA 98937	(509)453-8731	1500	8	20	60	20	10560	125

IDAHO

NAME OF AREA / LOCATION	TELEPHONE #	VERTICAL DROP	NUMBER OF SLOPES	% BEGINNER	% INTERMEDIATE	% EXPERT	LONGEST RUN	ANNUAL SNOWFALL
1. Bald Mountain, Orofino, ID 83544	(208)476-4942	975	5				5280	
2. Bear Gulch, St. Anthony, ID 83445	(208)527-3359	1240	7				5280	
3. Blizzard, Arco, ID 83255	(208)527-3357	900					4000	
4. Bogus Basin, Boise, ID 83702	(208)336-4500	1800	43	21	43	36	8000	100
5. Brundage Mountain, McCall, ID 83638	(208)634-2244	1800	18				10560	
6. Cottonwood Butte, Cottonwood, ID 83522	(208)962-3624	640	4				3000	
7. Kelly Canyon, Idaho Falls, ID 83401	(208)538-6261	900	7				6800	
8. Lookout Pass, Wallace, ID 83873	(208)744-1301	700	4				3960	
9. Magic Mountain, Albion, ID 83311	(208)638-5555	900					7920	
10. North-South Bowl, Emida, ID 83828	(208)335-2651	450	3				1500	
11. Pebble Creek, Pocatello, ID 83201	(208)234-0271	1650	20				6336	
12. Pomerelle, Albion, ID 83311	(208)638-5555	1000	16					
13. Schweitzer, Sandpoint, ID 83864	(208)263-9555	2000		20	50	30	11880	180
14. Silverhorn, Kellogg, ID 83837	(208)786-9521	2000	14				10560	
15. Snowhaven, Grangeville, ID 83530	(208)983-2155	400		30	70		1760	
16. Soldier Mountain, Fairfield, ID 83327	(208)764-2300	1400	36				5280	
17. Sun Valley, Sun Valley, ID	(800)635-8261	3400	64	25	50	25	15840	120
18. Taylor Mountain, Idaho Falls, ID 83401	(208)524-0202	750					2850	

MONTANA

NAME OF AREA	LOCATION	TELEPHONE #	VERTICAL DROP	NUMBER OF SLOPES	% BEGINNER	% INTERMEDIATE	% EXPERT	LONGEST RUN	ANNUAL SNOWFALL
1. Beef Trail,	Butte, MT 59701	(406)792-2242	2600	5				3650	
2. Belmont,	Helena, MT 59601	(406)442-8246	1500	9				5280	
3. Big Mountain,	Whitefish, MT 59937	(406)862-3511	2130	35	25	55	20	13200	300
4. Big Sky,	Big Sky, MT 59323	(406)995-4211	2500	221	25	50	25	16000	400
5. Bridger Bowl,	Bozeman, MT 59715	(406)586-2787	2000		25	45	30	13200	400
6. Deep Creek,	Butte, MT 59701	(406)839-2129	1000	5					
7. Discovery Basin,	Anaconda, MT 59711	(406)563-2184	1300	3		70		9240	
8. Lost Trail,	Darby, MT 59829	(406)821-3495	650					6600	
9. Marshall Mountain,	Missoula, MT 59801	(406)258-6619	1500	7				6000	
10. Maverick Mountain,	Polaris, MT	(406)834-2412	1655					13200	
11. Montana Snow Bowl,	Missoula, MT 59801	(406)549-9777	2600					18480	
12. Red Lodge Mountain,	Red Lodge, MT 59068	(406)446-2288	2016	21	15	60	25	10600	244
13. Showdown,	Neihart, MT 59465	(406)236-5522	1400	21				11000	
14. Teton Pass,	Choteau, MT 59422	(406)466-2672	1010	21				5000	
15. Turner Mountain,	Libby, MT		2165						
16. Wraith Hill,	Anaconda, MT 59711	(406)563-2357	450	5				5280	

OREGON

NAME OF AREA	LOCATION	TELEPHONE #	VERTICAL DROP	NUMBER OF SLOPES	% BEGINNER	% INTERMEDIATE	% EXPERT	LONGEST RUN	ANNUAL SNOWFALL
1. Anthony Lakes,	North Powder, OR 97867	(503)856-3277	800	15	25	50	25	7500	120
2. Cooper Spur,	Hood River, OR 97031	(503)386-3381	500	8				2500	
3. High Wallowas,	Joseph, OR 97846	(503)432-5331	3700	1				18480	
4. Hoodoo,	Sisters, OR 97759		1035	19				5280	
5. Mt. Ashland,	Ashland, OR 97520	(503)482-2897	1156	22	10	25	65	4000	100
6. Mt. Bachelor,	Bend, OR 97701	(503)382-8334	1700	36	30	20	20	6200	192
7. Mt. Hood Meadows,	Mt. Hood, OR 97041	(503)337-2222	2777	46	30	40	20	10560	200
8. Multopor-Ski Bowl,	Government Camp, OR 97028	(503)272-3522	1400	19	20	50	30	7950	300
9. Spout Springs,	Weston, OR 97886	(503)566-2015	1600	11				4000	
10. Summit,	Government Camp, OR 97028	(503)272-3351	400	3				3000	
11. Timberline,	Government Camp, OR 97028	(503)272-3311	3000	22	30	50	20	10560	252
12. Willamette Pass,	Cascade Summit, OR		800	10	40	40	20	10560	

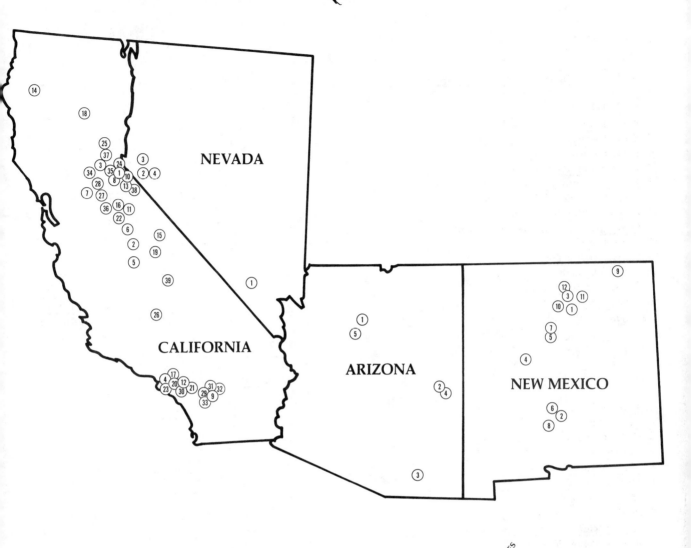

CALIFORNIA

NAME OF AREA / LOCATION	TELEPHONE #	VERTICAL DROP	NUMBER OF SLOPES	% BEGINNER	% INTERMEDIATE	% EXPERT	LONGEST RUN	ANNUAL SNOWFALL
1. **Alpine Meadows**, Tahoe City, CA 95730	(916)583-4232	1700		25	35	40	10560	180
2. **Badger Pass**, Yosemite, CA 95389	(209)372-1330	900	10	30	50	20	5300	300
3. **Boreal**, Truckee, CA 95734	(916)426-3666	600	36	20	60	20	5280	
4. **Buckhorn**, Whittier, CA		700	5				1760	
5. **China Peak**, Lakeshore, CA 93634	(209)893-3316	1679					15310	
6. **Dodge Ridge**, Pine Crest, CA	(209)965-3474	1000		20	60	20	4200	450
7. **Donner Ski Ranch**, Norden, CA 95724	(916)426-3578	825	25				4000	
8. **Echo Summit**, South Lake Tahoe, CA	(916)659-7154	575					5280	
9. **Goldmine**, Big Bear Lake, CA 92315	(714)585-2517	1500	20	30	40	30	13200	80
10. **Granlibakken**, Tahoe City, CA 95730	(916)583-4242	280	1	50	50		900	
11. **Heavenly Valley**, South Lake Tahoe, CA 95705	(916)541-1330	4000	64	25	50	25	36960	400
12. **Holiday Hill**, Wrightwood, CA 92397	(714)249-3256	1600	14	30	30	40	6000	100
13. **Homewood**, Homewood, CA 95718	(916)525-7256	1670	72	20	50	30	10560	96
14. **Horse Mountain**, Eureka, CA 95501	(707)443-6464	600					4000	
15. **Iron Mountain**, Kirkwood, CA	(209)258-8543	1200	14				10600	
16. **June Mountain**, June Lake, CA 93529	(714)648-7733	2500	30	30	45	25	10560	200
17. **Kirkwood**, Kirkwood, CA 95646	(209)258-6000	2000	50	25	50	25	13200	450
18. **Kratka Ridge**, La Canada, CA 91011	(213)790-4683	700					3000	
19. **Lassen National Park**, Mineral, CA 96063	(916)595-3306	500	6				2700	

continued . . .

NAME OF AREA	LOCATION	TELEPHONE #	VERTICAL DROP	NUMBER OF SLOPES	% BEGINNER	% INTERMEDIATE	% EXPERT	LONGEST RUN'	ANNUAL SNOWFALL"
20. **Mammoth Mountain,** Mammoth, CA 93546		(714)934-2571	3100	80	30	40	30	13200	600
21. **Mountain High,** Wrightwood, CA 92397		(714)249-3226	1100					1100	
22. **Mt. Baldy,** Mt. Baldy, CA 91750		(714)982-4208	2100						
23. **Mt. Reba at Bear Valley,** Bear Valley, CA 95223		(209)753-2301	2100	21	25	50	25	15840	450
24. **Mt. Waterman,** La Canada, CA 91011		(213)790-2002	1200	15				4000	
25. **Northstar-at-Tahoe,** Truckee, CA 95734		(916)562-1010	2200	41	33	50	17	15323	400
26. **Plumas-Eureka Ski Bowl,** Quincy, CA 95971		(916)836-2317	650					5280	
27. **Shirley Meadows,** Wofford Heights, CA 93285		(714)379-2871	400	6	40	30	30	2600	
28. **Sierra Ski Ranch,** Twin Bridges, CA 95735		(916)659-7475	1585	27	20	50	30	13200	475
29. **Signal Hill,** Norden, CA 95724		(916)426-3632	350	1					
30. **Ski Green Valley,** Green Valley Lake, CA 92341		(714)867-2238	300	15				2000	
31. **Ski Sunrise,** Wrightwood, CA 92397		(714)249-6150	800	18				5280	
32. **Snow Forest,** Big Bear Lake, CA		(714)866-8891	300					1500	
33. **Snow Summit,** Big Bear Lake, CA 92315		(714)866-5766	1200	14	20	50	30	6600	72
34. **Snow Valley,** Running Springs, CA 92382		(714)867-3677	1100	12	30	40	30	6600	155
35. **Soda Springs,** Soda Springs, CA 95728		(916)426-3801	750		40	50	10	1500	
36. **Squaw Valley USA,** Olympic Valley, CA 95730		(916)583-0121	2700		30	40	30	15840	450
37. **Sugar Bowl,** Norden, CA 95724		(916)426-3651	1500	36	20	30	50	10560	500
38. **Tahoe Donner Ski Bowl,** Truckee, CA 95734		(916)587-6046	600	6	50	50		6280	
39. **Tahoe Ski Bowl,** Homewood, CA 95718		(916)525-5224	1630	22	40	40	20	14200	120
40. **Wolverton Ski Bowl,** Sequoia Natl. Park, CA 93262		(209)565-3381	175	3				1000	

NEVADA

NAME OF AREA	LOCATION	TELEPHONE #	VERTICAL DROP	NUMBER OF SLOPES	% BEGINNER	% INTERMEDIATE	% EXPERT	LONGEST RUN'	ANNUAL SNOWFALL"
1. **Lee Canyon,** Las Vegas, NV		(702)872-5462	1030	6				5000	
2. **Mt. Rose,** Reno, NV		(702)849-0704	1500	18				15840	
3. **Ski Incline,** Incline Village, NV 89450		(702)831-1821	900	20	20	40	40	5280	184
4. **Slide Mountain,** Reno, NV		(702)849-0303	1450	16				15000	

ARIZONA

NAME OF AREA	LOCATION	TELEPHONE #	VERTICAL DROP	NUMBER OF SLOPES	% BEGINNER	% INTERMEDIATE	% EXPERT	LONGEST RUN'	ANNUAL SNOWFALL"
1. **Arizona Snow Bowl,** Flagstaff, AZ 86001		(602)774-0562	2100		39	25	36	7920	250
2. **Greer Ski Area,** Greer, AZ		(602)735-7503	250	2				1000	
3. **Mt. Lemmon Ski Area,** Mt. Lemmon, AZ 85619		(602)791-9791	870		20	45	35	15840	
4. **Sunrise,** McNary, AZ 85930		(602)334-2122	1440	12	30	45	25	15840	250
5. **Williams Ski Area,** Williams, AZ 86046		(602)635-2633	450	5	20	70	10		

NEW MEXICO

NAME OF AREA	LOCATION	TELEPHONE #	VERTICAL DROP	NUMBER OF SLOPES	% BEGINNER	% INTERMEDIATE	% EXPERT	LONGEST RUN'	ANNUAL SNOWFALL"
1. **Angel Fire,** Angel Fire, NM		(505)377-2301	2180	18	35	47	18	18480	120
2. **Eagle Creek,** Ruidoso, NM 87558		(505)336-4211	500	12				8000	
3. **Red River,** Red River, NM 87558		(505)754-2223	1524		35	40	25	13200	155
4. **Sandia Peak,** Albuquerque, NM		(505)296-9585	1700	25	15	75	10	13200	150

continued . . .

NAME OF AREA / LOCATION	TELEPHONE #	VERTICAL DROP	NUMBER OF SLOPES	% BEGINNER	% INTERMEDIATE	% EXPERT	LONGEST RUN'	ANNUAL SNOWFALL"
5. **Santa Fe,** Santa Fe, NM 87501	(505)982-4429	1650	32	20	40	40	15840	160
6. **Sierra Blanca,** Ruidoso, NM 88345	(505)336-4356	1700	25	20	40	20	13200	170
7. **Sipapu,** Vadito, NM 87579	(505)587-2240	800	15				7100	
8. **Ski Cloudcroft,** Cloudcroft, NM 88317	(505)682-2587	500	19				5000	
9. **Sugarite,** Raton, NM 87740	(505)445-5000	825					10560	
10. **Taos Ski Valley,** Taos Ski Valley, NM 87571	(505)776-2291	2612	62	24	13	12	27720	324
11. **Val Verde Ski Basin,** Eagle Nest, NM 87718	(505)377-6011	350	12	65	35		1350	
12. **Woodlands Ski Basin,** Red River, NM 87558	(505)754-2941	100	2				600	

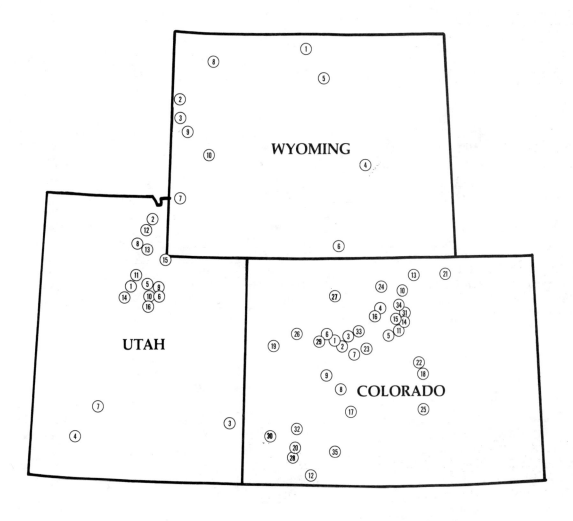

UTAH

NAME OF AREA / LOCATION	TELEPHONE #	VERTICAL DROP	NUMBER OF SLOPES	% BEGINNER	% INTERMEDIATE	% EXPERT	LONGEST RUN'	ANNUAL SNOWFALL"
1. **Alta,** Alta, UT 84070	(801)742-3333	2000		25	35	40	15840	500
2. **Beaver Mountain,** Logan, UT 84321	(801)753-0921	1600	16	25	35	40	11880	350
3. **Brianhead,** Cedar City, UT 84720	(801)586-4636	1800	32	20	60	20	7920	300

continued . . .

NAME OF AREA / LOCATION	TELEPHONE #	VERTICAL DROP	NUMBER OF SLOPES	% BEGINNER	% INTERMEDIATE	% EXPERT	LONGEST RUN	ANNUAL SNOWFALL
4. Blue Mountain, Monticello, UT	(801)587-2228	800						
5. Brighton, Brighton, UT 84121	(801)359-3283	1140	25	25	50	25	6500	428
6. Mt. Holly, Beaver, UT 84713	(801)438-5030	900	14				550	
7. Deer Valley, Park City, UT	(801)649-1000	2200	40	13	50	37		300
8. Nordic Valley, Eden, UT 84310	(801)745-3511	1000					5280	
9. Park City, Park City, UT 84060	(801)649-8111	3100	70	17	46	37	18480	300
10. Park West, Park City, UT 84060	(801)649-5555	3000	50	20	45	35	13200	275
11. Parley's Summit Resort, Park City, UT 84060	(801)649-9840	450	15				3500	
12. Powder Mountain, Eden, UT 84310	(801)745-3771	1300	35	10	70	20	15840	500
13. Snowbasin, Ogden, UT	(801)621-2234	2400	40	21	46	33	15840	400
14. Snowbird, Snowbird, UT	(801)742-2222	3100	32	20	30	50	13200	450
15. Snowland, Fairview, UT 84629	(801)427-3827	210	5				3500	
16. Solitude, Salt Lake City, UT	(801)534-1400	1600	34	25	42	33	7100	400
17. Sundance, Provo, UT 84601	(801)225-4100	1800	27	10	50	40	13200	60

WYOMING

NAME OF AREA / LOCATION	TELEPHONE #	VERTICAL DROP	NUMBER OF SLOPES	% BEGINNER	% INTERMEDIATE	% EXPERT	LONGEST RUN	ANNUAL SNOWFALL
1. Antelope Butte, Greybull, WY 82426	(307)765-2806	800	4				2300	
2. Grand Targhee, Alta, WY 83422	(307)353-2304	2200		10	70	20	13200	504
3. Jackson Hole, Teton Village, WY 82025	(307)733-2292	4139	67	10	35	50	39600	396
4. Hogadon, Casper, WY		650					2200	
5. Meadowlark, Worland, WY 82401	(307)366-2409	600	5				3960	
6. Medicine Bow, Centennial, WY 82055	(307)745-5750	600		30	40	30		
7. Pine Creek, Pine Creek Canyon, WY	(307)279-3201	1200	8					
8. Sleeping Giant, Cody, WY 82414	(307)587-4044	500	8				3960	
9. Snow King Mountain, Jackson, WY 83001	(307)733-2851	1571	7				5280	
10. White Pine, Pinedale, WY 82941	(307)367-4121	1000	8					

COLORADO

NAME OF AREA / LOCATION	TELEPHONE #	VERTICAL DROP	NUMBER OF SLOPES	% BEGINNER	% INTERMEDIATE	% EXPERT	LONGEST RUN	ANNUAL SNOWFALL
1. Aspen Highlands, Aspen, CO 81611	(303)925-5300	3800	66	30	40	30	3800	300
2. Aspen Mountain, Aspen, CO 81611	(303)925-1220	3300			25	75	15840	300
3. Berthoud Pass, Idaho Springs, CO 80452	(303)572-8014	972	16	40	40	20	6000	
4. Beaver Creek, Vail, CO 81657	(303)476-5601	3280		25	35	40		350
5. Breckenridge, Breckenridge, CO 80424	(303)453-2368	2390	80	30	45	25	13728	295
6. Buttermilk, Aspen, CO 81611	(303)925-1220	1972		49	32	19	10560	200
7. Copper Mountain, Copper Mountain, CO	(303)668-2882	4900	50	25	50	15	13200	250
8. Crested Butte, Crested Butte, CO 81224	(303)349-2333	2150	40	35	38	27	7920	300
9. Cranor Ski Hill, Gunnison, CO	(303)641-0073	400	4				1800	75
10. Eldora, Nederland, CO 80466	(303)447-8012	1100	20	16	64	20	5280	150
11. Geneva Basin, Grant, CO 80448	(303)674-4666	1250	16	25	45	30	5280	
12. Hesperus Family Ski, Durango, CO 81301	(303)385-4555	600	8				3500	
13. Hidden Valley, Estes Park, CO 80517	(303)586-4887	2000	14	30	30	40	7920	
14. Keystone/Arapahoe Basin, Keystone, CO	(303)468-2316	1670	22	10	50	40	15840	450
15. Keystone Mountain, Keystone, CO	(303)468-2316	2340		20	65	15	15840	200
16. Loveland, Georgetown, CO 80444	(303)569-2288	1430	50	25	50	25	7920	275
17. Monarch, Garfield, CO 83205	(303)539-3573	1000	25	20	52	28	9240	350

continued . . .

NAME OF AREA	LOCATION	TELEPHONE #	VERTICAL DROP	NUMBER OF SLOPES	% BEGINNER	% INTERMEDIATE	% EXPERT	LONGEST RUN	ANNUAL SNOWFALL
18. Pike's Peak,	Colorado Springs, CO 81416	(303)684-9968	1000		75	20	5	5280	
19. Powderhorn,	Grand Junction, CO 81501	(303)268-5482	1600	22	17	56	27	10560	
20. Purgatory,	Durango, CO 81301	(303)247-9000	1600	45	25	50	25	10560	300
21. Sharktooth,	Greeley, CO 80631	(303)353-2565	150	3				1000	
22. Ski Broadmoor,	Colorado Springs, CO	(303)634-7711	600		60	20	20	3960	
23. Ski Cooper,	Leadville, CO 80461	(303)486-2277	1200	21	40	50	10	7920	250
24. Ski Idlewild,	Winter Park, CO 80482	(303)726-5564	400	8	60	40		3000	
25. Ski San Isabel,	Wetmore, CO 81226	(303)784-6004	200	4	60	40		2640	
26. Snowmass,	Aspen, CO 81611	(303)923-2085	3600	12	10	67	23	18480	300
27. Steamboat,	Steamboat Springs, CO 80477	(303)879-6111	3600	62	23	49	28	13200	325
28. Stoner,	Cortez, CO 81321	(303)882-4437	1250	5	10	40	50	7800	
29. Sunlight,	Glenwood Springs, CO 81601	(303)945-7491	1850	22	24	48	18	13200	
30. Tamarron,	Durango, CO 81301	(303)247-8801	100	1	100			560	
31. St. Mary's Glacier,	Idaho Springs, CO	(303)567-2865						3960	
32. Telluride,	Telluride, CO 81435	(303)728-3856	3105	37	15	50	35	15050	340
33. Vail,	Vail, CO 81657	(303)476-5601	3050	89	30	40	30	23760	378
34. Winter Park,	Winter Park, CO 80482	(303)726-5514	2125	52	24	39	37	10560	250
35. Wolf Creek,	Pagosa Springs, CO 81147	(303)968-2533	1125	21	35	45	20	6864	435

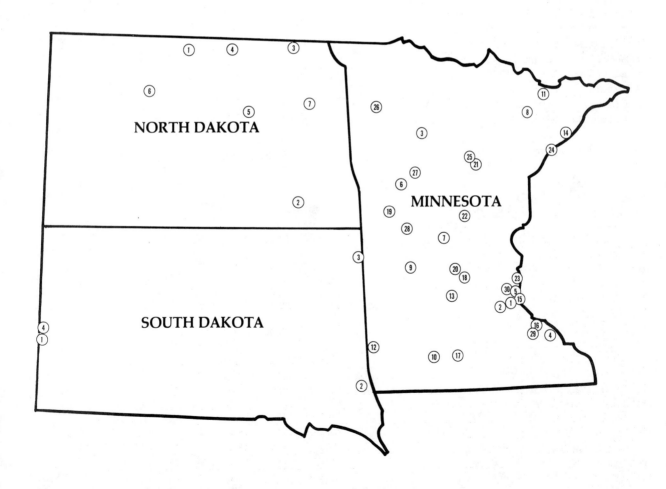

NORTH DAKOTA

NAME OF AREA / LOCATION	TELEPHONE #	VERTICAL DROP	NUMBER OF SLOPES	% BEGINNER	% INTERMEDIATE	% EXPERT	LONGEST RUN'	ANNUAL SNOWFALL"
1. **Bottineau,** Bottineau, ND 58318	(701)263-4556	200	8				1200	
2. **Ft. Ransom,** Ft. Ransom, ND 58033	(701)973-2711	300	6				2640	
3. **Frostfire,** Walhalla, ND 58282	(701)549-3600	350	6				2600	
4. **Rolla View,** Rolla View, ND	(701)477-5389	140	3				1200	
5. **Skyline Skiway,** Devils Lake, ND 58801	(701)766-4479	310	5				1750	
6. **Trestle Valley,** Minot, ND 58701	(701)839-5321	195	10				1400	
7. **Villa Vista,** Grand Forks, ND 58201	(701)594-4234	100	4				900	

SOUTH DAKOTA

NAME OF AREA / LOCATION	TELEPHONE #	VERTICAL DROP	NUMBER OF SLOPES	% BEGINNER	% INTERMEDIATE	% EXPERT	LONGEST RUN'	ANNUAL SNOWFALL"
1. **Deer Mountain,** Lead, SD 57732	(605)584-3230	600	25				5000	
2. **Great Bear,** Sioux Falls, SD	(605)338-1351	250	12				1500	
3. **Inkpa-Du-Ta,** Big Stone City, SD 57216	(612)839-3315	140	5	20	60	20	1000	
4. **Terry Peak,** Lead, SD 57754	(605)584-2165	1200	21	25	55	20	5200	150

MINNESOTA

NAME OF AREA / LOCATION	TELEPHONE #	VERTICAL DROP	NUMBER OF SLOPES	% BEGINNER	% INTERMEDIATE	% EXPERT	LONGEST RUN'	ANNUAL SNOWFALL"
1. **Afton Alps,** Hastings, MN 55033	(612)436-5245	330	32	20	60	20	3000	
2. **Buck Hill,** Burnsville, MN 55377	(612)435-7187	304	12	40	45	15	3000	42
3. **Buena Vista,** Bemidji, MN 56601	(218)243-2233	200	12				1600	
4. **Coffee Mill,** Wabasha, MN 55981	(612)565-4561	500					4000	
5. **Como Park,** St. Paul, MN	(612)489-1804							
6. **Detroit Mountain,** Detroit Lakes, MN 56501	(218)847-4703	235	13				2400	
7. **Eagle Mt.,** Grey Eagle, MN 56336	(612)285-4567	200	11				2000	
8. **Giants Ridge,** Biwabik, MN 55708	(218)865-6315	440	9				3800	
9. **Glenhaven,** Glenwood, MN 56334	(612)634-9912	150	7				950	
10. **Golden Gate,** Sleepy Eye, MN 56085	(507)794-6586	135	5	50	50		1350	
11. **Hidden Valley,** Ely, MN 55731	(218)365-3097	165	5				1800	
12. **Hole-In-The-Mountain,** Lake Benton, MN 56149	(507)368-9350	175	3				1400	
13. **Hyland Hills,** Bloomington, MN 55420	(612)835-4604	175	17	60	30	10	2000	50
14. **Lutsen,** Lutsen, MN 55612	(218)663-7281	650	20				7500	
15. **Marthaler,** West St. Paul, MN 55118	(612)455-9937	300	2				1000	
16. **Mt. Frontenac,** Red Wing, MN 55066	(612)388-5826	420	10				5280	
17. **Mt. Kato,** Mankato, MN 56001	(507)625-3363	240	14				5800	
18. **Mt. Wirth,** Minneapolis, MN	(612)522-4584	200	5	100			300	
19. **Old Smokey,** Fergus Falls, MN 56537	(218)736-2251	110	4				600	
20. **Powder Ridge,** Kimball, MN 55353	(612)398-7200	310	9				2600	
21. **Quadna Mountain,** Hill City, MN 55748	(218)697-2324	350	15				2640	
22. **Ski Gull,** Brainerd, MN 56401	(218)963-4353	285	12				1700	
23. **Snowcrest/Birch Park,** Stillwater, MN 55082	(612)439-2428	280	35				5280	
24. **Spirit Mountain Recreation Area,** Duluth, MN	(218)628-2891	610	14	25	50	25	3800	100
25. **Sugar Hills,** Grand Rapids, MN 55744	(218)326-9461	400	25	20	50	30	5000	85
26. **Timberlane,** Red Lake Falls, MN 56750		110	7				1200	
27. **Val Chatel,** Park Rapids, MN 56470	(218)266-3306	275	11				2200	
28. **Viking Valley,** Ashby, MN 56309	(218)747-2542		7				2200	
29. **Welch Village,** Welch, MN 55089	(612)222-7079	350	30	31	50	19	4000	50
30. **Wild Mountain,** Taylors Falls, MN 55084	(612)465-6365	300	14	30	40	30	4500	50

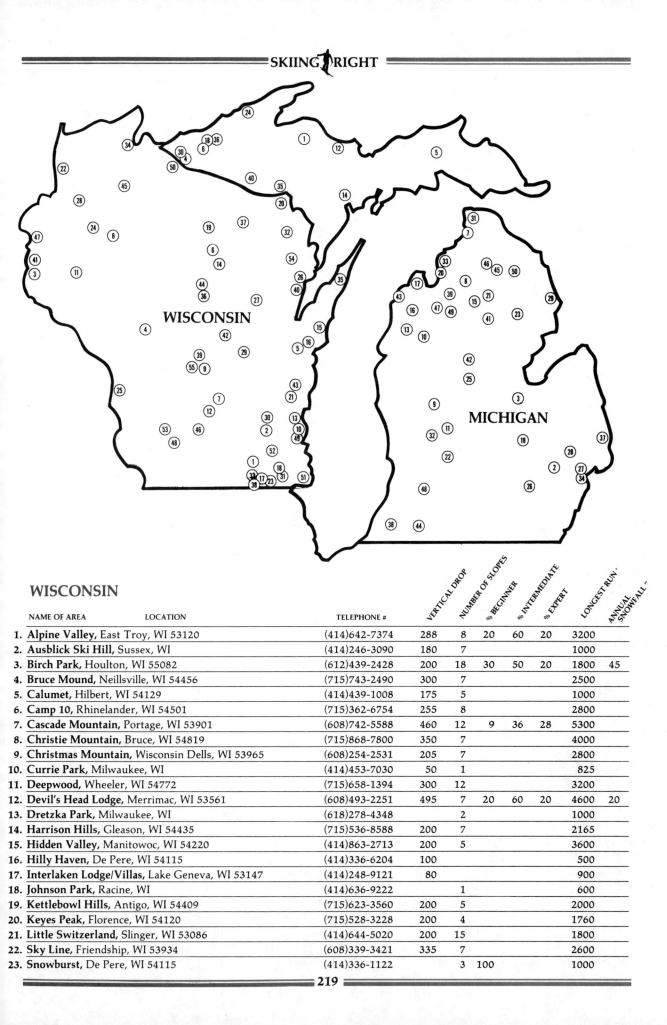

WISCONSIN

NAME OF AREA LOCATION	TELEPHONE #	VERTICAL DROP	NUMBER OF SLOPES	% BEGINNER	% INTERMEDIATE	% EXPERT	LONGEST RUN*	ANNUAL SNOWFALL**
1. **Alpine Valley,** East Troy, WI 53120	(414)642-7374	288	8	20	60	20	3200	
2. **Ausblick Ski Hill,** Sussex, WI	(414)246-3090	180	7				1000	
3. **Birch Park,** Houlton, WI 55082	(612)439-2428	200	18	30	50	20	1800	45
4. **Bruce Mound,** Neillsville, WI 54456	(715)743-2490	300	7				2500	
5. **Calumet,** Hilbert, WI 54129	(414)439-1008	175	5				1000	
6. **Camp 10,** Rhinelander, WI 54501	(715)362-6754	255	8				2800	
7. **Cascade Mountain,** Portage, WI 53901	(608)742-5588	460	12	9	36	28	5300	
8. **Christie Mountain,** Bruce, WI 54819	(715)868-7800	350	7				4000	
9. **Christmas Mountain,** Wisconsin Dells, WI 53965	(608)254-2531	205	7				2800	
10. **Currie Park,** Milwaukee, WI	(414)453-7030	50	1				825	
11. **Deepwood,** Wheeler, WI 54772	(715)658-1394	300	12				3200	
12. **Devil's Head Lodge,** Merrimac, WI 53561	(608)493-2251	495	7	20	60	20	4600	20
13. **Dretzka Park,** Milwaukee, WI	(618)278-4348		2				1000	
14. **Harrison Hills,** Gleason, WI 54435	(715)536-8588	200	7				2165	
15. **Hidden Valley,** Manitowoc, WI 54220	(414)863-2713	200	5				3600	
16. **Hilly Haven,** De Pere, WI 54115	(414)336-6204	100					500	
17. **Interlaken Lodge/Villas,** Lake Geneva, WI 53147	(414)248-9121	80					900	
18. **Johnson Park,** Racine, WI	(414)636-9222		1				600	
19. **Kettlebowl Hills,** Antigo, WI 54409	(715)623-3560	200	5				2000	
20. **Keyes Peak,** Florence, WI 54120	(715)528-3228	200	4				1760	
21. **Little Switzerland,** Slinger, WI 53086	(414)644-5020	200	15				1800	
22. **Sky Line,** Friendship, WI 53934	(608)339-3421	335	7				2600	
23. **Snowburst,** De Pere, WI 54115	(414)336-1122		3	100			1000	

continued . . .

NAME OF AREA / LOCATION	TELEPHONE #	VERTICAL DROP	NUMBER OF SLOPES	% BEGINNER	% INTERMEDIATE	% EXPERT	LONGEST RUN	ANNUAL SNOWFALL
24. Snowcrest, Somerset, WI 54025	(612)439-2427	290	18	25	50	25	3800	60
25. Standing Rocks, Stevens Point, WI 54481	(715)824-3949	100	5				1200	
26. Sunburst, Kewaskum, WI 53040	(414)626-4605	214	8				3000	
27. Sylvan Hill Park, Wausau, WI 54401	(715)842-0471	120	4				1800	
28. Telemark, Cable, WI 54821	(715)798-3811	370	10	40	40	20	1300	70
29. Timberline, Arena, WI 53503	(608)753-2315	390	7				2200	
30. Trollhaugen, Dresser, WI 54009	(715)755-2955	256	16				2600	
31. Tyrol Ski Basin, Mount Horeb, WI 53572	(608)437-3076	280	10				3600	
32. Whitecap Mountain, Montreal, WI 54550	(715)561-2227	400	29	25	50	25	5280	200
33. Whitnall Park, Milwaukee, WI	(414)425-1132	65	1				1100	
34. Wilmot Mountain, Wilmot, WI 53192	(414)862-2301	230	20	30	30	40	2500	
35. Wintergreen, Spring Green, WI 53588	(608)588-2124	400	9				4100	
36. Winter Haven, Delafield, WI 53018	(414)646-8418	188	7				1400	
37. Winterset, Crivitz, WI 54114	(715)854-7935	200	6				1800	
38. Woodside Ranch, Mauston, WI 53948	(608)847-4275	100	1	100			1200	
39. Mont Du Lac, Superior, WI 54880	(715)636-9991	300	7				2400	
40. Mt. Fuji, Lake Geneva, WI 53147	(414)248-6553	235	11				2700	
41. Mt. Hardscrabble, Rice Lake, WI 54868	(715)234-3412	350	8				4000	
42. Mt. La Crosse, La Crosse, WI 54601	(608)788-0044	516	13	20	50	30	5300	50
43. Mt. Le'Bett, Coleman, WI 54112	(414)897-2290	300	10				1500	
44. Navarino, Shiocton, WI 54170	(715)758-2211	106	11				1200	
45. Nest of Eagles, Spooner, WI 54801	(715)635-8447	160	3				1500	
46. Nordic Mountain, Wild Rose, WI 54984	(414)787-3324	240	7	15	50	35	3700	100
47. Olympia, Oconomowoc, WI 53066	(414)567-0311	196	10				2800	
48. Paradise Valley, Burlington, WI 53105	(414)763-5121	192	2				1750	
49. Paul Bunyan, Lakewood, WI 54138	(715)276-7143	150	6				1200	
50. Playboy, Lake Geneva, WI 53147	(414)248-8811	211		20	60	20	1320	46
51. Port Mountain, Bayfield, WI 54814	(715)779-3227	317	13				3200	
52. Potawatomi Park, Sturgeon Bay, WI 54235	(414)743-5123	120	2				500	
53. Rib Mountain, Wausau, WI 54401	(715)845-2846	600	8	25	50	25	3800	60
54. Sheltered Valley, Three Lakes, WI 54562	(715)546-3535	220	11				1600	
55. Ski Majestic, Lake Geneva, WI 52147	(414)248-6128	235	14				1400	

MICHIGAN

NAME OF AREA / LOCATION	TELEPHONE #	VERTICAL DROP	NUMBER OF SLOPES	% BEGINNER	% INTERMEDIATE	% EXPERT	LONGEST RUN	ANNUAL SNOWFALL
1. Al Quaal Recreation Area, Ishpeming, MI 49849	(906)486-6181	1000	3	50	50		1000	
2. Alpine Valley, Milford, MI 48042	(313)887-4183	250	17	30	40	30	1800	50
3. Apple Mountain, Freeland, MI 48623	(517)781-0170	200					1000	
4. Big Powderhorn Mountain, Bessemer, MI 49911	(906)932-4838	600	18	15	65	20	5280	200
5. Big Valley, Newbury, MI	(906)293-8785	140	2				800	
6. Blackjack, Bessemer, MI 49911	(906)229-5115	465	14	20	55	25	5280	180
7. Boyne Highlands, Harbor Springs, MI 48740	(616)526-2171	505		30	35	35	5200	150
8. Boyne Mountain, Boyne Falls, MI 49713	(616)549-2441	450	13	20	40	40	3960	145
9. Brady's Hills, Lakeview, MI	(517)352-7920		12					
10. Caberfae, Cadillac, MI 49601	(616)862-3301	350	36	30	50	20	5280	145
11. Cannonsburg, Cannonsburg, MI 49317	(616)874-6711	250		25	60	15	1800	68
12. Cliffs Ridge, Marquette, MI 49855	(906)225-1155	600	13	25	50	25	6600	150
13. Crystal Mountain, Thompsonville, MI 49683	(616)378-2911	375	20	25	45	30	2640	134
14. Gladstone Sports Park, Gladstone, MI 49837	(906)428-9130	110	4				1000	
15. Hanson, Grayling, MI 49738	(517)348-9266	3200	7				2500	
16. Hickory Hills, Traverse City, MI 49684	(616)947-8566	356	6				1800	

continued . . .

NAME OF AREA	LOCATION	TELEPHONE #	VERTICAL DROP	NUMBER OF SLOPES	% BEGINNER	% INTERMEDIATE	% EXPERT	LONGEST RUN	ANNUAL SNOWFALL
17. Hilton Shanty Creek,	Bellaire, MI 49615	(616)533-8621	227	16	20	60	20	5000	140
18. Indianhead Mountain,	Wakefield, MI 49968	(906)229-5181	638	15	25	50	25	5280	200
19. Kandahar Ski Club,	Fenton, MI 48430	(313)629-9109	260	10				2640	
20. Maplehurst,	Kewadin, MI 49648	(616)264-9675	250	10				2500	
21. Michawaye Slopes,	Gaylord, MI 49735	(517)939-8800	215	9				1200	
22. Middleville,	Middleville, MI 49333	(616)795-9872		8				1000	
23. Mio Mountain,	Ferndale, MI 48220	(517)826-5569	250	13				1500	
24. Mont Ripley,	Houghton, MI 49931	(906)487-2340	420					2200	
25. Mott Mountain,	Farwell, MI 48622	(517)588-2945	200	8				1800	
26. Mt. Brighton,	Brighton, MI 48116	(313)229-9581	230	19	30	45	25	1500	60
27. Mt. Grampian,	Oxford, MI 48051	(313)628-2450	200	12				1000	
28. Mt. Holly,	Holly, MI 48442	(313)634-8269	327	10				1800	
29. Mt. Maria,	Spruce, MI 48762	(517)736-8377	285	5				4500	
30. Mt. Zion,	Ironwood, MI 49938	(906)932-3718	300					3960	
31. Nub's Nob,	Harbor Springs, MI 49740	(616)526-2131	425	21	30	40	30	3960	120
32. Pando,	Rockford, MI 49231	(616)874-8343	125	7	34	33	33	1000	
33. Petoskey Winter Sports Park,	Petoskey, MI 49770	(616)347-4105			30	70			
34. Pine Knob,	Clarkston, MI 48016	(313)625-0800	300	14				3500	
35. Pine Mountain,	Iron Mountain, MI 49801	(906)774-2747	400	12	20	60	20	3600	80
36. Porcupine Mts. State Park,	Ontonagon, MI	(906)885-5798	544	10				5280	
37. Riverview Highlands,	Riverview, MI 48192	(313)479-2266	130	6				1000	
38. Royal Valley,	Buchanan, MI 49107	(616)695-3847	210	14	20	45	35	1800	120
39. Schuss Mountain,	Mancelona, MI 49659	(616)587-9162	400	13	25	40	35	4800	200
40. Ski Brule Mtn., Ski Homestead,	Iron River, MI 49835	(906)265-4957	420	10	30	40	30	5300	130
41. Skyline,	Grayling, MI 49738	(517)275-5445	210	10				2600	
42. Snowsnake Mountain,	Harrison, MI 48625	(517)539-6583	200	18				1800	
43. Sugar Loaf Mountain Resort,	Cedar, MI 49621	(616)228-5461	610	23	20	45	35	5300	180
44. Swiss Valley,	Jones, MI 49061	(616)244-5635	210	11				1800	
45. Sylvan Knob,	Gaylord, MI 49735	(517)732-4733	250	16				2600	
46. Thunder Mountain,	Boyne Falls, MI 49713	(616)549-2441	410	9				3000	
47. Timberlee,	Traverse City, MI 49684	(616)946-4444	385	16	25	50	25	4180	
48. Timber Ridge,	Kalamazoo, MI	(616)694-9449	240	11	40	40	20	2000	
49. Traverse City Holiday,	Traverse City, MI 49684	(616)938-1360	260	12					
50. Tyrolean Ski Resort,	Gaylord, MI 49735	(517)732-2743	270	12				2500	

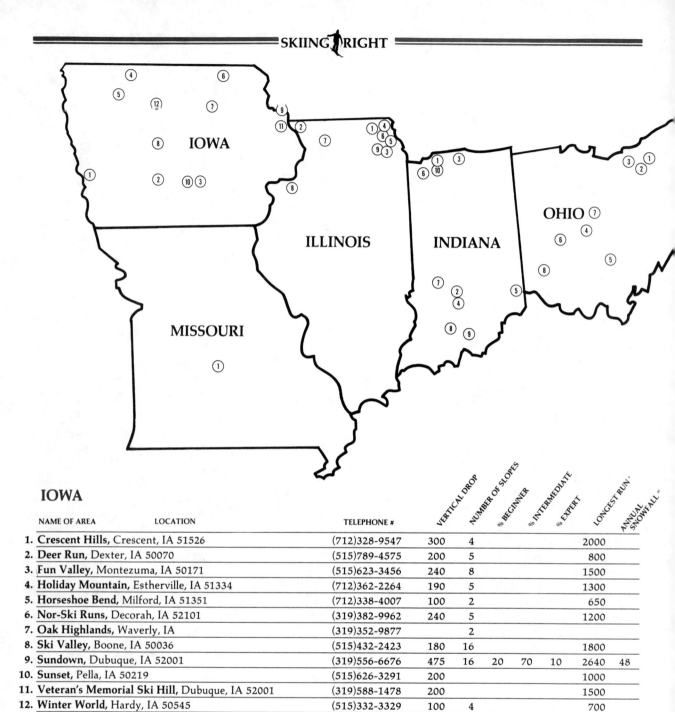

IOWA

NAME OF AREA / LOCATION	TELEPHONE #	VERTICAL DROP	NUMBER OF SLOPES	% BEGINNER	% INTERMEDIATE	% EXPERT	LONGEST RUN	ANNUAL SNOWFALL
1. **Crescent Hills**, Crescent, IA 51526	(712)328-9547	300	4				2000	
2. **Deer Run**, Dexter, IA 50070	(515)789-4575	200	5				800	
3. **Fun Valley**, Montezuma, IA 50171	(515)623-3456	240	8				1500	
4. **Holiday Mountain**, Estherville, IA 51334	(712)362-2264	190	5				1300	
5. **Horseshoe Bend**, Milford, IA 51351	(712)338-4007	100	2				650	
6. **Nor-Ski Runs**, Decorah, IA 52101	(319)382-9962	240	5				1200	
7. **Oak Highlands**, Waverly, IA	(319)352-9877		2					
8. **Ski Valley**, Boone, IA 50036	(515)432-2423	180	16				1800	
9. **Sundown**, Dubuque, IA 52001	(319)556-6676	475	16	20	70	10	2640	48
10. **Sunset**, Pella, IA 50219	(515)626-3291	200					1000	
11. **Veteran's Memorial Ski Hill**, Dubuque, IA 52001	(319)588-1478	200					1500	
12. **Winter World**, Hardy, IA 50545	(515)332-3329	100	4				700	

ILLINOIS

NAME OF AREA / LOCATION	TELEPHONE #	VERTICAL DROP	NUMBER OF SLOPES	% BEGINNER	% INTERMEDIATE	% EXPERT	LONGEST RUN	ANNUAL SNOWFALL
1. **Buffalo Mountain**, Algonquin, IL 60102	(312)426-7328	200	4				1000	
2. **Chestnut Mountain Resort**, Galena, IL 61036	(815)777-1320	465	14				3200	
3. **Four Lakes**, Lisle, IL 60532	(312)964-2550	130		20	80		1100	
4. **Holiday Park**, Ingleside, IL 60041	(312)546-8222	208	6				1400	
5. **James Park**, Evanston, IL	(312)869-9449	300	1				300	
6. **Marriott's Lincolnshire**, Lincolnshire, IL 60015	(312)634-0100	50	1	100				
7. **Plumtree**, Shannon, IL 61078	(815)493-2881	185		50	40	10		
8. **Snowstar**, Taylor Ridge, IL	(309)795-1600	200	3				1100	
9. **Villa Olivia**, Bartlett, IL 60103	(312)742-5200	125	12				800	

MISSOURI

NAME OF AREA LOCATION	TELEPHONE #	VERTICAL DROP	NUMBER OF SLOPES	% BEGINNER	% INTERMEDIATE	% EXPERT	LONGEST RUN'	ANNUAL SNOWFALL"
1. Marriott's Tan-Tar-A Res., Osage Beach, MO 65065	(314)348-3131 X266						1200	

INDIANA

NAME OF AREA LOCATION	TELEPHONE #	VERTICAL DROP	NUMBER OF SLOPES	% BEGINNER	% INTERMEDIATE	% EXPERT	LONGEST RUN'	ANNUAL SNOWFALL"
1. Bendix Woods County Park, New Carlisle, IN 46552	(219)654-3155	100	4				1000	
2. Long Mountain, Nashville, IN	(812)822-4708		5	60	40			
3. Mt. Wawasee, New Paris, IN 46563	(219)831-4112	190	9				1500	
4. Nashville Alps, Nashville, IN	(812)988-6638	240	6				2000	
5. Perfect North Slopes, Lawrenceburg, IN								
6. Pines, Valparaiso, IN 46383	(219)462-4179	170	8				1320	
7. Pleasant Run, Greencastle, IN 46552	(317)653-5994	135	8	35	65		900	
8. Ski Paoli Peaks, Paoli, IN 47454	(812)723-4696	300	9				3300	
9. Ski Starlite, Sellersburg, IN 47130	(812)246-5471	587	20	11	65	24	7000	
10. Ski Valley, La Porte, IN 46350	(219)362-1212	120	5				800	

OHIO

NAME OF AREA LOCATION	TELEPHONE #	VERTICAL DROP	NUMBER OF SLOPES	% BEGINNER	% INTERMEDIATE	% EXPERT	LONGEST RUN'	ANNUAL SNOWFALL"
1. Alpine Valley, Chesterfield, OH	(216)285-2211	250					1600	
2. Boston Mills, Peninsula, OH 44264	(216)467-2242	240	7	50	40	10	1600	53
3. Brandywine, Northfield, OH 44067	(216)467-8197	241	12	50	40	10	2000	
4. Clear Fork, Butler, OH 44822	(419)883-2000	300	7	30	40	30	5280	55
5. Echo Hills, Logan, OH 43138	(614)384-8760	310	5				2250	
6. Mad River Mountain, Bellefontaine, OH 43311	(513)599-1015	300	8				3000	
7. Snow Trails, Mansfield, OH	(419)522-7393	300		20	70	10	2000	39
8. Sugar Creek Ski Hills, Bellbrook, OH 45305	(513)848-6211	200	5	20	60	20	1600	

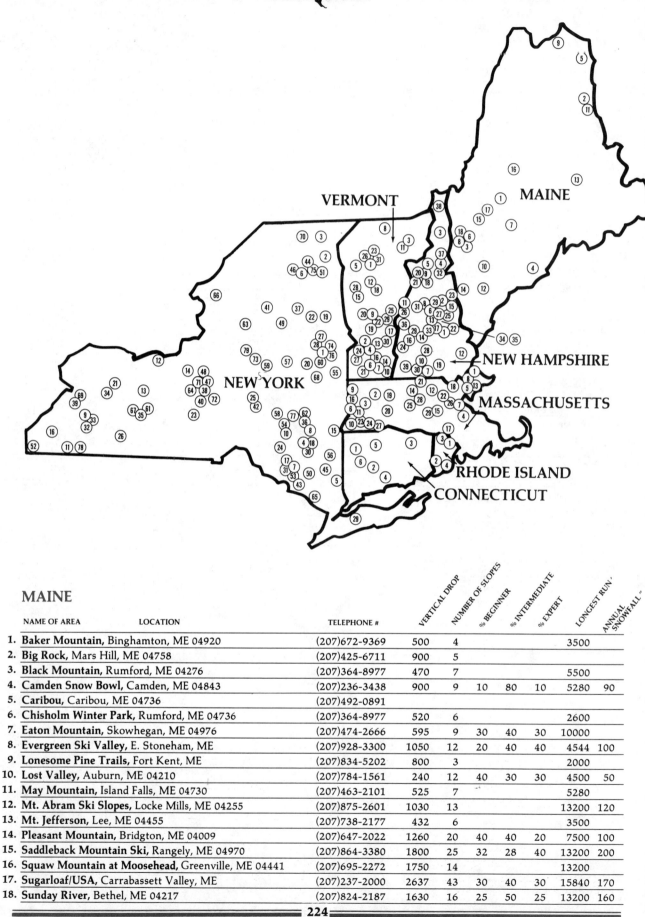

MAINE

NAME OF AREA	LOCATION	TELEPHONE #	VERTICAL DROP	NUMBER OF SLOPES	% BEGINNER	% INTERMEDIATE	% EXPERT	LONGEST RUN'	ANNUAL SNOWFALL'
1. Baker Mountain,	Binghamton, ME 04920	(207)672-9369	500	4				3500	
2. Big Rock,	Mars Hill, ME 04758	(207)425-6711	900	5					
3. Black Mountain,	Rumford, ME 04276	(207)364-8977	470	7				5500	
4. Camden Snow Bowl,	Camden, ME 04843	(207)236-3438	900	9	10	80	10	5280	90
5. Caribou,	Caribou, ME 04736	(207)492-0891							
6. Chisholm Winter Park,	Rumford, ME 04736	(207)364-8977	520	6				2600	
7. Eaton Mountain,	Skowhegan, ME 04976	(207)474-2666	595	9	30	40	30	10000	
8. Evergreen Ski Valley,	E. Stoneham, ME	(207)928-3300	1050	12	20	40	40	4544	100
9. Lonesome Pine Trails,	Fort Kent, ME	(207)834-5202	800	3				2000	
10. Lost Valley,	Auburn, ME 04210	(207)784-1561	240	12	40	30	30	4500	50
11. May Mountain,	Island Falls, ME 04730	(207)463-2101	525	7				5280	
12. Mt. Abram Ski Slopes,	Locke Mills, ME 04255	(207)875-2601	1030	13				13200	120
13. Mt. Jefferson,	Lee, ME 04455	(207)738-2177	432	6				3500	
14. Pleasant Mountain,	Bridgton, ME 04009	(207)647-2022	1260	20	40	40	20	7500	100
15. Saddleback Mountain Ski,	Rangely, ME 04970	(207)864-3380	1800	25	32	28	40	13200	200
16. Squaw Mountain at Moosehead,	Greenville, ME 04441	(207)695-2272	1750	14				13200	
17. Sugarloaf/USA,	Carrabassett Valley, ME	(207)237-2000	2637	43	30	40	30	15840	170
18. Sunday River,	Bethel, ME 04217	(207)824-2187	1630	16	25	50	25	13200	160

NEW HAMPSHIRE

NAME OF AREA, LOCATION	TELEPHONE #	VERTICAL DROP	NUMBER OF SLOPES	% BEGINNER	% INTERMEDIATE	% EXPERT	LONGEST RUN	ANNUAL SNOWFALL
1. Alpine Ridge, Laconia, NH 03246	(603)293-4304	800	10				8900	
2. Attitash, Bartlett, NH 03812	(603)374-2369	1550	20	25	50	25	10000	111
3. Balsams Wilderness, Dixville Notch, NH 03576	(603)255-3400	1000	19		65		10560	
4. Black Mountain, Jackson, NH 03846	(603)383-4490	1200	14				5320	
5. Bretton Woods, Bretton Woods, NH 03575	(603)278-5000	1100	10	33	45	22	6336	180
6. Brickyard Mountain Resort, Laconia, NH	(603)366-4316	420	6				3000	
7. Brookline, Brookline, NH 03033	(603)673-9892	600	12				1800	
8. Campton Mountain, Campton, NH 03223	(603)726-3082	400	3				3000	
9. Cannon Mountain, Franconia, NH 03580	(603)823-5563	2022	24	30	45	25	6500	156
10. Crotched Mountain, Francestown, NH 03043	(603)588-6345	900	25				5940	
11. Dartmouth Skiway, Lyme Center, NH 03769	(603)795-2143	900	12				5000	
12. Eastman Pond, Grantham, NH 03753	(603)863-4240	247	3				3000	
13. Gunstock, Laconia, NH 03246	(603)293-4341	1300	19	25	50	25	10500	100
14. Highland, Northfield, NH 03276	(603)286-4055	700	12				8300	
15. King Pine, East Madison, NH	(603)367-8897	350	12				3100	
16. King's Grant, Laconia, NH	(603)293-4431	100	5	100			3960	
17. King Ridge, New London, NH 03257	(603)526-6966	800	15	55	28	17	5000	90
18. Loon Mountain, Lincoln, NH 03251	(603)745-8111	1850	24	20	60	20	12000	125
19. McIntyre, Manchester, NH	(603)669-7931	169	3				1100	
20. Mittersill, Franconia, NH 03580	(603)823-5511	1600	17				5280	
21. Monteau, Haverhill, NH 03765	(603)787-2781	600	3	25	50	25	13200	
22. Moose Mountain, Brookfield, NH 03872	(603)522-3639	1220	3				5280	
23. Mt. Cranmore Skimobile, North Conway, NH 03860	(603)356-5544	1500	16	20	60	20	12000	100
24. Mt. Sunapee, Mt. Sunapee, NH 03772	(603)763-2356	1500	20				7920	
25. Mt. Whittier, West Ossipee, NH 03890	(603)539-7740	1900	10				2100	
26. Oak Hill, Hanover, NH 03755	(603)643-2226	300	3	50	50		1300	
27. Ossipee Mountain, Moultonboro, NH 03254	(603)476-8491	370	5				2640	
28. Pats Peak, Henniker, NH 03242	(603)428-3245	710	14	37	39	24	3960	102
29. Ragged Mountain, Danbury, NH 03230	(603)768-3971	1225	19				7500	
30. Temple Mountain, Peterborough, NH 03458	(603)924-6949	550	12				2200	
31. Tenney Mountain, Plymouth, NH 03264	(603)536-1717	1300	2				7920	
32. Tyrol, Jackson, NH 03846	(603)383-4315	1000	14				5280	
33. Veteran's Memorial, West Franklin, NH 03223	(603)934-3539	760	5					
34. Waterville Valley-Snow's Mtn., Waterville, Val., NH	(603)236-8391	583	3				4000	
35. Waterville Valley-Mt. Tecumseh, Waterville Val., NH	(603)236-8311	2020	33	30	40	30	15840	149
36. Whaleback, Lebanon, NH 03766	(603)448-2607	700	9				5280	
37. Wildcat Mountain, Jackson, NH 03846	(603)466-3326	2100	16	20	45	35	14520	174
38. Wilderness, Dixville Notch, NH 03576	(603)255-3400	1000	14				900	
39. Woodbound Inn, Jaffrey, NH 03452	(603)532-8341	600	2					

VERMONT

NAME OF AREA, LOCATION	TELEPHONE #	VERTICAL DROP	NUMBER OF SLOPES	% BEGINNER	% INTERMEDIATE	% EXPERT	LONGEST RUN	ANNUAL SNOWFALL
1. Bolton Valley, Bolton, VT 05676	(802)434-2131	1100	25	20	60	20	9000	275
2. Bromley Mountain, Manchester Center, VT 05255	(802)824-5522	1334	25	26	50	24	13200	150
3. Burke Mountain, East Burke, VT 05832	(802)626-3305	2000	27	38	38	24	18480	170
4. Carinthia, West Dover, VT 05356	(802)464-5461	800	8				4000	
5. Cochran, Richmond, VT 05477	(802)434-2479	500	9		66		3000	
6. Haystack, Wilmington, VT 05363	(802)464-5321	1400	24				10560	
7. Hogback Mountain, Marlboro, VT	(802)672-5152	1400	23				10560	
8. Jay Peak, Jay, VT 05859	(802)988-2611	2153	30	20	55	25	13200	275
9. Killington, Killington, VT 05751	(802)422-3333	3060	75	42	24	34	26400	300

continued . . .

NAME OF AREA / LOCATION	TELEPHONE #	VERTICAL DROP	NUMBER OF SLOPES	% BEGINNER	% INTERMEDIATE	% EXPERT	LONGEST RUN	ANNUAL SNOWFALL
10. Living Memorial Park, Brattleboro, VT 05301	(802)254-5808	204	1	100			1195	
11. Mad River Glen, Waitsfield, VT 05675	(802)496-3551	2000	25	20	40	40	18480	120
12. Magic Mountain, Londonderry, VT 05148	(802)824-5566	1600	27	25	50	25	13200	150
13. Maple Valley, West Dummerston, VT 05357	(802)254-6083	900	12				8000	
14. Middlebury College Snow Bowl, Middlebury, VT 05753	(802)388-4356	1100	13				6500	
15. Mount Snow, Mount Snow, VT 05356	(802)464-3333	1680	51	18	72	10	13200	200
16. Mt. Ascutney, Brownsville, VT 05037	(802)484-7711	1480	28	30	40	30	13200	100
17. Norwich University, Northfield, VT 05663	(802)485-9312	902	13				6864	
18. Okemo Mountain, Ludlow, VT 05149	(802)288-4041	2100	30	30	50	20	23760	126
19. Pico, Rutland, VT 05701	(802)775-4345	1967		20	60	20	13200	200
20. Prospect Ski Mountain, Bennington, VT 05201	(802)442-2575	700	14				5280	
21. Round Top, Plymouth, VT 05056	(802)672-5152	1300	14	30	35	35	8730	130
22. Smuggler's Notch, Jeffersonville, VT 05148	(802)644-8851	2610	36	25	41	34	18480	260
23. Snow Valley, Londonderry, VT 05148	(802)297-1000	900	10				5280	
24. Sonnenberg, Barnard, VT 05031	(802)234-9874	500	6				3500	
25. Stowe, Stowe, VT 05672	(802)253-7311	2150	35	10	70	15	23760	250
26. Stratton Mountain, Stratton Mountain, VT 05155	(802)297-2200	1900	51	47	28	25	22000	160
27. Sugarbush Valley, Warren, VT 05674	(802)583-2381	2600	73	24	45	31	13200	252
28. Suicide Six, Woodstock, VT 05091	(802)457-1666	650	18	30	40	30	5700	80
29. Timber Ridge, Windham, VT 05379	(802)824-6806	800	10				10560	
30. Underhill Ski Bowl, Underhill Center, VT 05490	(802)899-4677	150	7		100		3000	

NEW YORK

NAME OF AREA / LOCATION	TELEPHONE #	VERTICAL DROP	NUMBER OF SLOPES	% BEGINNER	% INTERMEDIATE	% EXPERT	LONGEST RUN	ANNUAL SNOWFALL
1. Adirondack, Porter Corners, NY 12859	(518)893-9484	1000	10				13200	
2. Bald Hill, Farmington, NY 11727	(516)732-4011	120	10					
3. Bassett Mountain, Jay, NY	(518)946-2272	730	15	40	50	10	2000	
4. Beartown, West Chazy, NY 12992	(518)563-2975	125	10					
5. Belleayre Mountain, Highmont, NY 12441	(914)254-5601	1265	30	24	59	17	10050	125
6. Big Birch, Patterson, NY 12563	(914)878-3181	500	16	40	30	30	5000	
7. Big Tupper, Tupper Lake, NY 12986	(518)359-3651	1152	26	60	30	10	9240	128
8. Big Vanilla, Woodridge, NY 12789	(914)434-5321	500	21				3900	
9. Blackhead Mountain, Round Top, NY 12473	(518)622-3157	110	2					
10. Bluemont, Yorkshire, NY 14173	(716)496-6041	800	12				6600	
11. Bobcat, Andes, NY 13731	(914)676-3143	1040	16				6600	
12. Bova, Salamanca, NY 14779	(716)354-2535	200	4				1000	
13. Brantling, Socus, NY 14551	(315)331-2365	240	8				1500	
14. Bristol Mountain, Canandaigua, NY 14424	(716)374-6331	1100	18	30	50	20	6600	90
15. Camillus Ski Association, Camillus, NY 13031	(315)487-2778	125	2				400	
16. Catamount, Hillsdale, NY 12529	(518)325-3200	1000	23	40	40	20	5280	55
17. Cockaigne, Cherry Creek, NY 14723	(716)287-3223	430	11				3100	
18. Concord, Kiamesha Lake, NY 12751	(914)794-4000	400	4	100			1245	
19. Cortina Valley, Haines Falls, NY 12436	(518)589-6500	625	12	20	60	20	5200	70
20. Dynamite Hill, Chesterton, NY 12817	(518)494-2711	80	1					
21. Eagle Mountain, Pettersonville, NY 12137	(518)887-2511	350	15				2400	
22. Frost Ridge, Le Roy, NY 14482	(716)768-9730	140	11				850	
23. Gore Mountain, North Creek, NY 12853	(518)251-2411	2100	30	20	50	30	8100	80
24. Greek Peak, Cortland, NY 13245	(607)835-6111	900	23	22	43	35	7920	110
25. Grossinger Ski Valley, Grossinger, NY 12734	(914)292-5000	190	3				1600	
26. Gunset Ski Bowl, Richfield, NY 13439	(315)858-1140	340	5				1400	
27. Happy Valley, Alfred, NY 14802	(607)587-8825	350	12				3000	

continued . . .

NAME OF AREA, LOCATION	TELEPHONE #	VERTICAL DROP	NUMBER OF SLOPES	% BEGINNER	% INTERMEDIATE	% EXPERT	LONGEST RUN	ANNUAL SNOWFALL
28. Hickory, Warrensburg, NY 12885	(518)623-9866	1200	13				5300	
29. Hidden Valley, Lake Luzurne, NY 12846	(518)696-2431	110	4				1000	
30. Hi Point, Huntington, NY 11743	(516)271-6690	115	3					
31. Highmount, Highmount, NY 12441	(914)254-5265	1050	11				8500	
32. Holiday Mountain, Monticello, NY 12701	(914)796-3161	400	12	30	40	30	3500	50
33. Holiday Valley, Ellicottville, NY 14731	(716)699-2345	750	31	25	50	25	4300	168
34. Holimont, Ellicottville, NY	(716)699-2320	600	15				3000	
35. Honey Hill, Warsaw, NY 14569	(716)786-5793	100	5				1500	
36. Hunt Hollow, Naples, NY	(716)374-5428	815	25	35	40		7920	
37. Hunter Mountain, Hunter, NY 12442	(518)263-4223	1600	37	20	40	40	10000	125
38. Indian Lake, Indian Lake, NY 12842	(518)648-5112	215	3					
39. Ironwood Ridge, Cazenovia, NY 13035	(315)655-9551	500	7				4750	
40. Kissing Ridge, Glenwood, NY 14069	(716)592-4963	500	43	30	50	20	3000	185
41. Labrador, Truxton, NY 13158	(607)842-6204	680	16				4500	
42. McCauley Mountain, Old Forge, NY 13420	(315)369-3225	633	9				3960	
43. Mt. Otsego, Cooperstown, NY 13326	(607)547-5447	425	7				3100	
44. Mt. Peter, Greenwood Lake, NY 10925	(914)986-4992	400	5	50	35	15	2500	35
45. Mt. Pisgah, Saranac Lake, NY 12983	(518)891-1990	300	5				2640	
46. Mt. Storm, Stormville, NY 12582	(914)226-4288	240	3				1450	
47. Mt. Whitney/Lake Placid Center, Lake Placid, NY	(518)523-3361	408	75				3960	
48. Mystic Mountain, New Woodstock, NY 13122	(315)662-3322	600	13				4500	
49. 90 Acres, Fayetteville, NY 13066	(315)637-9023	100	8	100			1500	
50. Oak Mountain, Speculator, NY 12164	(518)548-7311	650	12				6000	
51. Orange County, Montgomery, NY 12549	(914)457-3000	131	1	50	50		1850	
52. Otis Mountain, Elizabethtown, NY 12932	(518)873-6448	375			100			
53. Pines, South Fallsburg, NY 12779	(914)434-6000	270	6				2000	
54. Peak 'N Peak, Clymer, NY 14724	(716)355-4141	400	16	20	60	20	3000	200
55. Plattekill Mountain Ski Bowl, Roxbury, NY 12979	(607)326-7547	1000	14				7400	120
56. Rock Candy Mountain, Speigletown, NY 12180	(518)753-4814	200	4					
57. Rocking Horse, Highland, NY 12528	(914)691-2927	100	3	90	10		1000	
58. Royal Mount, Johnstown, NY 12095	(518)835-6445	550	7					
59. Scotch Valley, Stamford, NY 12167	(607)652-7332	750	12	20	60	20	5000	
60. Shu-Maker Mountain, Little Falls, NY 13365	(315)823-1111	750	13					
61. Ski Maple Ridge, Schenectady, NY 12306	(518)377-5172	225	6					
62. Ski Windham, Windham, NY	(518)734-4300	1550	20	30	45	25	13200	110
63. Ski Valley Club, Naples, NY 14512	(716)374-5157	700	11				7920	
64. Snow Ridge, Turin, NY 13473	(315)348-8456	550	13	20	60	20	2650	200
65. Song Mountain, Tully, NY 13159	(315)696-5711	700	18				5280	
66. Sterling Forest, Tuxedo, NY	(914)351-2163	450	6	20	70	10	3000	36
67. Sun-Burst Mountain, Watertown, NY	(315)782-2890	300	4					
68. Swain, Swain, NY 14884	(315)782-2890	650	10	40	45	15	6000	150
69. Taconic Trails, Petersburgh, NY	(518)658-3600	1606	18				5260	
70. Tamatack, Colden, NY 14033	(716)941-5654	500	10					
71. Titus Mountain, Malone, NY	(518)483-3740	600	11		80		6000	
72. Toggenburg, Fabius, NY 13063	(315)683-5842	600	12	40	40	20	6000	
73. Trainer Hill, Colgate Univ., Hamilton, NY 13346	(315)824-1000	370	4				2500	
74. Val Bialas, Utica, NY	(315)798-3294	380	6				2900	
75. West Mountain, Glens Falls, NY 12801	(518)793-6606	1010	19	15	70	15	8500	65
76. Whiteface Mountain, Wilmington, NY 12997	(518)946-2223	3216		23	33	44	13200	110
77. Willard Mountain, Greenwich, NY 12834	(518)692-7337	505	7				3000	
78. Windham Mountain Club, Windham, NY 12496	(518)734-4300	1500	11				11880	
79. Wing Hollow, Allegheny, NY 14706	(716)372-2288	813					10320	
80. Woods Valley, Westernville, NY 13486	(315)827-4721	500	7					

MASSACHUSETTS

NAME OF AREA, LOCATION	TELEPHONE #	VERTICAL DROP	NUMBER OF SLOPES	% BEGINNER	% INTERMEDIATE	% EXPERT	LONGEST RUN	ANNUAL SNOWFALL
1. Amesbury Ski Tows, Amesbury, MA 01913	(617)388-9205	330	3					
2. Berkshire East, Charlemont, MA 01339	(413)339-6617	1180	23	20	40	40	9800	93
3. Berkshire Snow Basin, W. Cummington, MA 01265	(413)634-8808	550	11				5280	
4. Blue Hills, Milton, MA 02186	(617)828-7490	365	7				3000	
5. Boston Hills, North Andover, MA 01845	(617)683-2733	210	7				2100	
6. Bousquet Ski Area, Pittsfield, MA 01201	(413)442-2436	750	16				7500	83
7. Boxboro Hills, Boxboro, MA 01720	(617)263-9005	130	5				1000	
8. Bradford, Haverhill, MA 01830	(617)373-0071	230	5				1400	
9. Brodie Mountain, New Ashford, MA 01237	(413)443-4752	1250	21	30	50	20	13200	85
10. Butternut Basin, Great Barrington, MA 01230	(413)528-3000	1000	16	15	60	25	7920	70
11. Eastover, Eastover, MA	(413)637-0625		2					
12. Groton Hills, Groton, MA 01450	(617)448-5214	150	7				1000	
13. Hamilton Ski Slopes, Hamilton, MA 01936	(617)468-4804							
14. Hidden Valley, Ashburnham, MA 01430	(617)827-6032	250	6				5280	
15. Jericho Hill, Marlboro, MA 01830	(617)485-9730	120	2				1000	
16. Jiminy Peak, Hancock, MA 01237	(413)738-5431	1140	25	30	30	40	10560	90
17. Klein Innsbruck, Franklin, MA 02038	(617)528-5660	200	5				1500	
18. Merrimac Valley, Methuven, MA 01844	(617)686-2021	200	2					
19. Mt. Mohawk, Shelburne, MA	(413)625-2643	400	11					
20. Mt. Tom, Holyoke, MA 01040	(413)536-0416	680	17	30	60	10	3600	
21. Mt. Watatic, Ashby, MA 01431	(617)386-7921	550	6	10	60	30	3960	85
22. Nashoba Valley, Westford, MA 01886	(617)692-3033	240	8	20	50	30	1500	
23. Oak 'N Spruce Resort, South Lee, MA 01260	(413)243-3500	100	1				1500	
24. Otis Ridge, Otis, MA 01253	(413)269-4444	375	14	25	45	30	4500	
25. Pine Ridge, Barre, MA 01005	(617)355-4306	210	3					
26. Prospect Hill, Waltham, MA 02154	(617)893-4837	90	8					
27. Springfield Ski Club, Blandford, MA	(413)848-2860	465	25				5000	
28. Wachusett Mountain, Princeton, MA 01541	(617)464-2355	650	7				4000	
29. Ward Hill, Shrewsbury, MA 01545	(627)842-6346	170	6				1500	

CONNECTICUT

NAME OF AREA, LOCATION	TELEPHONE #	VERTICAL DROP	NUMBER OF SLOPES	% BEGINNER	% INTERMEDIATE	% EXPERT	LONGEST RUN	ANNUAL SNOWFALL
1. Mohawk Mountain, Cornwall, CT 06753	(203)672-6100	640	23	20	40	40	7920	70
2. Mt. Southington, Southington, CT 06489	(203)628-0954	425	13	30	50	20	5000	32
3. Ohoho, Woodstock, CT 06281	(203)974-1040	300	10				3000	
4. Powder Ridge, Middlefield, CT 06455	(203)349-3454	500	15	30	50	20	5000	25
5. Ski Sundown, New Hartford, CT 06057	(203)379-0610	550	13	20	60	20	5100	32
6. Woodbury Ski and Racquet, Woodbury, CT	(203)263-2203	300	8				3960	

RHODE ISLAND

NAME OF AREA, LOCATION	TELEPHONE #	VERTICAL DROP	NUMBER OF SLOPES	% BEGINNER	% INTERMEDIATE	% EXPERT	LONGEST RUN	ANNUAL SNOWFALL
1. Diamond Hill, Cumberland, RI	(401)333-5400		1					
2. Pine Top, West Greenwich, RI 02827	(401)397-5656	280	6				2640	
3. Ski Valley, Cumberland, RI 02864	(401)333-6406	275	10				3000	
4. Yawgoo Valley, Exeter, RI 02822	(401)295-5366		4					

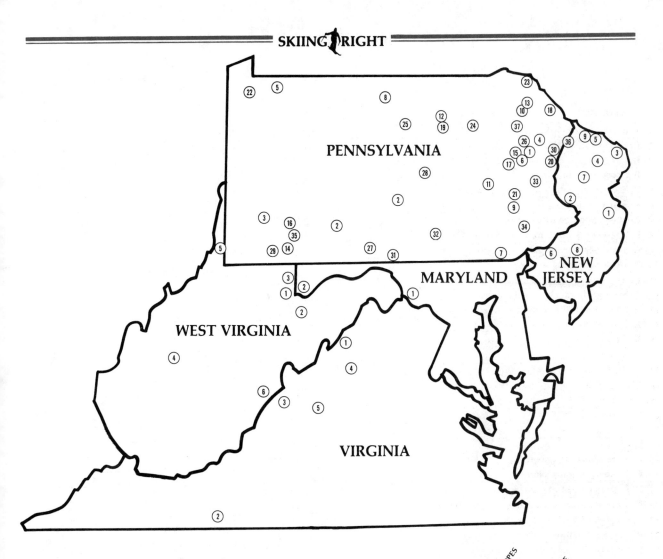

PENNSYLVANIA

	NAME OF AREA	LOCATION	TELEPHONE #	VERTICAL DROP	NUMBER OF SLOPES	% BEGINNER	% INTERMEDIATE	% EXPERT	LONGEST RUN	ANNUAL SNOWFALL
1.	**Big Boulder,** Lake Harmony, PA 19624		(717)722-0101	475	11	40	40	20	2900	60
2.	**Blue Knob,** Claysburg, PA 16625		(814)239-5111	1052	14	15	70	15	9200	100
3.	**Boyce Park,** Pittsburgh, PA		(412)325-1516	170	2				1200	
4.	**Buckaloons,** Youngsville, PA 16371		(814)563-9210	578	13				5280	
5.	**Buck Hill,** Buck Hill Falls, PA 18323		(717)595-7441	320	3					
6.	**Camelback,** Tannersville, PA 18372		(717)629-1661	800	20	40	40	20	6000	50
7.	**Chadds Peak,** Chadds Ford, PA 19317		(215)388-6476	283	4				1000	
8.	**Denton Hill,** Coudersport, PA 16915		(814)435-6372	660	13				5000	
9.	**Doe Mountain,** Macungie, PA 18062		(215)682-7109	500	5				4000	
10.	**Elk Mountain,** Union Dale, PA 18470		(717)679-2611	1000	16	30	30	40	10000	60
11.	**Hahn Mountain,** Kempton, PA 19529		(215)756-6351	500	7				2200	
12.	**Hanley's Happy Hill,** Eagles Mere, PA 17731		(717)525-3461	200	3				1000	
13.	**Hickory Ridge,** Honesdale, PA 18431		(717)253-2000	365	5				5280	
14.	**Hidden Valley Four Seasons Resort,** Somerset, PA 15501		(814)443-1414	450	9	25	50	25	3600	150
15.	**Jack Frost Mountain,** White Haven, PA 18661		(717)443-8425	500	12	25	50	25	2700	95
16.	**Laurel Mountain,** Ligonier, PA 15658		(421)238-6688	900	12	20	50	30	5500	
17.	**Little Gap,** Palmerton, PA 18071		(215)826-7700	300	8	20	40	40	1700	
18.	**Masthope,** Lackawaxen, PA 18435			650	5				5400	
19.	**Mont Saint Onge,** Hughesville, PA 17737		(717)584-2698	250	4				1300	
20.	**Mt. Airy Lodge,** Mt. Pocono, PA 18344		(717)839-8811	240	10					
21.	**Mt. Heidelberg,** Bernville, PA 19506		(215)488-7524	250	4				2500	
22.	**Mt. Pleasant,** Cambridge Springs, PA		(814)734-1641	350	11				3100	

continued ...

NAME OF AREA	LOCATION	TELEPHONE #	VERTICAL DROP	NUMBER OF SLOPES	% BEGINNER	% INTERMEDIATE	% EXPERT	LONGEST RUN	ANNUAL SNOWFALL
1. Mount Tone, Lake Como, PA 18437		(717)798-2707	450	9				2400	
2. North Mountain, Muncy Valley, PA 17758		(717)482-2541	175	2	100			1200	
3. Oregon Hill, Morris, PA 16938		(717)353-7521	515					7000	
4. Pocono Manor, Pocono Manor, PA 18349		(717)839-7111	250	4				1350	
5. Richmond Hill, Fort Loudon, PA 17224		(717)369-2673	125						
6. Saw Creek, Bushkill, PA 18324		(717)588-6611	300	7				2200	
7. Seven Springs Mtn. Resort, Champion, PA 15622		(814)352-7777	865	14	15	65	20	3685	130
8. Shawnee Mountain, Shawnee-on-Delaware, PA 18356		(717)421-7231	700	11				5000	
9. Ski Liberty, Fairfield, PA 17320		(717)642-8282	600	8	30	50	20	4800	24
10. Ski Roundtop, Lewisberry, PA 17339		(717)432-9631	550	10	40	30	30	4100	20
11. Split Rock, Lake Harmony, PA 18624		(717)722-9111	150	3				1400	
12. Spring Mountain, Spring Mountain, PA 19478		(215)287-7900	455	2				3000	
13. Sugarbush Mountain, Latrobe, PA 15650		(412)238-9655	200	5				1800	
14. Tamiment Resort & Country Club, Tamiment, PA 18371		(717)588-6652	125	2				1200	
15. Tanglewood, Tafton, PA 18464		(717)226-9500	417	7					

NEW JERSEY

NAME OF AREA	LOCATION	TELEPHONE #	VERTICAL DROP	NUMBER OF SLOPES	% BEGINNER	% INTERMEDIATE	% EXPERT	LONGEST RUN	ANNUAL SNOWFALL
1. Arrowhead, Marlboro, NJ 07746		(210)946-4598	100	1				100	
2. Belle Mountain, Hopewell, NJ 08525		(609)397-0043	190	5					
3. Campgaw Mountain, Mahwah, NJ 07430		(201)327-7800	270	5				2000	
4. Craigmeur, Newfoundland, NJ 07435		(210)697-4501	200	4				1900	
5. Hidden Valley, Vernon, NJ 07462		(201)764-6161	625	5				4000	
6. Holly Mountain, Salem County, NJ		(609)935-4600	150	6				1500	
7. Peapack, Brookside, NJ 07926		(201)543-4589	200	7				1200	
8. Ski Mountain, Pine Hill, NJ 08021		(609)783-8484	240	5				1800	
9. Vernon/Valley/Great Gorge, McAffee, NJ 07428		(201)827-2000	1000	53	25	45	30	7920	89

MARYLAND

NAME OF AREA	LOCATION	TELEPHONE #	VERTICAL DROP	NUMBER OF SLOPES	% BEGINNER	% INTERMEDIATE	% EXPERT	LONGEST RUN	ANNUAL SNOWFALL
1. Braddock Heights, Braddock Hgts., MD 21701		(301)371-7131	250	7				1250	
2. Wisp, Oakland, MD		(301)387-5503	610	16	25	55	20	10560	90

WEST VIRGINIA

NAME OF AREA	LOCATION	TELEPHONE #	VERTICAL DROP	NUMBER OF SLOPES	% BEGINNER	% INTERMEDIATE	% EXPERT	LONGEST RUN	ANNUAL SNOWFALL
1. Alpine Lake, Terra Alta, WV 26764		(304)789-2481	450	4	100			5000	
2. Canaan Valley, Davis, WV 26260		(304)866-4121	850	22	28	44	28	5280	185
3. Chestnut Ridge, Morgantown, WV 26505		(304)292-4773	170	2				1200	
4. Coonskin Park, Charleston, WV		(304)345-8000	125	1				600	
5. Oglebay Park, Wheeling, WV 26003		(304)242-3000	330	3				1600	
6. Snowshoe, Snowshoe, WV 26291		(304)799-6600	1598	18	25	55	20	8200	216

VIRGINIA

NAME OF AREA LOCATION	TELEPHONE #	VERTICAL DROP	NUMBER OF SLOPES	% BEGINNER	% INTERMEDIATE	% EXPERT	LONGEST RUN*	ANNUAL SNOWFALL**
1. **Bryce Resort**, Basye, VA 22810	(703)856-2121	500	5	34	33	33	3500	30
2. **Cascade Mountain Resort**, Fancy Gap, VA 24328	(703)728-3351	258	4				3000	
3. **The Homestead Ski Area**, Hot Springs, VA 24445	(703)839-5079	695	9	30	40	30	3500	60
4. **Massanutten**, Harrisonburg, VA 22801	(703)289-9441	795	9	25	50	25	5600	34
5. **Wintergreen**, Wintergreen, VA 22938	(804)325-2200	525	7	16	66	18	2755	46

NORTH CAROLINA, TENNESSEE, ALABAMA, GEORGIA

NAME OF AREA LOCATION	TELEPHONE #	VERTICAL DROP	NUMBER OF SLOPES	% BEGINNER	% INTERMEDIATE	% EXPERT	LONGEST RUN*	ANNUAL SNOWFALL**
1. **Appalachian Ski Mountain**, Blowing Rock, NC 28605	(704)295-7828	365	8				2700	
2. **Beech Mountain**, Banner Elk, NC 28604	(704)387-2011	809	18	50	30	20	7920	90
3. **Cataloochee**, Maggie Valley, NC 28751	(704)926-0285	740	8					
4. **Hounds Ear**, Blowing Rock, NC 28605	(704)963-4321	107	2				800	
5. **Mill Ridge Ski Mountain**, Boone, NC 28607	(704)963-4500	225	5					
6. **Sapphire Valley Resort**, Sapphire, NC 28774	(704)743-3441	425	4				1800	
7. **Scaly Mountain**, Scaly Mountain, NC	(704)526-3737	225	5	60	40		1500	
8. **Seven Devils Resort**, Banner Elk, NC 28604	(704)963-5665	619	6				3300	
9. **Sugar Mountain Resort**, Banner Elk, NC 28604	(704)898-4521	1200	12	35	30	30	7920	52
10. **Wolf Laurel**, Mars Hill, NC 28754	(704)689-4111	700	6				3500	
1. **Ober Gatlinburg**, Gatlinburg, TN 37738	(615)436-5423	275	4				3600	
1. **Cloudmont Ski Resort**, Mentone, AL 35984	(205)634-3841	150	3				1000	
1. **Sky Valley Resort**, Dillard, GA 30537	(404)746-5301	250	4				2200	

SOURCE DEVELOPMENT

PSYCHOLOGY-LEARNING THEORY

Helping Relationships, Combs, *Allyn & Bacon*
The Skilled Helper, Egan, *Brooks-Cole*
Drawing from the Right Side of the Brain, Edwards, *J.P. Tarcher, Inc.*
Inner Game of Tennis, Gallwey, *Random House*
The Positive Addiction, Feldenkrais, *Meta Publications*
How the Brain Works, Hart, *Basic Books, Inc.*
The Ultimate Athlete, Leonard, *Viking Press, Inc.*
Skiing from the Head Down, Loudis, *Lippincott Co.*
Golf in the Kingdom, Murphy, *Delta*
Centered Skier, McCluggage, *Vermont Crossroads Press*
The Psychic Side of Sports, Murphy & White, *Harper & Row Publishers, Inc.*
Superlearning, Ostrander & Schroeder, *Dell Publications*
Gestalt Therapy, Perls, *Bantam Books*
Piaget's Theory: A Primer, Phillips, *Freeman*
Myths and Truths in Psychology, Singer, *Harper & Row Publishers, Inc.*

MOTOR SKILL DEVELOPMENT

Motor Learning — Principles and Practices, Drowatsky, *Burgess*
Human Performance, Fitts & Pfosner, *Brooks/Cile*
Information Processing in Motor Skills, Marteniuk, *Holt, Rinehart & Winston, Inc.*
Motor Skills, Schmidt, *Harper & Row Publishers, Inc.*
Motor Learning and Human Performance, Singer, *MacMillan Publishing Co., Inc.*
Introduction to Motor Behavior — A Neuro-Psychological Approach, Sage, *Addison-Wesley*

SKI TECHNIQUE

Pianta Su, Ski Like the Best, Bear, *William C. Brown Co., Publishers*
Ski With the Big Boys, Campbell, *Winchester Press*
We Learned to Ski, Evans, *Martins' Press*
Teach Yourself How to Ski, Joubert, *Aspen Ski Masters*
Skiing, An Art, A Technique, *Poudre Publishing Co.*
How the Racers Ski, Witherell, *Norton & Co., Inc.*

World Cup Ski Technique, Major & Larson, *Poudre Publishing Co.*

SKI MECHANICAL RESEARCH

Zur Biomechanic des Schilaufs, Fetz, *Inn Verlag*
Basic Mechanics of Alpine Skiing, Glenne, *University of Utah Press*
Biomechanic Sportlicher Bewegung, Hochmuth, *Sportverlag*
An Instructor's Guide to Ski Mechanics, Holden, *PSIA*
Skiing Mechanics, Howe, *Poudre Publishing Co.*
Force and Torque Analysis of Simulated Downweighting and Pure Torque Turns in Skiing, Miller, *PSIA*
The Physiology of Alpine Skiing, Carlson, Eriksson, Forsberg, Carlberg & Tesh, *United States Coaches Association*
Belastung d. Menschlichen Bewegungapparatus b. Schilauf, Nigg, Neukomm & Leuthi, *University of Zurich*
A Search for Effective Stance, Twardokens, *PSIA*
Biomechanics of Skiing, Vagners, *PSIA*
Filmanalyse Biomechanischer Parameter beim Langlauf, Waser, *Zurich*

AVALANCHES

The ABC of Avalanche Safety, La Chapelle, *The Mountaineers*
The Avalanche Handbook, Perla & Martinelli, *Colorado Forest Service*

CONDITIONING AND EXERCISE

Stretching, Anderson, *Random House*
The Skier's Year 'Round Exercise Guide, Slusky, *Stein & Day*

SKI DIRECTORY

Ski Almanac, Miller, *Doubleday & Co., Inc.*
The Handbook of Skiing, Gamma, *Alfred A. Knopf*
The White Book of Ski Areas, Enzel, *Inter-Ski Services, Inc.*
Thomas & Leed Skier's Directory & Almanac, *Thomas & Leed Promotions, Inc.*